THE
DOMOSTROI

THE
DOMOSTROI

RULES FOR
RUSSIAN HOUSEHOLDS
IN THE TIME OF
IVAN THE TERRIBLE

EDITED AND TRANSLATED BY

Carolyn Johnston Pouncy

Cornell University Press

ITHACA AND LONDON

First published 1994 by Cornell University Press.

Printed in the United States of America

⊛ The paper in this book meets the minimum requirements of the
American National Standard for Information Sciences—Permanence
of Paper for Printed Library Materials, ANSI Z39.48-1984.

Library of Congress Cataloging-in-Publication Data
Domostroĭ. English.
    The "Domostroi" :   rules for Russian households in the time of Ivan the Terrible
/ Carolyn Johnston Pouncy editor and translator.
        p.   cm.
    Includes bibliographical references and index.
    ISBN 0-8014-2410-0 (cloth: alk. paper) — ISBN 0-8014-9689-6 (pbk.: alk. paper)
    1. Russia—Social life and customs—1533–1917.   2. Family—Russia.
I. Pouncy, Carolyn.   II. Title.
PG3300.D613   1994
640'.947'09031—dc20   93-48474

To the Pouncys—
Hillard, Mattie, Hillard, and Thomas—
for their help, love, and support

Contents

Acknowledgments

Twelve years of working on the *Domostroi* have engendered many debts. My thanks go to the Whiting Foundation, the International Research and Exchanges Board, and the Russian Research Center of Harvard University for financial support, research opportunities, and, in the case of the last, space in which to work. The staffs of the Academy of Sciences Library, the Russian National Library, the Russian State Archive of Ancient Acts, the State Historical Museum, and the Russian State Library were consistently helpful in uncovering previously unstudied manuscripts and in making available those already known. The Harvard, Stanford, Princeton, and Brandeis University libraries, the University of Pennsylvania Library, the Library of Congress, and the Swarthmore College Library have all, at one time or another, been mined for materials; I thank them all.

Dorothy Atkinson, Terence Emmons, Nancy Shields Kollmann, Edward Keenan, and many others read this work in its initial stages; without them, the project might never have been started, let alone finished. N. A. Kazakova, A. L. Khoroshkevich, M. V. Kukushkina, A. K. Leont'ev, and R. G. Skrynnikov guided the project at the very beginning, when I was still trying to find my way around Soviet archives. Many thanks, too, to Carol Leonard, who offered invaluable advice on how to gain access to those archives, and to Iu. K. Begunov, who ransacked secondhand bookstores to find a copy of A. S. Orlov's 1910 survey of Short Version manuscripts. Thanks are due also to the readers and editorial staff of Cornell University Press, who were consistently helpful and patient through what seemed at times innumerable delays.

To my in-laws, who cheerfully provided day care for my son during a crucial period, thank you. And most of all, my gratitude goes to my husband, who remained encouraging and full of useful suggestions even when I myself lost hope of finishing, and to my son, whose pleas that I stop "playing" with the computer reminded me that life did not end with the sixteenth century.

To anyone I may have omitted, my apologies: I appreciated your efforts nonetheless.

C. J. P.

THE
DOMOSTROI

Introduction

In the heart of present-day Moscow, on Razin Street heading out from Red Square, stands the stone house in which Michael, first tsar of the Romanov line (1613–1645), was born. This house is one of the few surviving examples of the world idealized in the sixteenth-century guide to good household management known as the *Domostroi*. Its padded benches, heavy oak furniture, cramped but luxurious women's quarters, and outdoor kitchens give substance to the *Domostroi*'s descriptions of the lives of wealthy nobles.

The *Domostroi* regulates the moral and civil obligations, the family relationships, and the physical needs of a large and varied household. The Romanov house illustrates many of its precepts. For example, the original household was, as the *Domostroi* prescribes, self-sufficient, with its own orchards, gardens, and storehouses.[1] It was wealthy, too: the taffetas, brocades, and velvets listed in the *Domostroi* are in evidence throughout. The book gives instructions on trading with foreign merchants; the Romanovs' interest in foreign lands is revealed by the presence of a globe—an unusual gadget in these times. The exquisite, cluttered rooms in some measure explain the *Domostroi*'s obsession with order (the word *domostroi* means exactly that: "house order").

---

1. Unfortunately, several of the outbuildings and gardens were destroyed to build the Rossiia Hotel. The main house is operated as a museum and has received good care; other outbuildings still stand but have not been maintained.

1

In other ways, the house exhibits features that the *Domostroi* takes for granted. Particularly striking is the way the builders fortified it for defense, separating the third-floor entrance from the street by a short bridge and a heavy oak door studded with nails. The physical structure also demonstrates the need for warmth: small, almost windowless rooms with low ceilings conserve heat. Preserved too are the separate spheres occupied by men and women. Quite literally, the house is split in two, emphasizing the strictly defined bounds within which elite women lived.

The proximity of the house to the Kremlin reflects another reality of sixteenth-century life. Moscow then was very small, barely extending beyond Red Square (although fields and shacks stretched past the protective city walls). People still called the region adjoining Red Square the "New Town."[2] The Kremlin, political and administrative heart of Muscovy, housed not only the tsar but the head of the Russian Orthodox church, the metropolitan of Moscow, as well as priests and high nobles. A monastery and a convent ministered to those who had retired from the world, and government offices watched over the concerns of the laity. Petitioners, clerics, merchants, and civil servants bustled about their business, while outside, in Red Square, crowds gathered to shop in the market, witness executions, and hear royal decrees. The Romanov house, then as now, stood right in the center of the activity.

The city itself, however, looked quite different then. Stone buildings were unusual, and houses, churches, streets, and shops were made mostly of wood. Because of the vulnerability of wood to fire, rot, and other forms of destruction, the old city survives for the most part only

2. See, for example, *Akty istoricheskie* (Moscow, 1836), t. 1, No. 164. Now this region is called the Kitaigorod.

"Every Christian must know how to live according to God in the Orthodox Christian faith" (Chapter 2). Here the patriarch (in the sixteenth century it would have been the metropolitan) of Moscow blesses the tsar while the court looks on. St. Basil's Cathedral, built in the second half of the sixteenth century to commemorate Ivan the Terrible's victories over the Mongols, can be seen in the background. From Adam Olearius, *Voyages en Moscovie, Tartarie et Perse* (Amsterdam, 1727). Courtesy of the Division of Rare and Manuscript Collections, Cornell University Library.

in its street plan. Beyond the familiar red brick walls and a few stone structures, even the Kremlin bears little resemblance to its sixteenth-century self. Some of the best-known landmarks—for example, St. Basil's Cathedral—either had not appeared or had not reached their present form at the time the *Domostroi* was written. The *Domostroi* opens a window on a world that—culturally, socially, even physically—has long since vanished.

Politics and Society in Muscovy

Although St. Basil's, built to commemorate emergent Moscow's victory over the Tatars (i.e., Mongols) of Kazan in 1552, was not completed until later, it nonetheless aptly symbolizes the period in which the *Domostroi* began to circulate. The colloquial Russian in which most of the text was written dates no earlier than the accession to the throne of Ivan III in 1462 and probably not much later than the death of his grandson Ivan IV in 1584. For several reasons—including terminology used, customs described, and the inclusion, in early manuscripts, of a chapter written by Sil'vestr, a priest who served in the Kremlin Cathedral of the Annunciation from 1545 to 1556 (approximately)—it most likely appeared sometime in the 1550s.[3] Overall, the years between 1462 and 1584 were prosperous and stable, the 1550s particularly so. The Muscovite government expanded and consolidated, confirmed its ascendancy over the other Russian principalities, achieved its final liberation from Mongol control, and began its reintegration into European politics. Although the 1530s and the last third of the sixteenth century were plagued by political and economic crises, as a whole the period was marked by the attainment of the goals of the early Moscow princes. Italian architects in the Kremlin, Russian diplomats in the Vatican, and English ships in the White Sea attested to Russia's renewed vitality. The parochialism of the thirteenth and fourteenth centuries began to disappear as Muscovy defined its imperial mission—

---

3. For example, the *Domostroi* mentions people sleeping on the stove, hardly possible before the mid-sixteenth century, when flat-topped stoves replaced the older round ones. It also mentions distilling vodka (or brandy, the usage is unclear), a process introduced in the sixteenth century. Other examples appear in notes to the translation.

Moscow the Third Rome, heir of Byzantium, head of the One True Church.

The *Domostroi* thus reflects the life enjoyed by the fortunate few of a new nation at a time of relative calm and comfort. This group made up only a small part of a complex social hierarchy. The rules of the system determined both the privileges and the obligations by which they lived; these same rules in turn underlie the principles expressed in the *Domostroi*. To evaluate the *Domostroi*, therefore, we must first understand the system.

The political and social system that became Muscovy evolved under unfavorable circumstances: in response to the need to create a viable, independent state in a northern land where agriculture operated at a subsistence level, politics were fragmented, and the country was subject to a foreign overlord (the Mongols). Although it drew on Kievan, Byzantine, and even Mongol sources, Muscovy seems to have developed for the most part in isolation. The fundamental assumptions in its political culture included the absolute centralization of authority in Moscow, government by consensus among a small and select group headed by the grand prince (later tsar), a political hierarchy based on birth and personal ties, control of information about how the system operated, and intense concentration on the performance of limited goals.[4] The government was supported by a strict social hierarchy in which, with rare exceptions, a man's father's profession determined his own and a woman's status depended on her husband's. By the middle of the fifteenth century, the bases of this system were in place. Through it and a combination of luck, ruthlessness, and quick thinking, the Muscovite princes had expanded their tiny original holding to encompass most of Russia, in the process forcing or persuading each new neighbor to adhere to their system. By the 1560s, Moscow had expanded still further, into the lands of its erstwhile conquerors, absorbing the Khanates of Kazan' (1552) and Astrakhan (1556); by 1582 Siberia too had fallen, at least nominally, under Russian control. As Moscow's hold over the Eurasian landmass strengthened, however, its administrative problems increased.

4. On the genesis of the Muscovite political system, see Edward L. Keenan, "Muscovite Political Folkways," *Russian Review* 45 (1986): 115–181. For a different interpretation, placing more stress on Mongol influence, see Charles J. Halperin, *Russia and the Golden Horde: The Mongol Impact on Russian Medieval History* (Bloomington: Indiana University Press, 1985).

The linchpin of the political system was the tsar, a member of the Daniilovich clan, connected through Daniil's father, Alexander Nevsky, to Riurik, semilegendary Viking conqueror of Russia.[5] For much of the sixteenth century (1533–1584), the throne was occupied by Ivan IV, known popularly as "the Terrible"—a ruler who moved from brilliance to ineffectuality to cruelty and paranoia, then back again. Although no one has yet advanced an explanation for Ivan's behavior on which everyone can agree, it is clear that his unpredictable temperament caused a progressive disintegration in society that culminated in civil war and chaos.[6] Military success and government reform in the 1550s gave way to military defeats and internal terror in the 1560s, setting up the conditions for social unrest and dynastic instability after Ivan's death. At the same time, and despite his apparently determined efforts to destroy the Muscovite political system at its roots, Ivan offers an example of its strength, for the system survived both him and the interregnum to return stronger than ever.

The system survived because the tsar relied on the corps of elite cavalrymen known as boyars.[7] Not quite an aristocracy but certainly more than the "tsar's slaves" that contemporary Western observers often called them,[8] boyars earned their standing through hereditary

5. According to the Russian Primary Chronicle (also known as the *Tale of Years Gone By*), Riurik accepted an invitation to rule Novgorod in 862. His lieutenants and descendants extended Riurik's principality, considered the first Russian state, by uniting Novgorod and Kiev in 882. See Samuel Hazzard Cross and Olgerd P. Sherbowitz-Wetzor, trans. and eds., *The Russian Primary Chronicle, Laurentian Edition* (Cambridge, Mass: Medieval Academy of America, 1953), pp. 59–61.

6. For biographies of Ivan IV, expressing various points of view, see Edward L. Keenan, "Vita: Ivan Vasilevich, Terrible Tsar: 1530–1584," *Harvard Magazine* 80, no. 3 (1978): 48–49; S. F. Platonov, *Ivan the Terrible*, trans. and ed. J. L. Wieczynski (Gulf Breeze, Fla.: Academic International Press, 1974); R. G. Skrynnikov, *Ivan the Terrible*, trans. and ed. Hugh Graham (Gulf Breeze, Fla.: Academic International Press, 1981).

7. For more on the boyars, see Nancy Shields Kollmann, *Kinship and Politics: The Making of the Muscovite Political System, 1345–1547* (Stanford: Stanford University Press, 1987); Robert O. Crummey, *Aristocrats and Servitors: The Boyar Elite of Russia, 1613–1689* (Princeton: Princeton University Press, 1983); Ann M. Kleimola, "Patterns of Duma Recruitment, 1515–1550," in *Essays in Honor of A. A. Zimin* (Columbus: Ohio State University Press, 1985), pp. 232–258; and Gustave Alef, *Rulers and Nobles in Fifteenth-Century Muscovy* (London: Variorum Reprints, 1983). A good overview of Muscovite social hierarchies and their interrelationships can be found in Richard Hellie, *Slavery in Russia, 1475–1725* (Chicago: University of Chicago Press, 1982), pp. 4–18.

8. See, for example, Giles Fletcher, "Of the Russe Commonwealth," in Lloyd Berry and Robert O. Crummey, eds., *Rude and Barbarous Kingdom: Russia in the*

service to the crown. They, and only they, counseled the tsar on a regular basis and participated in royal decision making. Scions of families who, through farsightedness or luck, chose to ally themselves with the Moscow princes in the fourteenth century, or of families that once had owned independent principalities, the boyars ruled Russia when the tsar was too young, too sick, or otherwise incapable. Although most lacked any formal education, they seem to have competently fulfilled their main functions: to command the cavalry and to set government policy. Their commitment to government service was lifelong, for their careers usually began at fifteen and ended only with incurable illness, extreme old age, or death. Their numbers were small, for like most European monarchies before 1800, the Muscovite government operated on personal relationships and recognition by the sovereign. Yet without them, Muscovy would not have survived, for the accidents of succession by primogeniture left the government vulnerable for long periods. Although in theory an autocratic tsardom, in practice Muscovy functioned as an oligarchy, with the ruler apart and above, moderating the fierce competition for power among the elite.

Boyars competed, first and foremost, for the survival and advancement of their *rod* (clan, lineage group: the descendants of a common ancestor). Individual abilities and preferences played a decidedly secondary role in their lives. Marriage alliances, essential for the propagation of the clan, also served political purposes. Here, too, families expected their individual members to bow to the needs of the lineage.

Because marriage and family ties determined political alliances, the Muscovite political system in large measure depended on the seclusion of elite women to prevent personal attachments between men and women and maximize the clan's freedom to arrange politically and economically appropriate marriages. Except on special occasions, women ate and lived apart, leaving the house only to attend church or to visit other women. Women played an important role within the household, managing its numerous and varied operations, running both urban and rural estates single-handedly while the men waged

---

Accounts of Sixteenth-Century English Voyagers (Madison: University of Wisconsin Press, 1968), p. 138. Fletcher echoes the views of most European visitors when he classifies the Russian government as "plain tyrannical" (p. 132). In this, he adhered to the propaganda assiduously disseminated by the Muscovite government and described by Keenan ("Muscovite Political Folkways").

war, producing new heirs for the clan, and maintaining the emotional links between families on which the political system depended, at times even venturing into the women's quarters of other families to approve or veto a prospective bride.[9] They had, however, no public role.

Social mobility within the Muscovite elite depended on a combination of talent, skillfully arranged marriage alliances, patronage networks (in part determined by marital ties), and the ability to attract favorable attention from the tsar. The ultimate political prize was marriage into the royal family. In keeping with the personal nature of Muscovite politics, the tsar's in-laws had the greatest access to the ruler and consequently benefited the most from royal patronage. The royal connection made members of their family desirable political and marriage partners and assured them high status among the elite. The sixteenth century experienced extremes of political stability and crisis. When marriage alliances were clear, the boyars could moderate their rivalries and maintain stability. When Ivan IV ascended the throne at the age of three, however, crisis ensued; power struggles among noble families waged unabated during the decade that passed before his marriage could be negotiated. Stability returned when the elite consolidated around the Romanov (also called Iur'ev or Zakhar'in) family after the tsar's marriage to Anastasia Romanovna in 1547, only to be threatened by Anastasia's death in 1560.[10] Ivan married six more times; boyar infighting preceded each wedding, leading to renewed crises that Ivan's bizarre policies only exacerbated. The century ended in social, economic, and dynastic chaos, from which the Romanovs emerged after a fifteen-year civil war to forge a new coalition, again solidified through royal marriage.

9. On women in Russia in pre-Petrine times (before 1682), see Barbara Evans Clements, Barbara Alpern Engel, and Christine D. Worobec, eds., *Russia's Women: Accommodation, Resistance, Transformation* (Berkeley: University of California Press, 1991), pp. 17–95 (articles by Pushkareva, Levin, Kollmann, and Kivelson); the special issue of *Russian History* 10, no. 2 (1983); and Dorothy Atkinson, Alexander Dallin, and Gail Warshofsky Lapidus, eds., *Women in Russia* (Stanford: Stanford University Press, 1977).

10. The composition of the boyar elite did not change much after Anastasia's death, and the Romanovs continued to be an important political force. Ivan IV's various attempts to break out of the system and establish an area in which he had complete control, however, unsettled the elite and effectively canceled attempts at reform—inflicting tremendous personal and economic suffering on his subjects as well.

Although marriage alliances among the royal and noble families were perhaps the most important determinants of status, the boyars' concern for clan advancement expressed itself in other areas as well. It lay behind, for example, their preoccupation with honor, exemplified by a system of precedence called *mestnichestvo*. Only the elite participated in the system, which ranked clans in relation to one another and the male members of the clan in relation to their fathers and brothers. Because of *mestnichestvo*, a Russian nobleman could not accept a court position lower than that to which his rank entitled him, lest he and his descendants be permanently dishonored. Disputes over these and similar issues (for example, seating at court functions and attendance at royal weddings) led to endless squabbling among families and between individuals over precedence. Precedence not only affected one's "honor" in terms of reputation and position but also provided economic privileges to accompany position: ownership of land and people to cultivate it.

Less privileged and wealthy were the cavalrymen known as "boyars' sons" (*deti boiarskie*) and *dvorianstvo* (usually translated "gentry" to distinguish them from their more aristocratic colleagues), who assisted the boyars in their military duties. Scholars once saw gentry and boyars as locked in an irreconcilable competition for power, in which the boyars represented the old feudal order and the gentry the new absolutist one, but the reality seems to have been more complex.[11] The boyars had little difficulty retaining control over Muscovite politics through the end of the seventeenth century, and the gentry devoted more energy to becoming boyars than to destroying the existing political system. Whatever issues may have divided them, boyars and gentry had much in common; both served the state on which they depended.

Within the ranks of the gentry, however, social position and economic resources varied greatly. Although in general less well-off than boyar families, some had considerable means; others lived hardly better than the peasants on their lands. Their importance lay in their numbers: they provided a kind of "middle management" for the army in a period when cavalry was still crucial; by the time artillery and infantry replaced the cavalry units, the gentry's virtual monopoly on military command experience ensured that, with retraining, they con-

11. For more information, see the works listed in note 7.

tinued to provide most of the officers the new standing army required. They had by then also acquired a social role (controlling the now enserfed peasantry) and an administrative role (the state needed more people to staff its growing bureaucracy). Tsar and boyars formed the government, and together they made use of the gentry, denying them the ultimate rewards of status and a say in policy making but granting them land for subsistence and peasants to work it.[12] Whereas boyars had always been largely Moscow-oriented, the gentry became increasingly provincial during the seventeenth century. Even they, however, could not afford to separate themselves entirely from urban life, for Russians typically divided their property equally among their children, and in a few generations even vast landholdings could dwindle to nothing. Acquiring new properties depended on connections with the capital, usually obtained through service to the central government.

The gentry had their civil counterparts in those who staffed the Muscovite chancery system.[13] The chancery system began as the private administration of the royal estates, staffed by elite slaves, and expanded steadily, if in a somewhat piecemeal fashion, throughout the sixteenth and seventeenth centuries. As it expanded, free labor replaced slaves; the resulting demand for literate personnel severely taxed Moscow's limited educational resources. In its way, however, the chancery system represented the triumph of ingenuity over nearly impossible odds. Completely informal, it benefited from extreme flexibility: chanceries appeared and disappeared as needed, some lasting no more than a few months, others—such as the Treasury or Foreign Office—enduring for centuries. The apparent disorganization allowed the government to target specific populations and goals and to concentrate its resources on those areas that seemed most likely to yield results, a pragmatic approach that permitted Moscow to control vast territories despite the difficulties created by poor transportation and communications.

In the sixteenth century, literacy was the most important character-

12. On the gentry, their part in enserfment, and the impact on both of changes in military technology, see Richard Hellie, *Enserfment and Military Change in Muscovy* (Chicago: University of Chicago Press, 1971).

13. On the chancery system in the sixteenth century, see Peter Bowman Brown, "Early Modern Russian Bureaucracy: The Evolution of the Chancery System from Ivan III to Peter the Great, 1478–1717" (Ph. D. dissertation, University of Chicago, 1978).

istic used in selecting the career bureaucrats who organized the collection of taxes, reports of military campaigns and genealogical records.[14] Muscovy still had no formal educational system to draw on, and the demand for personnel was pressing, so a candidate's abilities loomed larger than his social origins. Former slaves, priests' sons who did not wish to take orders, and foreigners with shady pasts were all welcome in Muscovite administrative service as long as they could read and write a fair hand. In this traditional, hierarchical society, chancery service offered one of the few paths to upward mobility: with enough talent, discretion, and luck a man could begin life as an apprentice and end it as the Muscovite equivalent of secretary of state.[15] This freedom lasted only a short time: as soon as the system became firmly established, those families who had discovered chancery service first began to exclude others. Eventually, the bureaucracy too became a closed caste.

In the early years, however, it was quite fluid. The bureaucrats, as a nouveau-riche group of mongrel origins in a well-defined and vertically organized society, were placed in a curious position. Chancery officials, for example, could own populated rural lands (a privilege they shared with other state servitors), but few of them did, presumably because owning rural landholdings was closely associated in the public mind with gentry status, which they lacked. Unlike their military colleagues, therefore, chancery personnel were predominantly urban, living by preference in Moscow and visiting the provinces only for the duration of a particular post. Within their own setting, they lived luxuriously; they may even have surpassed many of their social superiors in wealth, but they could never equal the elite cavalrymen in social standing. This ambiguity appears also in their official duties: they carried out policy but did not decide it, for the power to make decisions lay with the tsar and the boyars. Yet their input must often have been influential, for they held the knowledge and the experience on which good decisions depended.

14. For more information, see Borivoj Plavsic, "Seventeenth-Century Chanceries and Their Staffs," in Walter M. Pintner and Don Karl Rowney, eds., *Russian Officialdom: The Bureaucratization of Russian Society from the Seventeenth to the Twentieth Century* (Chapel Hill: University of North Carolina Press, 1980), pp. 19–45.

15. See, for example, the Iudins and the Gur'evs, both of whom began as merchants in chancery service and ended as gentry. Both families owned copies of the *Domostroi*. See Carolyn Johnston Pouncy, "The *Domostroi* as a Source for Muscovite History" (Ph.D. dissertation, Stanford University, 1985), pp. 269–270.

In addition to those actively involved in administration, elite merchants often served the state. Merchants turned up with particular frequency in the Treasury and the Foreign Office, where their expertise clearly served state interests. Informally as well, however, wealthy merchants often operated on behalf of the state. Out of their ranks came the *gosti*, a handful of privileged servitors who controlled international trade and administered the royal monopolies on such items as vodka, salt, and copper.[16] Great fortunes were made in the international trade, for it concentrated almost entirely on luxury goods: exchanging furs and wax, for example, for rare and expensive fabrics, unusual foods, precious metals, or jewelry.

Those who traded domestically in food and handicrafts were more diverse. The vast majority of Russian merchants typically came from the peasant and artisan classes. Peasant and urban traders at times found themselves in conflict, for the peasants needed trade to supplement their subsistence income from farming, and the urban traders feared that the sheer number of peasant entrepreneurs undercut their prices and ruined the sales on which their lives depended. Occasional outbreaks of animosity, however, had no significant impact on the number of peasants trading in the cities, for without food from the countryside no city could survive. The two groups therefore had little choice but to accept each other, however grudgingly.

Contemporary accounts portray Russian merchants of all levels as illiterate but shrewd, notorious for their dishonesty (caveat emptor!) and fond of bargaining.[17] The *Domostroi* explicitly argues that merchants should be both honest and fair, although most people of the time do not seem to have considered the traditional practices to be flaws of either character or judgment. More serious to the long-term health of the merchant classes were the destabilizing effects of illiteracy, the absence of any commercial credit or banking system, and the inherent dangers of sixteenth-century life. Many a prosperous commercial house collapsed because it lacked heirs, failed to pass on in time the details of its business ventures, or suffered a series of disasters (ships lost, crops failed, and the like) which its economic resources

16. On the *gosti*, see Samuel H. Baron, *Muscovite Russia* (London: Variorum Reprints, 1980).

17. On Russian trading customs, see, for example, Fletcher, "Of the Russe Commonwealth," pp. 245–246. Fletcher's attitude is more disapproving than those of Westerners who themselves engaged in commerce.

could not withstand. Even excessive government attention could prove catastrophic. When such misfortune struck, the members of a merchant family could quickly disappear among the artisans from whom they sprang.

Artisans occupied the lowest levels of the free urban population and practiced many trades. The *Domostroi* mentions, among others, carpenters, bootmakers, ironmongers, masons, icon painters, gold- and silversmiths. Women practiced dressmaking and related trades such as embroidery and weaving. Training occurred through apprenticeships, but unlike their Western counterparts, Russian artisans had no formal contracts or intricate guild structure to protect their interests.[18] They depended on their wits, their connections, their ability to attract patronage, and their trading skills to survive. Without these, they might be forced to sell themselves into slavery and practice their trade on behalf of a great lord, for slavery was the social welfare program of the day.

The rural counterparts of the artisans were the peasants. Although reliable population figures for the sixteenth century do not exist, peasants made up the overwhelming majority of the populace—easily 70 to 80 percent of the whole. (For comparison, in the eighteenth century, when the government began to take censuses, peasants were counted as more than 90 percent of the population, but by then the categories of slave and peasant had merged.) Despite their numbers, the peasants' social and economic status declined steadily between the fifteenth and the seventeenth centuries. As Moscow consolidated its hold on the other Russian principalities, the government's demands for military recruits and money to support them increased. So did its ability to collect what it demanded. To reward its military servitors, the state offered populated land; to nobles who had no interest in agriculture, unpopulated land had little value. Peasants who had known freedom thus became subject to boyars and gentry, forced to pay both state taxes and private dues. As the century progressed, state and lords increasingly required payment in cash, severely straining the resources of peasant households in cash-poor Russia.

For most of the sixteenth century, peasants still held a legally guaranteed right to leave their landlords once a year, during the two weeks

18. The few guilds that existed were for merchants: the *gostinnaia sotnia, sukonnaia sotnia,* and others.

"Such irrational people [who do not pay their debts] live in slavery, in fear of rightering, and in debt" (Chapter 62). The person seen in the lower right is suffering rightering, whether for indebtedness or some other crime (graft, for example), while an indifferent crowd mills around him. Behind them, Moscow towers within its protective walls. From Adam Olearius, *Vermehrte Moscowitische und Persianische Reisebeschreibung* (Schleszwig, 1656). Courtesy of the Princeton University Library, Department of Rare Books and Special Collections.

around the autumn St. George's Day (November 25), if they had paid all their dues. For practical reasons, many peasants did not choose to leave their homes at the beginning of the Russian winter; others who might have wished to do so could not afford to pay their obligations. Many, however, apparently did take the opportunity to move to larger (or simply more congenial) estates whose owners paid the necessary sums; the most fortunate and adventurous could leave altogether to start a new life.

Gradually, however, the government curtailed the right to leave. The economic disaster that followed Ivan IV's decision to terrorize his own subjects and the costly yet ultimately futile war against Livonia (1558–1583) sent many peasants in flight to the fertile southern steppes.

Faced with a dwindling labor supply, the nobles demanded state decrees to tie the remaining peasants to the land. In 1649, the state removed the statute of limitations that had to some extent protected peasants from recovery by their landlords and effectively made all peasant movement illegal.[19] By 1700, the legal distinction separating peasants from slaves had disappeared; both were designated serfs.

In the sixteenth century, however, slavery still filled several rungs on the social ladder, for not all slaves held equal status. Slavery existed in Russia from earliest times, although the country never had a major slaveholding system comparable to that of Classical Rome or the American antebellum South.[20] Slaves made up about 10 percent of the population (in contrast, Mississippi in 1860 had a slave population of 55 percent).[21] Some of these, such as the estate stewards and highly trained military slaves, had considerable value and prestige. Most benefited to some extent from the social standing of their masters, since slavery tended to be concentrated among the Muscovite elite; all, however, also suffered from the limitations imposed by slavery, for their status could never approximate that of free men with equal responsibility or resources.

Muscovite slavery differed in several respects from the American slave system with which most of us are more familiar. Slaves in Muscovy served primarily as domestic servants, not in a productive capacity; owners saw them as dependent family members, not as chattel. Because slaves often ate more than they produced, slavery served in part, as Richard Hellie has noted, as a welfare system for Muscovites with no other means of support.[22] As well as a flexible and undemanding work force, the slave owner received psychological and social

19. Within the vast literature on enserfment, historians generally fall into two camps, one holding that peasants were enserfed by state decree beginning around 1582 and ending with the 1649 Law Code, the other arguing that enserfment resulted from a long, slow deterioration in the peasants' economic position. For an example of the "decree" school, see Hellie, *Enserfment and Military Change*, introduction. For the economic argument, see Jerome Blum, *Lord and Peasant in Russia from the Ninth to the Nineteenth Century* (Princeton: Princeton University Press, 1961), pp. 219–276.

20. The most extensive discussion of Russian slavery is Hellie, *Slavery*. Hellie also compares and contrasts Muscovite slavery with other slave systems. For an analysis of slavery as an institution, see Orlando Patterson, *Slavery and Social Death* (Cambridge, Mass.: Harvard University Press, 1982).

21. The estimate of Russian slaves comes from Hellie, *Slavery*, pp. 681–689; the data for Mississippi from Patterson, *Slavery*, p. 483.

22. Hellie, *Slavery*, pp. 692–695.

benefits: honor among his peers (who valued the conspicuous consumption exemplified in supporting many underemployed servants), the opportunity to exercise authority within his household, and appreciation of his own freedom from control.[23]

Muscovite slavery also differed from American slavery because it depended on people from its own culture who sold themselves into slavery to escape hard times.[24] Russian slaves shared their masters' ethnicity, religion, and culture. This similarity lessened the social distance between the two groups and seems to have ameliorated, at least to some extent, the harshness inherent in slavery.

Perhaps for this reason, Muscovite slavery was relatively mild compared to other slave systems. Slaves had certain legal rights; slave marriages were honored and their families generally kept intact; as far as we can tell, society expected masters to feed and clothe their servants adequately and not to punish them too severely (by Muscovite standards, which tolerated corporal punishment even for the elite).[25] At the same time, slaves remained subject to abuses of power. Because most slaves were domestic servants, for example, free domestic servants could be forcibly converted into slaves.[26] Certain occupations, such as estate stewardship, required that the holder become a slave. Throughout the sixteenth century, moreover, most were still full, hereditary slaves; only toward the end of the century did the more limited debt service contract, which bound the signers for the life of the lender and prohibited sale or transfer, predominate.[27]

Women's roles in Muscovite society were determined by a combination of gender and social status. Women among the gentry, chancery personnel, and elite merchants tried as far as possible to imitate the

23. Both Hellie and Patterson mention these often overlooked rewards of slavery for the master—particularly obvious in a domestic slavery system like the Muscovite one, in which slaves provided few economic benefits and, in fact, were economic burdens. See Hellie, *Slavery*, pp. 690–692; and Patterson, *Slavery*, pp. 77–101.

24. Muscovy fit Patterson's definition of an extrusive slave system (*Slavery*, pp. 38–45).

25. On the treatment of servants, see Hellie, *Slavery*, pp. 503–510.

26. The legal right to convert slaves postdates the *Domostroi*, for it was only after 1597 that a master had the legal right to convert anyone who served him for six months or longer into a limited service contract slave, even against the servant's wishes. Records, however, indicate that the practice was not new. See Hellie, *Slavery*, pp. 39–41; Patterson, *Slavery*, p. 34.

27. Hellie tracks the shift from full to contract slavery in Russia between 1450 and 1725. The shift presaged the eventual abolition of slavery or, more accurately, its merging with the institution of serfdom. See *Slavery*, passim.

life-style of the boyar elite (sometimes to the latter's distress). These richly dressed and lavishly painted women lived largely private lives, although the wives of military servitors, in particular, might find themselves responsible for managing the family estates for long periods while their husbands waged war. Widows, too, enjoyed a certain independence, and married women retained their right to own property.

Peasants and artisans, however, could not afford to seclude their wives; women among them had a broader range of responsibilities, although a sexual division of labor prevailed and women bore primary responsibility for tasks within the home. Slave women, like slave men, worked mostly as domestic servants; most slave women in Muscovy seem to have been spared the degradation of serving as concubines (the Orthodox church severely condemned such practices), but they did suffer in comparison with their male counterparts: Richard Hellie has found a significant discrepancy in the sex ratio between male and female slaves, suggesting both a preference for males and the possibility of female infanticide. Prices were lower for female slaves than for male ones.[28]

Marriage and childbearing formed the common boundaries of women's existence. Up and down the social pyramid, women married young in arranged matches, bore children as frequently as nature would permit, and took primary responsibility for child care, at least in the early years. Society considered the virginity of brides, like their "honor" (chastity) after marriage, to be crucial; at all levels, a woman's health, character, disposition, and family connections took precedence over issues of personal compatibility. Older women—mothers, grandmothers, and widows—acted as matchmakers and so controlled the destiny of the young. Women also achieved prestige through their children, especially their sons.

The cloister offered the only exception to women's almost universal dedication to marriage and the family. Unlike their contemporaries in western Europe, the Russian nobility do not seem to have used convents as dumping grounds for unwanted or unmarriageable daughters, although unwanted wives sometimes "discovered," against their wills, a religious vocation that freed their husbands to seek a younger, more fertile, or more congenial bride. Russian convents did not match West-

---

28. On male-female ratios, price differentials, and possible female infanticide, see ibid., pp. 415–422, 442–459.

ern ones as places of learning, nor did they offer women a national platform; in accord with the principles of female seclusion, the cloister was always strictly enforced. Nevertheless, at least until well into the seventeenth century, Russian nuns enjoyed considerable freedom from supervision, so that within their small communities, individual women could wield extensive authority as abbesses. In this way, the convent, in Muscovy as elsewhere, offered women a rare, if limited, alternative to the patriarchal society that surrounded it.[29]

Outside and above the cloister, and separate as well from the secular hierarchy, stood the male clergy. These men were divided by their marital status. The vast majority of clerics were parish priests, almost invariably married.[30] Most lived in small, remote villages and supplemented their incomes with farming. Parish priests were generally dependent on their parishioners for their livelihood, which made them reluctant to oppose the villagers who supported them. Often barely literate, acting much like the peasants they served, parish priests made at best poor instruments for enforcing church policy.

The most highly educated and best-connected priests attained places in urban cathedrals or as private chaplains. These men lived more relaxed and secure lives than village priests and had more opportunities to augment their salaries with trade or book-copying. Still, they remained low in the church hierarchy; although Orthodox clerics need not be celibate, the prelates must. Priests who became monks, usually because their wives died,[31] could continue their old duties as monastic priests.

29. For more on women within the Muscovite family, see Christine D. Worobec, "Accommodation and Resistance," in Clements, Engel, and Worobec, eds., *Russia's Women*, pp. 17–28; and N. L. Pushkareva, "Women in the Medieval Russian Family of the Tenth through Fifteenth Centuries," ibid., pp. 29–43.

30. Byzantine canon law stipulated that priests and deacons could not marry after ordination. In the Slavic world, this ordinance became a requirement that all priests and deacons be married, on the grounds that they lived in the world and were subject to temptation. Thus all priests and most deacons had to marry before ordination (some deacons married after their ordination as deacon but before they were ordained as priests). On Russian Orthodox attitudes toward clerical marriage, see Jack Edward Kollmann, "The *Stoglav* Council and Parish Priests," *Russian History* 7 (1980): 65–91, pp. 69–74; and Eve Levin, *Sex and Society among the Orthodox Slavs* (Ithaca: Cornell University Press, 1989), pp. 248–253.

31. The Slavic Orthodox churches did not permit second marriages for priests until 1667. The Orthodox church viewed marriage as a concession to human weakness and held that its servitors should not receive multiple concessions but instead offer a good example to the laity. The church's attitude toward widowed priests

Monks applied skills developed in the secular world to the administration of their communities and lands. But becoming a monk was only a first, if necessary, step to advancement. Most monks lived quiet lives in small communities, although monks in urban monasteries sometimes played active roles in the outside world. The most ambitious and gifted eventually became bishops, archbishops, even metropolitan of Moscow. Through these leaders, especially the metropolitan, the church fulfilled its traditional functions in Muscovite politics. It provided a place of exile for barren wives and uncooperative nobles; it legitimized the claims of the Moscow princes; it influenced, or tried to influence, the tsar through confession, pleading, and threats. Some metropolitans maintained independence from state control; others did more or less what the tsar required. Except for humanitarian concerns or in its own interests, however, the church had little impact on policy making and enforcement. It supported the government but did not try to rule it; its influence was more cultural than political.

The church, for example, supervised and funded the great literary and artistic projects of the sixteenth century. These projects, in turn, illustrate both the strengths and weaknesses of the Russian church's approach to culture—in a phrase, "more is better." The creations of the sixteenth century generally took older art forms (chronicles, hagiography, icon painting) to their greatest extent, with little latitude for interpretation or innovation. Metropolitan Makarii of Moscow (1542–1563) exemplified the spirit of the age with his *Illustrated Chronicle Codex* (*Litsevoi svod*) and his *Great Lexicon* (*Velikii Chet'i Minei*), which compiled as many chronicles and saints' lives, respectively, as his assistants could find.

At the same time, new technology and ideas, if accepted only begrudgingly by the ecclesiastical powers, began to arrive in the sixteenth century. They accompanied the foreigners who started to appear during Ivan III's reign and whose numbers grew along with Muscovy's emergence onto the European stage. A printing press opened briefly in Moscow in 1564, publishing a Gospel and an *Apostol* (Acts and Epistles of the Apostles) before a local mob, believing the press the work of the Devil, burned it. New forms of icon painting brought

---

who remained in the world, however, was suspicious in the extreme; in the Russian church, especially, priests whose wives died were barred from singing mass and pressured into finding a monastic vocation. See Kollmann, "*Stoglav* Council," pp. 70–71; and Levin, *Sex and Society*, pp. 264–269.

charges of heresy in their wake, embroiling, among others, Sil'vestr, priest of the Annunciation Cathedral in the Kremlin and contributor to the *Domostroi*.[32] Herbals, agricultural manuals, and other secular works were translated from various European languages, particularly Latin and Polish. I. S. Peresvetov and others began to theorize about the proper form and function of government. Old genres, unused for many years, were revived, resulting in, for example, the 1497 and 1550 law codes. The church produced a similar code of conduct for its own employees and, by extension, believers, with the recommendations of the "Hundred Chapters" (*Stoglav*) Council in 1551. Within this peculiar mix of new and old, this fascination with categorization, encyclopedic knowledge, and order, belongs the *Domostroi*.

Domestic Life and the *Domostroi*

To the *Domostroi*'s author, life was simple: "a place for everything, and everything in its place." Didactic, in love with detail, he exemplified the legalistic mind. In his view, belief in the Trinity, the cross, Mary, and the saints—along with regular church attendance, frequent confession, and communion—marked the good Christian. Obedience to superiors (tsar, princes, boyars, husbands, parents, masters, priests) made a good citizen. Paternalistic kindness to inferiors characterized a good master or mistress; abundant household supplies, a good manager. Care for the poor and the clergy, avoiding sorcery and "the Devil's games" (that is, folk medicine and popular entertainment) were considered the signs of a good person.

Depending on their station, people incurred additional responsibilities. A good wife, for example, was chaste, modest, abstemious, quiet, and obedient to her husband, firm and knowledgeable with children and servants. These same children and servants had to do what they were told, be content with what they had, and protect the interests of their households by refraining from gossip, theft, bad manners, drunkenness, promiscuity, and other sins.

32. The dispute over the icons focused on renovations to the Annunciation Cathedral, supervised by Sil'vestr. It is known as the "Viskovatyi Affair," after the chief complainant, I. M. Viskovatyi. For more on this controversy, see David B. Miller, "The Viskovatyi Affair of 1553–1554: Official Art, the Emergence of Autocracy, and the Disintegration of Medieval Russian Culture," *Russian History* 8 (1981): 293–332; and Pouncy, "*Domostroi* as a Source," pp. 232–240.

Together, these well-ordered people created a good house: clean, well-stocked, neatly organized ("like entering Paradise," as the author says in a rare lyric moment—Chapter 38). For in the *Domostroi*'s universe, pickled mushrooms and clean straw reflected the soul as clearly as acts of charity. Everyday details became symbols of one's moral state, bringing concomitant rewards or punishments. "If everything," says the author—whether he means dowering a daughter, stocking the larder, or professing one's faith—"is done in accordance with these recommendations," the family with all its dependents can look forward to eternal happiness; if not, eternal damnation will surely follow.[33]

Imperfections, individuality, and the complexity of human experience the *Domostroi* honors mostly in passing. Thieving servants, ladies dabbling in sorcery, dishonest tradesmen, disobedient sons, drunken guests, and negligent masters offer sometimes welcome relief from the relentless advice giving. The *Domostroi* does not say which behaviors were more typical of Muscovite households; it expresses ideals, not reality. Its definitions of good and evil, however, expose the foundations of its culture, a perspective fundamentally different from our own. This worldview prizes religious orthodoxy, reliance on tradition, absolute interpretations of virtue and vice, hierarchy, obedience, and the subordination of the individual to family and state—ideals to which most sixteenth-century Muscovites unquestionably subscribed.

The *Domostroi*, then, reveals much about how Muscovites translated the general principles of their culture into an ideal of family life. It also provides a wealth of domestic detail unparalleled in other sources. Principles and details together yield a composite—not, perhaps, of a typical household, but one to which sixteenth-century Russians aspired.

The Household

This household was, above all, large and self-sufficient. It included a main house and numerous outbuildings, surrounded by a high fence that supplied privacy and, if necessary, defense.[34] Care of these struc-

---

33. For examples of this philosophy, see Chapters 1, 15, 39, and 64 and the additions to chapter 17.

34. Such a conglomeration of buildings is more like an urban estate than the compact structure evoked by the word "household." Nonetheless, I used "household" or "homestead" throughout the translation to distinguish these urban struc-

tures, made mostly of wood, required constant vigilance, particularly to prevent and control fires. Heat came from a clay stove (the *pech'* of Russian folktales), situated on an earthen floor and large enough to sleep on during cold winter nights—a relatively new invention in the sixteenth century, replacing the older round-topped stove. If the owner were lucky, a well in the courtyard provided water; if not, servants with buckets hauled it from the river each day. The river also doubled as a site for doing laundry.

Ground-floor storerooms occupied the lowest levels of the main house, while the upper floors held living areas, bedrooms, and separate women's quarters. An outdoor staircase, roofed to protect the steps from snow, allowed visitors to bypass the storerooms and enter the main receiving area. A foyer led off the staircase, insulating the family rooms from winter's cold. The living chambers were richly decorated and often contained a particularly opulent "beautiful corner," a shrine with icons and candles, to which all visitors paid obeisance on entering. Glass was introduced to Russia only in the seventeenth century, so windows gave little light, especially in winter, when they had to be shuttered against the cold. Candles—mostly made from tallow but occasionally wax—and torches provided most illumination.

Furniture was heavy and serviceable and, among the elite, richly decorated with brocades and jewels. The *Domostroi* mentions beds, benches, tables, and chests as major items of furniture. Chairs were still scarce in this period; only the master, and only in the most elite households, would have one. Carpets (probably Oriental), pillows, throw rugs, tablecloths, and napkins added a luxurious touch. Sideboards and cupboards held dishware: goblets, platters, tureens, and serving utensils made mostly from pewter, copper, or wood. Dishes and utensils were large and intended for sharing; individual plates and cutlery, except for spoons, had not yet come into fashion.

Such great houses with their sumptuous furnishings belonged only to the uppermost circles of the Muscovite social hierarchy: boyars, gentry, chancery personnel (state secretaries and above), wealthy merchants, and prelates. Russians below these groups lived in small wooden houses not unlike peasant huts, with one, or at most two,

---

tures from rural estates (*pomest'ia* and *votchiny*—see glossary for explanation of these terms).

rooms, an entrance hall, and a stove.[35] The *Domostroi*'s author had something much grander in mind.

Within the large and affluent household lived a large, extended, and not always clearly defined group, which historians, for lack of a better word, call the family. The *Domostroi* at times limits its understanding of family to people related by blood who share a residence, at times broadens it to include all people within the household, regardless of blood relationship. This variation is typical of the sixteenth century in Western sources as well as Russian ones. At the same time, however, it confirms the *Domostroi*'s social origins, for among people of limited resources, the nuclear family still predominated in the sixteenth century (the extended peasant family apparently developed later, in response to changes in the tax structure). Boyars and gentry, in contrast, favored large, extended families; merchants and chancery personnel, eager for advancement, consistently sought to emulate their betters.

In the uppermost circles, teenage marriages easily led to three-generation families, despite an infant mortality rate of around 50 percent and, by modern standards, relatively low life expectancy, especially for women. But the definition of family also extended to numerous dependents: for example, poor, orphaned, or widowed kinsfolk and, of course, slaves. Furthermore, nobles often gave charity to certain nonresident poor people and slaves who were also considered part of the family. Sometimes slave artisans lived on the top floor of the main building, sometimes in separate quarters of their own. Some lived completely apart from the family, supporting themselves on meager allowances. Altogether, such a home might include anywhere from fifty to two hundred people; even larger households were not unknown.[36]

The daily life of the household occurred mostly outside the main building, in the stand-alone kitchens, bakeries, breweries, smokehouses, icehouses, drying rooms, granaries, barns, and stables. Here

35. For descriptions of these huts as they appeared in the nineteenth century, see Mary Matossian, "The Peasant Way of Life," in Wayne S. Vucinich, ed., *The Peasant in Nineteenth-Century Russia* (Stanford: Stanford University Press, 1968), pp. 2–8.

36. On the size of boyar households, see Crummey, *Aristocrats and Servitors*, pp. 145–146.

servants prepared food, performed their crafts, raised plants and animals for the family to eat, brewed beer, stacked lumber, and washed clothes. The *Domostroi* provides copious instructions for such tasks; it portrays a self-contained village—a mini-corporation, almost—running under the iron rule of its master and mistress.

The homestead supported animals for its own use: horses, pigs, dogs, ducks, geese, chickens, and occasionally cows.[37] The *Domostroi* suggests that only homes sporting ponds in their courtyards should breed waterfowl, but it considers pigs and horses essential to any homestead. Many animals ate table scraps (see Chapter 42), but large beasts (cows, horses) foraged outside the city walls in summer and lived inside on oats or hay in the winter. Most fish seems to have been purchased; Russian rivers yielded an ample and varied supply, and in this period fresh fish was probably easy to obtain near Moscow. Other food needs were met by orchards and vegetable gardens, which provided apples, pears, melons, cherries, carrots, beets, cabbage, and other produce. Grain, yeast, oils, and a dizzying variety of other staples came from the market.

Whether produced at home or purchased, food in season was eaten fresh. September, however, brought a whirlwind of salting, smoking, pickling, making into broth or juice, and immersing in syrup. For the rest of the year, preserved food ruled the kitchen. Russia, fortunate in one respect in its northern climate, had natural refrigerators as soon as the snows started to fall. People generally used icehouses only for cooling aspic, drinks, and similar items, however; frozen foods remained undiscovered. Preserving food to last a household of several hundred people for eight months or so constituted a major undertaking, but failure to perform it adequately carried great costs—literally as well as figuratively. As the *Domostroi's* author says on more than one occasion, "if you find you need something that is out of season, you will pay three times the price," and for inferior goods at that.

Overall, the *Domostroi* maintains an ambivalent attitude toward the marketplace: on one hand, it encourages self-sufficiency; on the other, it recognizes the impossibility of achieving complete independence without the benefit of rural estates (see, for example, Chapter 42). It

37. No cats, for some reason.

compromises by recommending bulk purchases, even "go[ing] in with one or two friends" (Chapter 43) to buy a case of fish, and storing food bought in season as well as commodities produced within the homestead.

The *Domostroi* also offers insights into the extent and nature of commercial transactions in sixteenth-century Muscovy. It mentions peasants hauling meat carcasses and timber into the city, merchants selling imported luxury goods (lemons, wine, brocade, and the like), householders stocking up on groats, salmon, caviar, and other items. Overall, the *Domostroi* indicates a vibrant (although not necessarily large) commercial sector in the towns. It illustrates, for example, established links between town and countryside, a monetary economy, ample food and clothing for the rich, and an adequate, if monotonous, diet even for slaves. It assumes that its readers have mercantile interests—instructing them on granting and repaying loans, urging them not to incur excessive debts. To some extent, therefore, the *Domostroi* contradicts the once widespread view that sixteenth-century Russia was a stagnant rural economy, for it portrays the towns as centers of a thriving domestic and international trade.[38] In its exploration of commercial ethics, however, the *Domostroi* seems more medieval than mercantilist in its attitude: it promotes (from all other sources, a wholly uncharacteristic) concern with honesty and straight dealing; it deplores usury and excessive gain.

The links between household and market were several and various: household products were sold in the market and others' goods purchased. Many households also employed one or more merchants in their service; the *Domostroi* provides instruction in selecting and disciplining such commercial agents (Chapter 60). The elite urban homestead of this time and place was not a simple dwelling but a full-scale economic operation. The person in charge of this operation was, first and foremost, the lord (*gosudar'*: the word means slave owner, sovereign, one whose power is absolute), assisted, perhaps, by wife and steward, but holding ultimate responsibility.

38. See, for example: Alexander Gerschenkron, *Continuity in History and Other Essays* (Cambridge, Mass.: Belknap Press, 1968), p. 416. For more positive views of the sixteenth-century economy, see Blum, *Lord and Peasant*, pp. 199–218; and Robert O. Crummey, *The Formation of Muscovy, 1304–1613* (New York: Longman, 1987), pp. 21–22.

Husband, father, master, patriarch: religion and custom supported the master's position. According to the *Domostroi*, every family member owed him deference and obedience; he made all decisions; he bore sole responsibility—not only for the results of his choices but even for the souls of his dependents, should they fall because he failed to instruct them.

The master's character determined the family's success. He had to fulfill the duties of a good citizen: loyalty, piety, honesty, and deference to those in power. He had to worship God in Orthodox ritual several times each day, attend church regularly, manage his professional concerns between calls to prayer, conduct home services, entertain guests, monitor even the smallest domestic details, and supervise the morals and performance of his dependents. He had to direct the production and storage of alcohol personally, meet with his servants and commercial agents at least once a week, consult with his wife and his steward every day, and tour the premises each night before retiring to ensure that all gates were locked and all fires banked.

Although burdened by many duties, he enjoyed as many privileges. In theory, at least, his slightest wish evoked instant obedience. He determined whom the family would honor and to what extent. He decided what the household would produce, conducted all purchases, reviewed all accounts, assigned clothes and jobs, rewarded and punished as he saw fit. No one was supposed to take so much as a piece of bread from the larder without his consent.

Although this formulation worked well in theory, in real life servants and children were not always obedient, nor were men uniformly endowed with managerial skills. Even men who had the ability to fulfill their roles as envisioned in the *Domostroi* might be prevented from doing so by the demands of government service or commercial ventures, which required them to spend long periods away from home. In practical terms, therefore, wives and stewards often took on the master's role within the household; the conflicting summonses of ideal and practicality left a certain confusion within the *Domostroi* and some latitude for families to work out individual solutions. Still, the overriding principles of female seclusion and patriarchal authority gave men in general, and the master of the house in particular, a broader role in domestic management than modern Westerners would generally expect.[39]

A man depended on his wife for assistance in fulfilling his domestic responsibilities. She supervised the training of daughters and female servants, entertained women guests, and in general made sure that the rest of the household faithfully carried out her husband's orders. Together, husband and wife provided for the family's physical well-being and moral education—contributing protection, food, clothing, religious instruction, training in an appropriate craft, and, in due course, a suitable marriage partner.

The mistress of the house occupied an anomalous position within the family: neither master nor slave, she constantly balanced superior and subordinate roles. Sixteenth-century Europeans, including Muscovites, did not consider women the moral or intellectual equals of men. Husbands expected obedience, conciliation, and passivity from their wives. Society required that women not show (or even feel) anger toward their spouses, that they make no demands; Eve's disobedience had brought humanity's downfall, but Christ had been born through the body of a woman who bowed meekly to the will of her Lord. All women, first and foremost, held a responsibility to preserve their chastity and protect their family's honor from the shame that could result from bold glances or heedless words.

This standard of feminine behavior, endorsed by the Orthodox church, remained the ideal in Russia for many centuries.[40] Diatribes, usually written by monks, against evil women condemn them for rebelliousness, pertness, gossiping, vanity, and promiscuity—exact opposites of the feminine virtues of submissiveness, silence, decorum, and chastity.

The *Domostroi* takes a more moderate view of women. Its advice to

39. For modern examples of burdens placed on men by the seclusion of women, see Sandra Mackey, *The Saudis: Inside the Desert Kingdom* (New York: Signet, 1990), pp. 130–182.

40. For some other examples, see Kallistrat Druzhina-Osoryin, "The Life of Yuliana Lazarevsky," in Serge A. Zenkovsky, trans. and ed., *Medieval Russia's Epics, Chronicles and Tales*, rev. and enl. ed. (New York: Dutton, 1974), pp. 391–399; and the description of Archpriest Avvakum's wife, Anastasia Markovna, in "The Life of Archpriest Avvakum by Himself," ibid., pp. 401, 420, 429–430. For a different, but biased, view of Russian womanhood, see Adam Olearius, *The Travels of Olearius in Seventeenth-Century Russia*, trans. and ed. Samuel H. Baron (Stanford: Stanford University Press, 1967), pp. 168–170.

women begins with the famous passage from Proverbs 31:10–31 ("Who shall find a capable wife?") and in general portrays women as good, not evil. If wives had to demonstrate suitable awareness of their inferior status, woman as mistress of the household gained rewards through her industry, competence, firmness, fairness, and initiative (within the confines of her husband's orders). According to the *Domostroi*, women should know how to bake and brew, wash and clean, pickle and poach, knead and stitch (Chapters 29, 33). The author did not expect elite women actually to perform these chores, but the knowledge supposedly allowed them to maintain control over their servants. The master bore responsibility for the behavior of his entire household, but he held his wife accountable for those beneath her: if she did not punish her servants for wrongdoing, he would punish her (Chapter 38).

Of the various sins a housewife might commit, the *Domostroi* concentrates on gossip, secrecy, and tolerance of sorcery. The author did not, however, consider any of these unique to women. The dislike of gossip apparently stems from the author's preoccupation with family honor and its vulnerability to rumor; he advises servants and children as well as wives to refrain. Prohibitions against sorcery, too, apply to all classes, although the author apparently sees women as peculiarly vulnerable to folk magicians—perhaps because women did in reality stay attached to the pagan tradition longer than men.[41] The concern over secrecy is really an issue of control: it extends as well to children and servants and is intended to prevent clandestine attempts to evade the master's authority. As applied specifically to women, however, the prohibitions against secrets uncover a contradiction inherent in the practice of female seclusion: the very structures that confined women freed them, in some ways, from male interference; albeit within narrow limits, women lived separate lives.

Because the *Domostroi* adopts the male viewpoint, it gives at best a distorted picture of how women lived. It barely mentions, for example, the relationship that most affected a woman's happiness: the bond between mother-in-law and daughter-in-law. In this sex-segregated

41. For some examples of this, and speculations on the psychology behind it, see Joanna Hubbs, *Mother Russia: The Feminine Myth in Russian Culture* (Bloomington: Indiana University Press, 1988), pp. 14, 24–27, and passim; Pushkareva, "Women in the Medieval Russian Family," pp. 34–36, 39–40; and Eve Levin, "Childbirth in Pre-Petrine Russia: Canon Law and Popular Traditions," in Clements, Engel, and Worobec, eds., *Russia's Women*, pp. 45–56.

society, husbands and wives usually saw each other under limited circumstances and had few emotional ties. Young wives and mothers-in-law, by contrast, interacted daily in restricted surroundings. The imbalance of power clearly favored the older generation: the bride, still in her teens, entered a new family that expected her to comply with its own (probably unspoken) rules. But the *Domostroi* provides no clues to how this worked in practice.[42] Only the wedding rituals (Chapter 67) even mention this vital bond, and then merely to recommend that the older woman extend a warm welcome to the new bride.

These few examples illustrate the complexity of elite women's lives in sixteenth-century Russia. On one hand, women did not engage in professions, serve the government, or perform any public role. They lived under the control of their male relatives and of women older than themselves. On the other, they played a vital role in the private sphere, not only by running the household (no mean accomplishment) but in defining and maintaining the emotional links between clans that allowed Muscovite politics to function. Female skills were respected, and at least in the mind of the *Domostroi*'s author, women themselves were seen generally in a positive light. Although dependent, they were not despised, for they performed numerous functions indispensable to the clan. Of all the contributions women made, however, none was more critical than the bearing of children, without whom the family could not survive.

Children

Although the *Domostroi* clearly values children, it has curiously little to say about them, less than about almost any other topic. There is nothing on childbirth, breast-feeding versus wetnursing, weaning, early childhood, fostering, or any form of education. Apparently the author assumed that his reader already knew all he needed to know about these subjects. Because girls, as everywhere in early modern

---

42. That brides often anticipated a miserable life (until they too became mothers-in-law) is suggested by the laments traditionally sung at weddings. (For examples of laments, see N. A. Kolpakova, *Lirika russkoi svad'by* [Leningrad, 1973], nos. 199–203.) The laments probably exaggerate the situation, however, for one of their purposes was to honor the bride's parents by emphasizing the contrast between her life as a maiden and the future she envisions.

Europe, lived almost exclusively under their mothers' care, it is perhaps understandable that the author summarizes the father's responsibilities toward his daughters in a single chapter (16) on planning ahead for a dowry. But the training of boys receives no more attention, only a passing recommendation that the father "teach his sons whatever trade they can learn. God gives each person some capacity" (Chapter 15). Occasionally the author mentions using a servant or a son to run an errand (Chapter 35), notes that children deserve care instead of neglect (Chapter 1), or acknowledges special needs—for example, recommending that small children should be fed on demand, not made to wait until the rest of the family can eat (Chapter 13). Otherwise, the injunctions are sternly biblical ("A man who loves his son will whip him often. . . . Have you daughters? See that they are chaste," Chapter 17, quoting Jesus ben Sirach)[43] and preoccupied with child mortality ("that [dead] child is a bloodless sacrifice from the parents," Chapter 15; "if . . . a dowered daughter should die," Chapter 16). As a result, no clear picture of childhood emerges. The author has more to say about the care of horses than about raising one's sons.

Other sources reveal resemblances between childhood in sixteenth-century Russia and childhood in the Christian countries of western Europe (probably because both derived independently from biblical and patristic sources). It is too soon to say definitely whether medieval Russian parents recognized stages in child development comparable to the ones that Shulamith Shahar has delineated in Western sources,[44] but some general patterns can be observed.

Infants were born into a world of women; not even a priest attended the birth except in an emergency, to provide extreme unction. In Russia, women bore their babies in the bathhouse (warm, dark, and humid—an excellent place for newborns), attended by midwives, as well as female friends and relatives. Semipagan ritual surrounded the event, and the midwife immediately placed the child under the protection of ancient clan spirits (*Rod* and *rozhanitsy*).[45] In contrast to many of their

43. That is, the Book of Ecclesiasticus, or the Wisdom of Jesus ben (son of) Sirach. This collection of proverbs by a Diasporan Jew who lived during the second century B.C. is included in the Catholic and Eastern Orthodox Bibles but considered deuterocanonical by the Protestant churches. A good English translation of the Greek text (from the Septuagint) can be found in *The New English Bible with the Apocrypha* (New York: Oxford University Press, 1976), pp. 115–175.
44. Shulamith Shahar, *Childhood in the Middle Ages* (London: Routledge, 1990).
45. Levin, "Childbirth," pp. 47, 52–54.

Western counterparts, most Muscovite mothers, even among the elite, seem to have breast-fed their infants, although a wetnurse might substitute during the forty days following childbirth during which the church considered the mother ritually impure (according to custom, no one, not even the newborn baby, could eat in the presence of a woman considered impure). How the break in nursing affected lactation is unclear.

Children of both sexes remained primarily their mothers' responsibility during early childhood. The sources give little sense of how people treated them (in western Europe, parents generally indulged small children; the harsh discipline for which this period is known started later).[46] In general, however, the evidence—even in the *Domostroi*, despite ben Sirach—indicates that parents loved their children, grieved when infants died, and tried to make adjustments (in feeding and in dress, for example) suitable to a small child's needs.[47]

At some point—perhaps around the age of seven, like their Western counterparts—boys moved from their mothers' orbit to their fathers'. The *Domostroi* indicates that boys began at this time to train for their future professions (which would be the same as their fathers'); in the absence of any formal school system, training seems to have been entirely at the father's discretion. During this period of childhood, discipline probably included corporal punishment, especially for boys. The *Domostroi* does, however, recommend strict limits on such punishment; the restrictions make good sense, but no one knows whether people followed them. The *Domostroi* also suggests allocating to (presumably older) sons responsibility for supervising servants and questioning commercial agents about their activities, to acquaint them with the family business. Again, other sources do not confirm this practice. In order of importance, the father's responsibilities can be summarized as follows: provide your sons with a good moral upbringing; discipline them well; teach them a trade; endow them with worldly goods and, if you have them, good connections; arrange a good marriage for them.

While boys went with their fathers, girls remained with their moth-

46. Shahar, *Childhood*, pp. 98–100, 172–174.

47. On the love of Western parents for their children, see ibid., which contradicts the argument advanced by Philippe Ariès, *Centuries of Childhood: A Social History of Family Life*, trans. by Robert Baldick (New York: Vintage Books, 1982) and adopted by many others. For Russian examples, see *Domostroi*, Chapters 1, 13, 15, 16, and 64; "Life of Avvakum," pp. 415, 417, 420–421.

ers to receive training as wives. To an even greater extent than for boys, the moral education of girls seems to have taken precedence over other forms of instruction. Because so much depended on female chastity and on the family's marital plans, the seclusion of young unmarried girls was particularly strict.[48]

The training of girls presumably included the instruction in baking, brewing, and the like that the *Domostroi* so strongly endorses, but as before, other sources yield no detailed information. Literacy was not a requirement for either sex, unless a boy trained for the priesthood, in which case his father would teach him whatever formal educational skills he himself possessed.

Childhood was also, however, a time of play. Hagiography, for example, reveals that ordinary, worldly children played games from which the saint, by tradition, abstained.[49] Large families and a plentiful supply of servants made playmates readily available. Even in her teens, the blessed Yuliana Lazarevsky, according to her son, had to fight off her cousins' invitations "to take part in games and frivolous songs," preferring as she did the saintly (female) pursuits of spinning, embroidery, and plain sewing.[50] The sad tale of Prince Dmitrii Ivanovich, youngest son of Ivan the Terrible, illustrates the prevalence, and at the same time points up the dangers, of unsupervised play: Dmitrii reportedly died of a knife injury sustained during a game similar to mumblety-peg.[51]

Whether happy or grim, the typical sixteenth-century Russian childhood was brief. For boys, childhood ended abruptly at fifteen, when service careers typically began. Girls might be wrenched from their homes into marriage even earlier.[52] These sudden transitions were

48. A preoccupation with female chastity typifies societies like Muscovy that place so much emphasis on male honor. For non-Russian examples, see Mackay, *The Saudis*, pp. 133–135; Shulamith Shahar, *The Fourth Estate: A History of Women in the Middle Ages* (London: Methuen, 1983), pp. 109–110. The Wisdom literature of the Bible is also replete with such concerns. On Muscovite interpretations of female honor, see Nancy Shields Kollmann, "Women's Honor in Early Modern Russia," in Clements, Engel, and Worobec, eds., *Russia's Women*, pp. 60–73.

49. See, for example, the lives of St. Theodosius, St. Sergius of Radonezh, Yuliana Lazarevsky, all in Zenkovsky, trans. and ed., *Medieval Russia's Epics, Chronicles and Tales*.

50. Ibid., p. 392.

51. On Dmitrii's death and contemporary rumors that he did not die by accident but was murdered on the orders of Boris Godunov, see Jerome Horsey, "Travels," in Berry and Crummey, eds., *Rude and Barbarous Kingdom*, p. 358.

52. Legally, girls could marry at twelve. Probably most elite brides were older

buffered, to some extent, by the extended family. Apprenticeship continued, but in greater earnest, as the young master and mistress began to assume family responsibilities, eventually stepping into their parents' shoes.

Masters and Servants

The master and mistress were responsible for training slaves, on which topic the *Domostroi* has plenty of advice. In some ways, the master's obligation differed little from the father's. Keep your servants, the author says, "like children—rested, well-fed and clothed, in a warm house and under good governance" (Chapter 1).

Although people sometimes treated their slaves like children, the *Domostroi* has more to say about problems they presented as adults. Masters might, for example, find it difficult to dismiss slaves once they had acquired them, for slaves were legally entitled to food and clothing. The government forbade lords to free slaves to avoid feeding them during a famine, and society as a whole frowned on those who mistreated their servants.[53] Slaves typically stayed with the family for a long time, and the *Domostroi* emphasizes the need to choose people of good character, competent and hardworking, well-trained in a craft and free from such vices as drinking, gambling, and carousing (that is, enjoying a good time, Chapter 22). It demands that masters feed, clothe, and house their slaves adequately so they will not turn to theft to meet their needs (Chapters 22, 28); it requires owners to arrange marriages for their servants, lest passion undermine their morals (Chapter 22). The paternalism inherent in these instructions reflects the extreme hierarchical sense and veneration of male authority characteristic of the *Domostroi* and the society that produced it.

In return for sufficient maintenance, slaves owed honest, faithful, and obedient service, which the master secured through a simple reward/punishment system. In the imposition of this system he recruited the assistance of his wife and steward (Chapters 38, 58, and passim),

---

than this, but not much, for the *Domostroi*, for example, talks about making clothes that will fit "a young bride" as she grows (Chapter 31). Girls in lower strata married later, around nineteen or twenty, to grooms four or five years older than themselves. See Hellie, *Slavery*, pp. 437–442.

53. See Hellie, *Slavery*, pp. 123–125, 127–129, 504.

the latter himself a slave.[54] The steward occupied an even more anomalous position than the mistress of the house; even an elite slave is a slave, but a steward substituted in many respects for his master, with equivalent control over his fellow slaves. In many families, the steward ran the household; his subjection to his master was then little more than nominal, especially when the latter spent much time away from home. But slavery left him always in a precarious position. A death or shift in family fortune could radically change his situation.

The *Domostroi* includes four chapters (48–51) that discuss the responsibilities of a steward. All emphasize the need for obedience; otherwise most of the instructions are self-evident (assign food to the kitchens, check it before having it placed on the table, distribute alcohol as the master has ordered, and so on). A few points are more revealing. Theft during a banquet, for example, apparently seemed a real threat to the *Domostroi*'s author, so he advised the steward to station guards in the courtyard to prevent guests and their servants from stealing household possessions (Chapter 50). Drinking was another major concern: the steward had to watch for drunkenness among the guests, prevent quarrels, and take care of anyone who became intoxicated, while simultaneously deterring his fellow servants from overindulgence (Chapters 49, 50). The *Domostroi* also tells the steward to examine each dish after the feast, giving the smallest leftovers to those who served at table, serving the larger "broken" (cut) pieces later to the family and keeping the "unbroken" pieces for the master and mistress.

Except for the steward, the *Domostroi* makes little distinction among servants. It lists numerous crafts—carpentry, bootmaking, baking, brewing, sewing—and discusses such general household tasks as laundering and cutting out clothes. The third "instruction to a steward" distinguishes between an upper group (seamstresses, merchants) and other servants, recommending that the first eat with the master and mistress of the house while the others share meals primarily composed of rye bread, cabbage soup, kasha (simmered buckwheat groats), and low-alcohol beer. On Sundays and holidays, pies, pancakes, and different soups provided some variety. Those who prepared and served food sometimes enjoyed special privileges: they ate before the banquet

54. From the ninth to the seventeenth centuries in Russia, "he who holds the keys is a slave," said the proverb, and accepting the job of steward was equivalent to accepting full slavery. See ibid., p. 37.

"so they will not suffer" while waiting at table (Chapter 49) and shared those leftovers considered suitable for servants after the feast was done (Chapter 50). Otherwise, the shared status of slave seems to have overridden other distinctions within the household.

The *Domostroi* shows the same lack of discrimination when it describes clothing. Servants generally did not wear livery in the sixteenth century, but the *Domostroi* seems to assume that servants of all ranks would dress similarly. The text does distinguish, however, between garments suitable for everyday work and those for holidays; it devotes much attention to making servants presentable, insisting that clothes be appropriate to the occasion and that both clothes and their wearers appear clean and neat (Chapter 22). It also emphasizes the master's obligation to furnish clothing to his slaves, which in real life was, like the duty to provide food and shelter, often evaded by paying the slave a minuscule allowance, which could not possibly meet all his needs. The *Domostroi* accepts the allowance system, telling slaves to be content with whatever funds their master chooses to grant them (Chapter 22), but unequivocally condemns its abuses, for the master who fails to provide for his slaves bears responsibility if they steal out of need (Chapter 28).

The concern for hygiene, evident in the discussion of clothing, extends to a minimal interest in manners, particularly among servants. The text discourages sneezing or coughing at table (Chapter 49) or while engaged on an errand (Chapter 35); it reminds visiting slaves to knock before entering another's house (Chapter 35); and it emphasizes cleanliness of person, especially among the waiters and kitchen staff (Chapters 48, 49). It recommends polite and deferential speech for everyone and condemns gossiping, rudeness, and other sources of conflict. The *Domostroi* is, however, curiously quiet concerning more complicated issues of etiquette—for example, precedence, which one would expect would provoke an in-depth discussion, is dismissed in a phrase ("send something . . . according to the recipient's worth or rank," Chapter 10). Instead, the author discusses general rules of moral behavior and matters of practical concern to the master, such as ensuring that cheese dispatched to one's neighbor arrives in one piece.

The slaves depicted in the *Domostroi* led far from glorious lives. The text endorses tight control over their existence and harsh discipline if their performance fell below its standards. In households that followed its recommendations, however, servants could be assured adequate food and clothing, a roof over their heads, and fair treatment (the *Domostroi* prohibits, for example, punishing anyone before the master personally investigates the accusations and confronts the accused; Chapters 38, 58). People sold themselves into slavery to escape destitution, and the *Domostroi* accepts this situation; it does, however, try to mitigate the miserable conditions that slaves often suffered in real life.

The Household and the World Outside

Among their other responsibilities, servants and male children acted as liaisons among households. The *Domostroi* also occasionally mentions banquets, weddings, and visiting among women. Overall, however, it has little to say about relationships among families or with neighbors and friends. The church ruled people's lives and probably provided a meeting place, especially for men. The marketplace also apparently depended on connections (as it still does); granting loans on good terms is counted a sign of neighborliness (Chapter 25), gifts promote friendships (Chapter 64), merchants make goods available because of past favors (Chapter 64). Men developed other business and career connections as well. Women were less fortunate: seclusion limited their opportunities to form friendships—except for family ties, passed on through relatives or deriving from the needs of the male members of their families for politically astute associations. Less often than for men, the church probably became a meeting ground for women, too.

Chapter 36 spells out the author's ideal concerning women's behavior toward their friends (avoid drunkenness, gossip, and secrets; speak demurely, asking deferentially for advice on good household management). On male friendships, the *Domostroi* is virtually silent, although these, along with kinship ties, largely determined the political and economic structure of Muscovy. Sil'vestr, claiming friendship with people of all ranks (Chapter 64), furnishes the sole exception, and even he has little to say about friendship itself; he sees it as useful, not as innately worthwhile. But perhaps this has more to do with the nature of the *Domostroi* than with the concerns of the society that read it, for those times when the text does mention friends tend to be specifically tied to household concerns. Neighbors, for example, are people against whose animals one erects fences to protect the vegetables; friends require banquets, a special grade of beer, a gift to honor them, a written contract to prevent enmity should a pledged item come back damaged, a private word so they will not depart grumbling from a feast. The spirit of hospitality undoubtedly lies behind this very down-to-earth advice, but family, not friends, attract most of the author's attention.

Lords and ladies, husbands and wives, parents and children, masters and servants reach across the four hundred years separating the *Domostroi* from the present. Some of the advice holds the immediacy of yesterday's newspaper column, some suggests a vast gulf in time and space. Some alienates and disgusts, some draws the reader in. Yet throughout a single clear ideal emerges: a neat, orderly world ruled by religious principles, in which human and material spheres ring in harmony and no discordant note is permitted to sound. It is a curious ideal—in step, perhaps, with the great compilation projects of the 1550s, with their obsession for detail, but in contrast with a reign that knew much conflict and chaos. Who, one wonders, was this person who valued order above all else?

The Text of the *Domostroi*

Authorship

The *Domostroi*, like many texts of its time and place, has no clearly identified author. For more than a century, people have associated it with Sil'vestr, a priest in the Kremlin Cathedral of the Annunciation, because his name begins Chapter 64 in some manuscripts. In discussions of the *Domostroi*, Sil'vestr appears sometimes as author, sometimes as editor, but inevitably he does appear. This section takes on three tasks: (1) evaluating Sil'vestr's participation; (2) sketching the text's evolution; and (3) examining other evidence that may shed light on who wrote the *Domostroi*.

Of the three, the second is the most fundamental. Typically, people who consider the manuscripts with Sil'vestr's name in them to be original also consider Sil'vestr the author of the *Domostroi*.[55] Those

55. On Sil'vestr as the author of the *Domostroi*, see D. P. Golokhvastov, "Domostroi blagoveshchenskogo popa Sil'vestra," *Vremennik Imperatorskogo Obshchestva Istorii i Drevnostei Rossiiskikh* [OIDR] (1849), bk. 1; A. V. Mikhailov, "K voprosu o redaktsiiakh Domostroia, ego sostave i proiskhozhdenii," *Zhurnal Ministerstva Na-*

who think that these manuscripts preserve a reworked text logically conclude that Sil'vestr could not have been the original author but believe that he produced (edited) the later version.[56] Although they reach opposite conclusions, these two schools of thought share the belief that Sil'vestr's role can be determined by proving which version came first. Here I briefly present an alternate view of the *Domostroi*'s textual development, indicating a much more peripheral role for Sil'vestr while upholding the primacy of the manuscripts that bear his name.[57]

The *Domostroi* has survived in forty-three handwritten copies. It was not printed until 1849—partly because printing did not become established in Russia until the 1630s, at least fifty years after the *Domostroi*,[58] partly because when printing *was* introduced, the church controlled the presses for its own use. A relatively secular text like the *Domostroi* did not attract the patriarch's interest. By the time private presses became established (after 1775), public interest had passed the *Domostroi* by; translations of Erasmus and other Western writers prevailed.

The reliance on hand-copying meant, among other things, that no standard text existed. Production depended on a copyist having access to one or two manuscripts—which might contain any number of errors, additions, or lost pages—and transcribing them in a way that the copyist found acceptable. Within this framework, the *Domostroi* demonstrates a remarkable consistency. Nevertheless, over time, the text changed. Errors crept in, accretions adhered, losses occurred. Tracking these changes reveals the history of the *Domostroi*.

---

rodnogo Prosveshcheniia [ZhMNP] (1889), nos. 2:294–324 and 3:125–176, and "Eshche k voprosu o Domostroe," *ZhMNP* (1890), no. 8:332–369.

56. For arguments that Sil'vestr edited the *Domostroi*, see, among others, I. S. Nekrasov, "Opyt istoriko-literaturnogo issledovaniia o proiskhozhdenii drevnerusskogo Domostroia," *Chteniia OIDR*, 1872, bk. 3:1–184; A. A. Zimin, *I. S. Peresvetov i ego sòvremenniki* (Moscow, 1957), pp. 41–70; M. A. Sokolova, *Ocherki po delovykh pamiatnikov XVI v.* (Leningrad, 1957). The conclusion is also implicit in A. S. Orlov, *Domostroi. Issledovanie* (Moscow, 1917).

57. The reasons for preferring this particular evolutionary path are examined in Carolyn Johnston Pouncy, "The Origins of the *Domostroi*: An Essay in Manuscript History," *Russian Review* 46 (1987): 357–373; abridged from Pouncy, "*Domostroi* as a Source."

58. Watermarks in two manuscripts (older part of State Historical Museum [GIM], Sobr. Barsova, No. 368 [MS 368A] and Russian State Archive of Ancient Acts [TsGADA], f. 188, No. 1380 [MS 1380]) date from the 1560s. For specifics, see Pouncy, "Origins," pp. 361–362.

The *Domostroi* manuscripts divide into four distinct types, here called Short, Intermediate, Mediate, and Long.[59] The four groups clearly share a core text, which varies little among the manuscripts. To create the different versions, the editors added or deleted whole sections, moved passages around and renumbered them, but made few alterations in wording or style.[60] The *Domostroi* probably evolved roughly as follows.

First came the Short Version. It was compiled by a single male author, who used a basic text—either his own or one compiled from other works, supplemented with biblical and other religious passages. In its original form the Short Version probably contained only sixty-three chapters, but Sil'vestr's "Epistle" soon became attached to it. Sil'vestr, himself a book copyist, probably reproduced this original text as a gift to his son Anfim.[61] The "Epistle" perhaps first appeared as a cover letter or summary that accompanied this copy when Sil'vestr sent it to Anfim.

Within a relatively short period of time, probably no more than ten to fifteen years, the original *Domostroi* was expanded and reorganized.[62] During copying, a page was lost in one of the manuscripts, leaving confusion in Chapters 10 and 11. The "Epistle" also disappeared around the same time, although for a while copyists continued to list it in the table of contents. Someone created a new version, the Intermediate, dropping the title and all mention of the vanished "Epistle," leaving the first chapter unnumbered, redoing Chapters 10 and 11, shifting Chapter 39, and adding numerous religious passages. The additions disturbed the original progression of ideas. A third version, the Mediate, solved this problem through a thorough reorganization, including again numbering the first chapter and adding more quota-

59. Not two, as thought by Nekrasov ("Opyt") or three, as argued by Orlov (*Domostroi. Issledovanie*). In my dissertation, the Mediate Version was called the Transitional Version. The other three correspond to Orlov's first (long), second (short), and third (intermediate) editions.

60. For visual representation of these and the other textual changes described here, see Pouncy, "*Domostroi* as a Source," pp. 329–349.

61. This theory receives support from two seventeenth-century Short Version manuscripts (Russian National Library [GPB], Sobr. Pogodina, No. 1137 and GIM, Sobr. Zabelina, No. 446), where the names of Sil'vestr, Anfim, and Anfim's wife, Pelageia, appear in the first chapter. The latter also names Tsar Ivan (IV) and his first wife, Anastasia, in chapter 10. Both include the "Epistle."

62. The alterations had to have been completed in time to produce MSS 368A and 1380 (watermarks from 1564 and 1560s–1570s, respectively). If in fact the *Domostroi* originated in the 1550s, that means a span of twenty years at most.

tions from religious literature, among them St. Basil of Caesaria's "Admonition to the Young" (Russian version).[63]

Finally, the creator of the Long Version added a preface and three long discourses, fairly secular in tone, on such topics as the evils of drunkenness and preventing slave flight. Between 1600 and 1625, three unrelated chapters with menus and recipes, possibly translations from another European language, became associated with the Long Version; shortly thereafter they received numbers and became Chapters 64–66.[64] The wedding rituals (Chapter 67) became attached in the same way somewhat later. During the seventeenth century, the Long Version developed still further: an abridged subtype seems to have been particularly popular.

Sil'vestr thus assumes a relatively minor position as author/compiler of the "Epistle" and copyist of the *Domostroi*. This argument has several advantages over those that assign him a more active role. It explains, for example, why the *Domostroi* text shows little evidence of editing.[65] It accords with Sil'vestr's known skills as a copyist; he has left numerous volumes and, according to the "Epistle," ran workshops to train others in the copyist's art.[66] It matches—but this is more equivocal, for the *Domostroi* is itself a source—current theories about the place of the church in Muscovite culture, which preclude clerical participation in producing such a secular work. Last but not least, it explains why Sil'vestr's writing style—orthographically pure, grammatically precise, and heavily influenced by Slavonic—differs dramatically from the colloquial language found in much of the *Domostroi*, with its Muscovite dialect and echoes of the bureaucratese found in chancery documents.[67]

63. The Russian version is really excerpts from Basil's *Discourses on the Ascetical Life*; only the title comes from his "Admonition to the Young." See Chapter 17.

64. In MS 1380, the oldest copy to contain them, only the first sixty-three chapters form a unit; the others were written on separate quires at various times, all later than the original. The best description of this manuscript is Orlov, *Domostroi. Issledovanie*, pp. 26–47. (In Orlov's time, the manuscript was designated Moskovskogo Obshchestva Istorii i Drevnostei Rossiiskikh, otd. 1, No. 340.)

65. Pointed out first by Sokolova, *Ocherki*.

66. See, for example, the six books he left in the library of the Solovetskii Monastery (M. V. Kukushkina, "Biblioteka Solovetskogo monastyria v XVI v.," pt. 2 [*Arkheograficheskii ezhegodnik*, 1970], pp. 349, 351, 353). Sil'vestr gave many books to monasteries over the course of his career, but it is unclear how many, other than these six, came from his own hand or workshops.

67. For example, he distinguishes between aorist (simple past) and past perfect (now used as the only past tense in Russian, but in Slavonic mixed with a form of the verb "to be"; by the sixteenth century the modern form was already widely

As author of the "Epistle," and probable reader and copyist, Sil'vestr still merits attention, but for now, eliminating him as author brings us back to the third question raised at the beginning of this discussion: what information does the *Domostroi* itself provide about the person (or persons) who wrote it?

First, it was, almost certainly, written by a single person. With the exception of passages devoted to religious topics—which, following the standards of his time, the author would have copied from applicable sources—the text manifests throughout a single, consistent style.[68]

Second, this author was surely a man. The *Domostroi* addresses the married male head of a large household and on every occasion adopts the male point of view. Although much of the text concerns women's roles within the household, the author does not address women directly, but rather instructs men on what they can expect of their wives and daughters and how to ensure that the women in their lives conform to those expectations. Issues of importance only to women receive at best an abrupt dismissal. Muscovite women were not, in any case, sufficiently well educated to write books, but even if they had been, the content virtually eliminates any possibility of a female author.

Besides the gender of the author, the content of the *Domostroi* also reveals other details about him. He supported, for example, numerous children and servants, was wealthy, and lived in an urban environment. Although his property included gardens, orchards, stables, and animals (Chapters 45, 56), he bought on the market because he had few or no rural landholdings (Chapter 43). His wife moved in social circles in which she could expect to hear gossip about "princesses and boyars' wives," but she was clearly not their social equal (Chapter 34). The author presumes that his reader can write and keep written accounts, that he employs servants who can do the same (Chapters 52–

---

used). Some other works attributed to Sil'vestr, such as a letter to Prince A. B. Gorbatov-Shuiskii, demonstrate even greater command of Slavonic forms, including the difficult dative absolute, but I consider these attributions still unproven.

68. Sokolova (*Ocherki*) postulated a split between the first twenty-five chapters and the remainder. This idea can be dismissed, both because she studied the Long (latest) Version and because she failed to note that the difference corresponds to the shift from Slavonic, used in the religious section, to colloquial Russian. Sokolova did, however, effectively demolish earlier arguments for a division into three parts, proposed by I. S. Nekrasov ("Opyt").

54), that he has little interest in war but much in trade (Chapter 60), that he values thrift and self-sufficiency (Chapters 40–43). The author both believed in and observed the rituals of Orthodox Christianity (Chapters 2–3, 12–13). He had to pay taxes; he knew the procedures for borrowing and lending money (Chapter 62). He lived in a world where brides joined their new families before they finished growing (Chapter 31), where dowering one's daughters could cause serious financial strain (Chapter 16), where men and women lived largely separate lives (Chapter 34), and where servants might be slaves but were nonetheless entitled to support (Chapters 22, 28).

The trouble lies in finding someone to match these criteria. Boyars and gentry do not fit, for most sixteenth-century nobles could neither read nor write, and almost all spent their careers in the cavalry and owned rural estates that supplied them with food, soldiers, and horses. Hereditary nobility, too, probably needed no books to instruct them in running a household, for they (particularly the wives) acquired such skills from their parents. Merchants seem a little more promising, for successful merchants could rise quickly, if they were lucky and talented, and might find themselves in charge of a much larger household than their parents had trained them to administer. But those who actually did so were few in number, and even they seldom knew how to read and write.

Clerics, by contrast, had to show at least minimal literacy to qualify for ordination. Monks lived in large communities but did not marry or set up families; their "households," however similar in some ways, were organized around a different principle. Parish priests invariably had wives and usually children but often lacked economic resources.[69] In many cases, as well, parish priests had learned only enough to pass their ordination examination and were functionally illiterate, sometimes saying the rites purely by rote.[70] They, too, seldom held household on the scale described in the *Domostroi*.

Discounting peasants, artisans, and slaves—because they had neither need, education, nor resources—that leaves personnel from the chancery system. The chanceries did, on one hand, consistently employ literate urbanites, often skilled in commerce, who were married

69. Some priests, probably including Sil'vestr, ran commercial enterprises; they were exceptions to the rule of poverty among the married clergy.
70. See, for example, Gary J. Marker, "Primers and Literacy in Muscovy: A Taxonomic Investigation," *Russian Review* 48 (1989): 1–19.

as a matter of course, wealthy enough to support large households, eligible to own populated land, but without, for the most part, rural villages to supply their food. Because these men generally stayed out of the spotlight, little is known about their private lives; even speculation cannot fill the vacuum. On the other hand, the chancery system was very small at this time, perhaps no more than two hundred people in all ranks and offices. Still fewer of them (perhaps one or two) showed any literary skills.[71] Officials in the chanceries were not, moreover, subject to taxation (although they associated socially and professionally with people who were). So although chancery officials meet the criteria for authorship most closely, even they do not match the *Domostroi* exactly.

Perhaps the *Domostroi* did not originate in Russia at all. Someone—such as an official in the Foreign Office, which had most contact with foreigners—could have found it abroad and translated it for his personal library.[72] The *Domostroi* does manifest similarities in topic and style to Western domestic books, but it covers far more ground than most.[73] It does not quote verbatim from Western works, but it could descend from a now vanished predecessor. Books of this type were extremely numerous in the sixteenth century; many have received little or no scholarly attention, and still more can never be studied because all copies have disappeared. Borrowing without attribution, moreover, characterized domestic handbooks both within and across national borders—to the point that one must prove originality, not the reverse. But a clear link between the *Domostroi* and any other book of this type still awaits proof.

The authorship question, therefore, can be answered only in probabilities, with the most likely candidates an as yet unknown chancery

71. For example, Fedor Kuritsyn, a diplomat who has been credited with producing, among other works, *The Tale of Dracula*.

72. The descriptions of author and importer match, in many respects, the career of Sil'vestr's son Anfim who, through his contacts with Livonia and Poland-Lithuania, could have had access to one or more Western sources. In this case, the "Epistle" became attached by chance to a *Domostroi* already owned by Anfim. Not enough is known about him, however, to prove involvement on his part.

73. The closest Western equivalent, in style and breadth of material covered, is *Le Ménagier de Paris*, written by an elderly Parisian merchant for his fifteen-year-old wife sometime in the fourteenth century. This book, however (like the *Domostroi* itself), remained unpublished until the nineteenth century; even in manuscript, it existed in only a few copies; there seems to have been no way in which it could have influenced the *Domostroi*.

official, an unexpectedly literate merchant, or an unidentified foreigner. Although hardly satisfactory, for an author's social standing discloses much about the sources and the probable range of acceptance of his ideas, such an answer is unfortunately all too typical of sixteenth-century sources. The possibility of foreign authorship, in particular, raises the issue of whether, in fact, the *Domostroi* genuinely does reflect Russian culture. Fortunately, the extensive reworking to which people subjected the *Domostroi* in the 1560s and 1570s disposes of this objection. Although these people made no major changes in wording, they repeatedly went over the text, adding passages and rearranging where they felt necessary. It seems reasonable to assume that during this process anything glaringly inappropriate to Russian culture would have been weeded out, for only religious works were sacrosanct. What came down to the present, therefore, apparently met more or less with the editors' approval.

As with the author, information about the editors is limited, and the *Domostroi* itself again remains the only source. Still, some conclusions can be drawn.

The religious passages, both those borrowed from other sources and apparently original ones describing Russian customs, were added during the first two revisions. They point to editors familiar with the Gospels, the Pauline Epistles, and the *Prolog* (a collection of daily readings used in the Russian church)—most likely churchmen, but potentially any knowledgeable Orthodox Christian.[74] The diatribes speak of a secular author, a landowner or wealthy householder similar to the person who wrote the original text. The menus and wedding ceremonies likewise appeared in two stages; their authors demonstrate a greater appreciation for luxury, which suggests a more elevated social

74. Did many of these exist? Edward Keenan, for example, has argued that there were two, not one, literate cultures in Muscovy (*The Kurbskii-Groznyi Apocrypha: The Seventeenth-Century Genesis of the "Correspondence" Attributed to Prince A.M. Kurbskii and Tsar Ivan IV* [Cambridge, Mass.: Harvard University Press, 1971] and "Putting Kurbskii in His Place, or: Observations and Suggestions Concerning the Place of the 'History of the Grand Prince of Moscow' in the History of Muscovite Literary Culture," *Forschungen zur osteuropäischen Geschichte* 24 [1978]: 131–161). According to this argument, people who learned to read and write exclusively within the chancery system knew little about Slavonic literature, whereas the clergy knew little else. In the sixteenth century, however, there were some overlaps. Anfim, for example, learned to read from his father, who encouraged him (Chapter 64) to read the Scriptures and church literature; other priests' sons probably had similar experiences.

standing than that of others associated with the *Domostroi*—boyars, or more likely people writing on behalf of boyars.[75] The menus, which appeared first as a separate text and later attached themselves to the Long Version, probably have a foreign origin, for one is identified as "In perevod" ("Another translation") and the details throughout do not correspond exactly with Russian dietary customs of the period; although interesting, they have less to recommend them as examples of Muscovite practice.

Boyars, gentry, clergy, chancery personnel: within one generation, the *Domostroi* had attracted attention from all sectors of Muscovite high society. By 1575 at the latest, it had become a genuine mirror for this vanished world.

Readership

Readership, in the case of a text like the *Domostroi*, actually means people, primarily owners, who signed their names in those manuscripts that have survived to the present day. How many people read copies that have not survived or borrowed the extant manuscripts and returned them without noting the fact obviously cannot be determined or even estimated. Nor can we know how many people owned manuscripts and never opened them. Still, people who bothered to leave their names in the record—whether as copyists or in marginal notes—did demonstrate interest in the manuscript. Certainly anyone who copied the book by hand for his own use or the use of his family must have done so because he was interested in its contents. We can only assume that these last two groups were typical of people who read the *Domostroi*.

Those who signed copies of the *Domostroi* were a disparate group.[76] Information about the earliest owners is hard to find, but around 1675 the circle included the boyar Prince G. G. Romodanovskii, a famous general; several members of the Dement'ev family, relatively insignificant Moscow merchants; several members of the Iudin family, who began as merchants and worked their way up through the chancery system to merge with the gentry; various parish priests and the archimandrite of the Alexandrov Siiskii Monastery (in northern Russia).

75. See, for example, the descriptions of clothing: black fox fur hats, robes made from cloth-of-gold, and so on.
76. See Pouncy, "Origins," pp. 361–366; "*Domostroi* as a Source," pp. 267–284

Fifty years later, the group had lost little of its diversity: an icon painter, a family of priests fighting over ownership of the manuscript, country gentry, and a cheese merchant.

Besides the diversity, several things stand out about those who owned copies of the *Domostroi*. First, most were not monks, for books preserved in monasteries had the highest rates of survival and the least vulnerability to fire. Second, they did not (before 1675 or so) originate within social groups particularly known for conservatism, as sometimes suggested.[77] The older the manuscript, the more likely it was owned by a government servitor, either in the chanceries or the military service classes (that is, the nobility and gentry). Beginning in the last quarter of the seventeenth century, parish priests became more interested in the text. By the time of the Petrine reforms, the *Domostroi* represented an older way of life and thus probably did appeal to the more conservative elements of Russian society, but these came from various classes: even at the end of the eighteenth century the text still, for example, found favor among the provincial gentry.

Some *Domostroi* readers moved in influential circles. Of them all, though, we know most about the priest Sil'vestr and his son—in part because of the "Epistle" that became Chapter 64 of the Short Version. Sil'vestr's "Epistle" reveals the process of assimilation in action: much of it mirrors ideas presented in the *Domostroi*, but in a way integrated with Sil'vestr's life and philosophy. This is important for two reasons: (1) because it offers an example of how at least one reader, undeniably a mid-sixteenth-century Russian, incorporated the *Domostroi* into his own life, and (2) because Sil'vestr himself is a curious historical figure.

First, a word on Sil'vestr. This priest, who served at the Cathedral of the Annunciation in the Kremlin from at least 1545 to sometime between 1556 and 1560, has acquired a reputation out of all proportion to the evidence about him.[78] A combination of mistake, apparent forgery, and faulty attributions led to his identification as father-confessor to Ivan the Terrible,[79] which in turn won him acclaim as architect of

77. That is, the text was not favored by Old Ritualists (those who resisted Patriarch Nikon's reforms during the 1660s).

78. For the sources available on Sil'vestr, with an assessment of their reliability, see Pouncy, "*Domostroi* as a Source," pp. 207–266.

79. The mistake seems to have originated in the account books of the Solovetskii Monastery for 1570–1575 (TsGADA, f. 1201/1, no. 207, f. 157v.). Whoever composed the *History of Ivan IV* perpetuated the error.

the 1550s reforms and contributor to most of the major sources of the period (*Domostroi, Stoglav* [Code of the "Hundred Chapters" Church Council in 1551], 1550 Law Code, and the like).[80] This view is almost certainly exaggerated.[81]

Sil'vestr served as but one among many priests in the Annunciation Cathedral during the 1550s.[82] He may have had a personal relationship with the tsar (this can be neither proven nor disproven), but not as his confessor. He probably, as the "Epistle" states, came from the once-formidable merchant republic of Novgorod, by the sixteenth century firmly under Muscovite control, and seems to have specialized in art and commerce. He wrote a very fine hand (at least half a dozen of his signatures survive) and employed it copying numerous books which he donated to monasteries. He supervised the renovation of the Kremlin cathedrals after the great Moscow fire of 1547. He ran workshops to train icon painters, book copyists, and specialists in many other crafts, all connected with church building, ornamentation, and restoration. (Whether he began these workshops in connection with the renovations, or was chosen to direct the renovations because of the workshops, the sources do not say.) To staff the workshops, he bought people out of slavery, trained them, and set them free. This brought him great satisfaction. He wrote proudly to Anfim, "Now our domestic servants are all free; they live with us of their own free will." But except for this one departure from custom, Sil'vestr seems otherwise to have observed convention.

The only evidence that Sil'vestr participated personally in commercial activity comes from the "Epistle," where he says, "If anyone bought an item from me in good fellowship and genuinely did not like it, I would take it back and refund his money. . . . I was never duped

80. The longest list of works attributed to Sil'vestr can be found in D. P. Golokhvastov and Archimandrite Leonid, "Blagoveshchenskii ierei Sil'vestr i ego pisaniia," *Chteniia OIDR*, 1874, bk. 1:1–110.

81. It still appears in historical literature, despite the efforts of several scholars to debunk it. For examples of the latter, see Antony N. Grobovsky, *The "Chosen Council" of Ivan IV: A Reinterpretation* (Brooklyn, NY: Theo Gaus's Sons, 1969); I. I. Smirnov, *Ocherki politicheskoi istorii russkogo gosudarstva 30–50kh godov XVI veka* (Moscow-Leningrad, 1958); and Pouncy, "*Domostroi* as a Source," pp. 204–266.

82. Sil'vestr had reached Moscow by 1545/1546, because in that year he gave an *Oktoikh* (order of weekly church services) to the Chudov Monastery in Moscow (Russian State Library [GBL], sobr. Tikhonravova, No. 629). He left Moscow after 1555/1556, but probably before 1560; Anfim moved to Smolensk in 1561, but according to the "Epistle," he was still in Moscow when Sil'vestr retired.

or enticed in anything by anybody, nor were payments due me delayed, either in handicraft production or in trade." His son Anfim, however, was definitely involved in commerce. By 1549, Anfim was already involved in trade with Livonia (now Estonia and Latvia), lending hundreds of rubles to Livonian merchants. By the 1550s, Anfim had attained the rank of state secretary in the Treasury Department, collecting customs duties for Ivan the Terrible. In 1560 he moved to Smolensk, on the Polish border, where he worked with the staff of the military governor (*voevoda*) receiving foreign envoys. As a state secretary, he attended a national council (*zemskii sobor*) in 1566. What happened to him after that is a mystery. Even without knowing his whole story, however, one can easily see why Anfim might have found a work like the *Domostroi* useful, perhaps in managing the household he reportedly maintained on Nikol'skaia Street in Moscow.

Anfim's reaction to the *Domostroi* remains unknown. He may have read it, as a gift from his father, without necessarily accepting its provisions—or not have read it at all. Sil'vestr, however, explicitly endorses the values expressed in the *Domostroi* by using its tenets in his "Epistle," the stated purpose of which was to provide a written substitute for his daily paternal presence. Compiled from several sources just before his departure from Moscow—that is, sometime between 1555/1556 and 1560—the "Epistle" nevertheless communicates Sil'vestr's personal values, for the priest himself selected the material.[83] In many respects, these values match the worldview proclaimed in the *Domostroi*.

Sil'vestr's views on the reciprocal obligations of parents and children, for example—as well as the proper roles of husbands and wives, the training of servants, the most desirable behavior toward guests and merchants, the evils of drunkenness, and the Christian's responsibilities toward his church and the poor—duplicate those expressed elsewhere in the *Domostroi*, although he demonstrates an unabashed affection for his son of which ben Sirach, at least, would not approve.[84]

83. Among other sources, he used Xenophon's *Admonition to My Two Sons* (published in Slavonic translation in *Izbornik 1076 g.* [Moscow, 1965], pp. 475–481).

84. In the opening sentences of the "Epistle," for example, he addresses Anfim as "my dear sweet child" and "my beloved only son." Compare to ben Sirach: "Pamper a boy and he will shock you; play with him and he will grieve you. Do not share his laughter, for fear of sharing his pain" (Ecclesiasticus 30:9–10).

The only major break between the "Epistle" and the rest of the *Domostroi* occurs in their views toward slavery; here Sil'vestr, not his fellow author, fell out of step with his times. The "Epistle" has a more personal tone than the other chapters, supplementing general moral advice with anecdotes; in this, too, it is unusual among documents created in the sixteenth century. In relation to the *Domostroi*, however, its importance lies in its confirmation that these values, regardless of their social or national origin, genuinely appealed to Muscovites.

Significance

Clearly, the *Domostroi* affected Sil'vestr. Many others, of various stations, also found it an important source of ideas on family life and organization. The impact of the *Domostroi* has, nonetheless, been somewhat exaggerated. Nineteenth-century scholars once confidently spoke of a *domostroinaia Rus'*, a pre-Petrine golden age when Muscovite civilization flowered free of Western influences. This seems unlikely. The *Domostroi* was inaccessible to the vast majority of the population (peasants, artisans, slaves) who could not read it and had no use for it.

This limitation in itself, however, does not invalidate the *Domostroi* as a source, any more than it invalidates *The Canterbury Tales* to say that most fourteenth-century Englishmen could not read them. The sixteenth-century Muscovites who encountered the *Domostroi* were the policy makers, the trendsetters, and the cultural determinists of their time. In this sense, the text had far more importance than sheer numbers of readers could impart.

The *Domostroi* reveals that, at least through the end of the sixteenth century, the elites remained very concrete in their thinking. Traditional Christian ethics influenced them greatly; no traces of secularism surface here. Ritualism, however—numerous arguments to the contrary notwithstanding—does not predominate: the theology is simplistic, without discussions of dogma or theoretical exegeses, but it does take precedence over purely ritualistic concerns.[85] This adherence to traditional (that is, medieval) Christianity manifests itself also in a hierarchical concept of society, similar to but not as elaborate as the

---

85. The great nineteenth-century historian V. O. Kliuchevskii, among others, saw Muscovy as ritualistic. See *A Course in Russian History: The Seventeenth Century*, trans. Natalie Dunnington, intro. Alfred J. Rieber (New York, Quadrangle, 1968), pp. 307–320.

Western Great Chain of Being, and in the denigration of women, which, although minor compared to the misogynistic diatribes produced by monks, elevates the male head of household to a kind of kingship within the family.

The influence of the church appears in some unexpected places. Medicine, for example, is evaluated entirely in spiritual terms: God sends illness as punishment for sin, so healing must come through prayer and ritual. The text barely mentions doctors, although some had reached Muscovy by then (for example, Eleazar Bomelius, a physician with a checkered past, had Ivan the Terrible as a patient before his ill-advised attempt to leave the country led to his execution by that far from forgiving prince). Herbal medicine, the only healing available to the general population—and probably more effective than the imported kind, still appallingly primitive in the sixteenth century—had associations with sorcery and therefore earned condemnation from the church, although Western herbals and medical manuals, too, began to appear in translation during this time. In this, the *Domostroi* was probably behind the times, but it reflected official ideology.

Even more telling is the reluctance of the *Domostroi*'s author to leave anything to chance. When he discusses washing dishes, he lists each item by name. When he describes storing fabrics, he names each fabric. In this he offers a perfect example of the bureaucratic mind in action.

The *Domostroi* demonstrates some specifically Muscovite concerns, as well as some typical of the European nobility of the time. Most of the former, such as female seclusion and slavery, have been discussed above. The latter include the emphasis on dishonor, which the author considers sufficiently appalling that fear of it can deter sin, the stress on almsgiving, and the value placed on conspicuous consumption as evidence of one's generosity of spirit. The *Domostroi* deplores this last (more evidence that the text did not arise in the highest social circles), except in the wedding rituals, which explicitly endorse it.[86] Although the text flies in the face of Russian practice when it recommends thrift and careful accounting, it offsets this advice by repeated encouragement to feed the poor, give alms to the churches, and provide adequate support to dependent members of the household.[87] Since he sought

86. See, for example, the last ritual, which advises people of lesser means on how to appear richer than they are.
87. This has sometimes been described as a "bourgeois" ethic, see, for example: Charles Halperin, "Master and Man in Muscovy," introduction to A. E. Presniakov,

to form ideals, not reflect reality, the author may, of course, have felt comfortable with both, in the way that politicians promise to balance the budget while they eliminate poverty.

On a more mundane note, the *Domostroi* reminds us how great and how complex were the problems of domestic management in the days before small families and household appliances made them routine. The planning, the organization, the quantity and variety of supplies, the number of people involved, the amount of storage required, the time taken even for apparently simple tasks like laundry—all make it clear why many men and almost all women did little else with their time.

Finally, the *Domostroi* had an impact far beyond its time. That *domostroinaia Rus'* may have existed primarily in the thoughts of nineteenth-century historians and philosophers, but it influenced them nonetheless. When Westernizers condemned and Slavophiles yearned for a Russia free of Peter's innovations, the *Domostroi* lay at the back of their minds. Some called it backward, reactionary, conservative—as it was, for them, but not for its own time. Some applauded its "organic" glorification of family and religious values, not considering that the *Domostroi*, too, may have crossed Muscovite borders at one time. Even today, when conservatives look back to a vision of Old Russia as a harmonious community of the faithful—autocratic but not oppressive, preserving tradition, free from foreign contamination, placing family above politics—the world of the *Domostroi* (as they understand it) is what they see. In this sense, the sixteenth century seems quite close after all.

The Translation

The present translation draws primarily on Short Version manuscript GPB, Q.XVII.149, published by A. S. Orlov as *Domostroi po Konshinskomu spisku i podobnym* (Moscow, 1908–1910; reprint, The Hague:

The Tsardom of Muscovy (Gulf Breeze, Fla.: Academic International Press, 1978), p. xvi. Compared to the limited interest in estate matters characteristic of Russian nobles, it is. But others have found evidence of similar views among, for example, provincial French nobles, who could not by any stretch of the imagination be described as "bourgeois" (Robert Forster, "The Provincial Noble: A Reappraisal," *American Historical Review* 68 [1962–1963]: 681–691). Since sixteenth-century Russians show no other evidence of developing a "bourgeois" mentality (whatever that may be), it probably reflects no more than the recognition of limited resources.

Europe Printing, 1966). The chapters are arranged in the order used in that manuscript. Some material, both whole chapters and parts of chapters, has been added from later versions of the text. The additions were translated from TsGADA, f. 188, No. 1380 (the oldest example of the Long Version), published by I. E. Zabelin as *Domostroi po spisku Imperatorskogo Obshchestva Istorii i Drevnostei Rossiiskikh [Domostroi OIDR]* (Moscow, 1882; reprint, Letchworth, Herts.: Bradda Books, 1971). The added chapters are listed in italics in the Contents and are identified in the text by a footnote at the beginning of the chapter. Other added passages are enclosed in {braces} to distinguish them from editorial insertions, which are indicated by standard [brackets].

The Contents applies to this reading version of the *Domostroi*; the original tables of contents for the Short and Long versions are given in the Appendix. (The Preface and Chapters 64–67, though found in the Long Version, are not included in its table of contents.)

Russian words have been translated wherever possible. Technical historical terms are given generally accepted English equivalents, with the Russian word provided in parentheses the first time it is used. Where no English equivalent exists, the word remains in the original Russian with definitions in notes and glossary.

Biblical passages come from *The New English Bible with the Apocrypha*, 2d ed. (New York: Oxford University Press, 1970). We do not know which specific biblical manuscripts were used in compiling the *Domostroi* (indeed, at times the author seems to be quoting from memory), but he does quote extensively from the Old Testament Apocrypha, which are accepted as canonical by the Orthodox church and included in the *New English Bible*. Where other, older versions of the Bible provide more exact parallels to the wording in the *Domostroi*, references appear in the notes. I have also added bracketed references to chapter and verse, not supplied in the original. Unless noted otherwise, and with the exception of biblical quotations, all translations are my own.

Throughout, I use the Library of Congress transliteration system. Spelling has been modernized and the hard sign omitted from the ends of masculine nouns. Names present special problems because some historical figures are generally known by Westernized names; others are not. For the most part, names are transliterated, not translated: for example, Ivan IV, not John IV; Nikon, not Nicon. Where the person referred to is not Russian, however, or where a standard Western name exists, I have used the more recognizable form: St. Nicholas, not Nikolai; Alexander Nevsky, not Aleksandr Nevskii; Sergius of Radonezh, not Sergei. For simplicity, female names ending in "-iia" are transliterated "-ia": hence, Anastasia, not Anastasiia.

Finally, a note on the use of "he" and "his" throughout the text: the structure of the *Domostroi* indicates that it was written by a man for other men, during a time when women's roles were strictly limited to the private sphere. Wherever the original Russian suggests the possibility that women may be included in indefinite phrases like "someone, anyone," I used plurals in the translation. Remaining "sexist language" reflects the prejudices of the sixteenth-century author.

T H E

DOMOSTROI

Contents

Most material is taken from the Short Version of the *Domostroi*; titles given in *italics* indicate material from other versions. The original tables of contents are given in the Appendix.

Preface

This is an admonition and instruction of father-confessors to all Orthodox Christians. It tells you how you must believe in the Holy Trinity, the Immaculate Mother of God, Christ's cross, and the heavenly powers and must make obeisance to holy relics and all other holy objects. It tells you to honor the tsar, his princes, and boyars.[1] For the apostle says:

> Discharge your obligations to all men; pay tax and toll,[2] reverence and respect, to those to whom they are due. [Romans 13:7]
> But if you are doing wrong, then you will have cause to fear them; it is not for nothing that they hold the power of the sword [Romans 13:4]
> You wish to have no fear of the authorities? Then continue to do right and you will have their approval [Romans 13:3]

The Preface is added from the Long Version of the *Domostroi*.

1. Boyar (*boiarin*, pl. *boiare*): officially, one of a small group of men chosen from among the heads of the oldest princely and nontitled service families to act as the tsar's closest counselors. There were about forty of these in the mid-sixteenth century. More generally, any senior male from these old and very elite families. There is no exact English equivalent to boyar. On the boyars, see Kollmann, *Kinship and Politics*, and Crummey, *Aristocrats and Servitors*.

2. The *Domostroi* has "*urok, urok*" (a lesson where a lesson is due) instead of the usual "*obrok, obrok.*" *Obrok*, here translated as "tax," is a rent paid in cash or kind.

62

That is why you are obliged to submit. It is an obligation imposed not merely by fear of retribution but by conscience. [Romans 13:5]

Then you will be a chosen vessel and will carry the King's name in your heart.[3] This book also tells you how you must honor bishops, priests, and monks. You should take advantage of their services, asking them for prayers to bless your house and seeking their advice on all issues, both sacred and profane. You should pay diligent attention to your confessors also, heeding their admonitions as though they came from God's own lips. Herein you will also find someone's discourse on secular life, how Orthodox Christians should conduct themselves in the world and with their wives, children, and servants.[4] You will learn how you should teach them and punish them, saving them with fear and weakening their resistance with dread.[5] You should watch over them always, that they may be pure both spiritually and corporally. You yourself should be their guard in all matters, and should worry about them as about your own limbs. For the Lord says, "The two shall become one flesh." [Matthew 19:5; Mark 10:8]. And the apostle says, "If one organ suffers, they all suffer." [1 Corinthians 12:26]. Therefore, you must worry not only about yourself, but about your wife, your children, your relatives, unto the least of your servants. For all are united by a single love of God, and by means of this good diligence of yours. Love all those who live according to God. You will be the eye of the heart, looking toward God. You will be a chosen vessel, bringing not only your own self to God but many.[6] And you will hear, as though in your own voice, the joyful cry of the good and faithful servant.[7]

3. A reference to Acts 9:15: "But the Lord said to him, 'You must go, for this man is my chosen instrument [King James version: "a chosen vessel"] to bring my name before the nations and their kings, and before the people of Israel.' "

4. *Domochadtsy*. The Russian word means "bondsman" or "slave."

5. Dread: *groza*. This Russian word means "thunderstorm," and by extension the awe-inspiring and unpredictable power of a strong ruler. Its best-known application is to Ivan IV, known in English as "the Terrible" (i.e., he who inspires terror). *Groznyi* has a positive connotation that the English equivalent has lost.

6. Another reference to Acts 9:15.

7. Reference to the parable of the ten talents (Matthew 25:14–30).

In addition, you will find in this book a treatise on domestic management, how to instruct your wife and children and servants, how to have in stock all necessary supplies—bread and meat, fish and vegetables—and how to keep order in the household, again, as among the heretics.[8] In all, you will find sixty-seven chapters.[9]

8. Probably Roman Catholics, as Russian heretics in the sixteenth century were neither numerous nor organized enough to be writing domestic literature.

9. Originally, the manuscript said "sixty-three chapters"; the 3 was scratched out and replaced by a 7, presumably when the last four chapters (written on separate quires in the oldest manuscript) were added to the book.

1. A Father's Instruction to His Son

I, sinful N., bless, teach, admonish, and instruct my son N., his wife,[1] their children, and domestic servants to live according to every Christian law and in all pure conscience and justice. Do God's will faithfully and keep His commandments. Always live lawfully, fearing God. Teach your wife to do this also. Admonish your servants—not with blows or hard labor, but by keeping them, like children, rested, well-fed and clothed, in a warm house, and under good governance.

I give you this work on the Christian life as a reminder, to instruct you and your children. If you do not heed my work, if you disobey our commands,[2] if you do not live according to these precepts or act on these recommendations, you will answer for yourselves on Judgment Day. I will not share in your guilt and sin, but will answer only for my own soul, for I have blessed, wept, prayed, and taught on this subject in all modesty and have offered you this work.

But if you accept this poor teaching and my crude instruction, then you need but say these things in prayer. Worship, and invite others to come to God for help; kiss the holy relics with faith and worship them.

1. In two seventeenth-century manuscripts (GPB, Sobr. Pogodina, No. 1137 and GIM, Sobr. Zabelina, No. 446), the names of the Annunciation Cathedral priest Sil'vestr, his son Anfim, and Anfim's wife, Pelageia, appear in place of the "N." On Sil'vestr as author of the *Domostroi*, see the Introduction.

2. It is unclear whom the author means by "our." Himself and his wife? Himself and the author of the rest of the work?

2. How Christians Should Believe in the Holy Trinity, the Immaculate Mother of God, the Cross of Christ, the Holy Heavenly Powers, and All Holy Relics, and Must Worship Them

Every Christian must know how to live according to God in the Orthodox Christian faith.[1a] To do this, you must first believe with your whole soul in Father, Son, and Holy Ghost, united in the Indivisible Trinity. Believe also in the incarnation of our Lord Jesus Christ, Son of God. Call on the mother who bore Him, the Virgin. Worship Christ's cross faithfully, for on it the Lord brought salvation to everyone. Honor the icons of Christ and His most holy Mother and of the heavenly powers and of all the saints, as you would offer love to your own.

3. How One Should Partake of the Divine Sacraments, Believe in the Resurrection of the Dead, Prepare for Judgment Day, and Treat Holy Objects

Believe in the divine sacraments;[1b] believe in His Blood and His Body. Partake of communion with fear. It brings about the purification and

---

1a. As I. S. Nekrasov noted long ago ("Opyt istoriko-literaturnogo issledovaniia o proiskhozhdenii drevnerusskogo Domostroia," *Chteniia OIDR*, 1872, bk. 3, pp. 102–118), this and the three following chapters draw to a small extent on the *Hundred Points* (*Stoslov*) by pseudo-Gennadius, a short moral treatise widely disseminated in medieval Russia. The parallels are exact where they occur, but the *Domostroi* elaborates considerably on the older work. For an overview of Gennadius's work, including examples, see Fedotov, *The Russian Religious Mind*, vol. I, p. 1:204–209.

1b. In the Orthodox church, these are called the "mysteries." The second part of this sentence refers to the Eucharist, greatest of the sacraments, during which the Orthodox, like Catholics, believe that bread and wine are miraculously transformed into Christ's body and blood. (Protestants hold that the bread and wine symbolize Christ's body and blood.) A good description of the Orthodox sacraments for non-Orthodox is Ware, *Orthodox Church*, pp. 281–303.

consecration of your soul, and of your body also, the remission of sins and eternal life. Believe in the resurrection of the dead and in life after death. Remember Judgment Day, when we shall be rewarded according to our deeds. Whenever you are spiritually clean, having achieved a pure conscience through prayer and petition,[2] you may kiss the life-giving cross, the holy, revered, miracle-working icons, and the healing relics. This is how you should touch them. First pray and cross yourself, then kiss the cross; hold your breath and do not part your lips.

God is well-disposed toward him who shares Christ's divine communion. Take the bread carefully from the priest's spoon into your mouth.[3] Do not snap at it with your lips, but take it in your hand and touch it to your chest like a Christian. Eat the communion bread and any holy food carefully. Do not drop the crumbs on the floor, nor chew the communion bread with your teeth as though it were ordinary bread.[4] Breaking off small pieces, put each in your mouth; eat it with your lips. Do not chew it; eat it carefully. You should not drink just any liquid with the bread; you may sip water or add dill to consecrated wine or eat it by itself, but use nothing else. Finish the communion bread before starting any other food, whether you are at church or at home. Do not drink commemorative beer with the bread, nor add it to frumenty for your evening meal.[5]

If you kiss someone in Christ's name, you should kiss him or her holding your breath, without sputtering. Remember human weakness:

---

2. See Hebrews 10:22, on partaking of communion: "Let us make our approach in sincerity of heart and full assurance of faith, our guilty hearts sprinkled clean, our bodies washed with pure water." In the medieval Russian Orthodox church, parishioners rarely achieved this state. Once-yearly communion was usual, and penances could exclude parishioners for years. See, for example, the additions to Chapter 23 and Levin, *Sex and Society*, pp. 140–142 and passim.

3. The Orthodox church, like the Protestant churches, uses leavened bread in its communion services. The bread is prepared by special bakers, usually widows who have had only one husband (based on 1 Timothy 5:9), and is offered by the priest to each communicant with a spoon. See Ware, *Orthodox Church*, p. 294.

4. Unlike Catholic wafers, the bread used in Orthodox services will not simply dissolve in the mouth; however, it cannot be chewed because to believers it has become, literally, the body of Christ—hence the special instructions.

5. Commemorative beer (*kanun/kanon*), frumenty (*kut'ia*): Special food and drink used in the Russian church for commemoration of the dead and church festivals. Frumenty is porridge mixed with fruit and spices; *kanun*, usually, beer mixed with mead or honey. These foods had their origins in pagan ancestor worship so the church at best accepted them reluctantly and at times condemned their use.

we disdain the uncouth spirit of garlic, intoxication, sickness, and all such odors. How foul must our stink be to God! Because of this, we must always be careful in how we act.

4. How One Should Love God with One's Whole Heart, and One's Brother Also. How One Should Fear God and Remember Death

" . . . and you must love the Lord your God with all your heart and soul and strength" [Deuteronomy 6:5, quoted in Matthew 22:37 and Luke 10:27]. You must fashion all your deeds, customs, and mores in a manner pleasing to our Lord. Likewise, love your neighbor who is made in the image of God—that is, every Christian.[1]

Always fear God in your heart and remember death. Always do the will of God and "walk according to His commandments."[2] For the Lord said, "I judge as I am bidden" [John 5:30]. Therefore every Christian must be prepared—through good deeds, chastity, repentance, and full confession—for the hour of death.

{On the same subject:[3] Love the Lord with your whole soul, and fear Him in your heart. Be righteous, honest, and humble. Turn your eyes toward the abyss, but your mind to the heavens.[4] Be loving toward God and affable to others. Comfort the grief-stricken. Be patient in misfortune, not fretful. Be generous and compassionate toward everyone. Become a person who feeds the poor and accepts the stranger,

1. A reference to Matthew 22:39 (the "Golden Rule") and Luke 10:27 (parable of the Good Samaritan).

2. In older translations of the Bible, such as the Douai Bible, this phrase directly quotes 2 John 1:6. The *New English Bible*, however, offers a slightly different, less poetic translation: "Let us love one another. And love means following the commands of God."

3. This passage seems to be based on the works of St. Basil of Caesaria. It resembles, for example, selections from his sermon "On Humility" (*Ascetical Works*, trans. Sister M. Monica Wagner, The Fathers of the Church, vol. 9 [Washington, D.C.: Catholic University of America Press, 1962], pp. 484–485.) Note also the resemblance to St. Basil's "Admonition to the Young," added to Chapter 17.

4. An Orthodox cliché, used twice elsewhere in the *Domostroi*, always in passages added to the original text, although not all the passages that use it were added at the same time.

who suffers for his sins but rejoices in God. Refrain from drunkenness and gluttony.[5] Be gentle, loving neither glory nor gold, but others. Do not be proud. Be fearful before the tsar, ready to serve him. Answer him softly. Pray often. Be wise. Labor for God, and judge no one. Defend the oppressed. Do not be hypocritical. Be a child of the Gospel, a son of the Resurrection, and one who will inherit the life hereafter, in Jesus Christ our Lord, may glory be unto Him forever.}

5. How One Should Revere Bishops, Priests, and Monks {and Use Their Help to Heal One of All Spiritual and Physical Ills}

Always approach bishops eagerly and offer them the honor that is their due. Request a blessing from them and instruction in spiritual matters. Fall at their feet and obey them in everything, as God commanded.

Be faithful, loving, and obedient when priests and monks command you. Submit to them completely. Pay heed when they offer spiritual help. {Inquire of them, without shame, if you do not understand something, or need spiritual counsel, or wonder whether something is a sin. If you are ever visited by some spiritual or physical scourge—an ache, a disease, fire, flood, theft, armed robbery, the tsar's condemnation,[1] a superior's wrath, if you are imprisoned or slandered, if sales are poor or you cannot find anything to trade—do not despair. Remember that you too have sinned before God and man. Weep hot tears to the compassionate King, the Immaculate Mother of God, and all the saints.[2] Run to the storm-free harbor, to these spiritual instruc-

5. The literal translation of this passage is "Thirst from drunkenness and hunger from gluttony," a neat parallel that cannot be captured in English. The phrase is also found in a letter to Prince Aleksandr Borisovich [Gorbatov-Shuiskii] (Golokhvastov and Leonid, "Blagoveshchenskii ierei Sil'vestr," p. 88), also attributed to Sil'vestr.

1. *Opala*: a punishment inflicted on unruly servitors by the tsar. Until released from his disgrace, the servitor would grow his hair as a visible symbol of his banishment from the royal presence (the sovereign's "bright eyes").

2. The ability to produce copious tears was considered a special sign of sanctity in the medieval Orthodox church.

tors. Confess your sinfulness and agony with love, with tears, and with tenderness of heart. They [the priests] can heal you of your ills and offer spiritual help. Fulfill the penances that they enjoin, as examples of divine correction.} For these are the servants and petitioners of the Heavenly King.[3] They have license from the Lord to ask for good and profitable things for our souls, for the remission of sins, and for eternal life.[4]

6. How One Should Visit Monasteries, Hospitals, Prisons, and the Unfortunate

Visit monasteries and hospitals, those living in the wilderness, and those incarcerated in prisons. Give alms (in accord with your means) to the needy, as much as they require. Care for them in their poverty and sorrow. Help them as much as possible. Do not neglect any unfortunate, troubled, needy, or poor person. Bring the poor into your home, offer them food and drink, warm them with clothing, giving with love and a pure conscience. By these things you do the work of the merciful God and will receive absolution.

When your parents die, make an offering to the church in memory of them and hold a feast for them in your home.

Treat the poor with compassion and you yourself will be remembered by God.[1]

3. There are echoes here of the Slavonic exhortation to confession, quoted in Ware, *Orthodox Church*, p. 296: "Therefore be not ashamed or afraid; conceal nothing from me, but tell me without hesitation everything that you have done, and so you shall have pardon from Our Lord Jesus Christ....I am but a witness, bearing testimony before Him of all the things which you have to say to me.... Take heed, therefore, lest having come to a physician you depart unhealed."

4. A reference to the Aitesis, sung during vespers and lauds. The priest chants: "For the forgiveness and remission of our sins and offenses, let us ask the Lord. ... For what is good and profitable to our souls, and for peace in the world, let us ask the Lord." See Archbishop Joseph Raya and Baron José de Vinck, eds., comps. and trans., *Byzantine Daily Worship* (Allendale, N.J.: Alleluia Press, 1969), pp. 52 and 196.

1. A reference to Ecclesiasticus 4:10: "Be a father to orphans and like a husband to their mother; then the Most High will call you his son, and his love for you will be greater than a mother's."

7. How One Should Honor Tsars and Princes, Obey Them in Everything, and Serve Faithfully. How to Act Toward All People—Whether Great or Small, Unfortunate, and Weak. How One Should Keep Watch Over Oneself

Fear the tsar and serve him faithfully.[1] Always pray to God for his health. Do not say anything false to him, but tell him the truth, deferentially, as though you spoke to God Himself. Obey the tsar in all things. If you serve the earthly king righteously and fear him, you will learn to fear the Heavenly King also. This ruler is temporary, but the heavenly one is eternal; He, the impartial judge, rewards each according to his deeds.

In the same way submit yourself to a prince and give him the honor due him. "[F]or they are God's agents of punishment, for retribution on the offender" [Romans 13:4], showering approval on those who do good [paraphrase of Romans 13:3].

Love your prince and your superiors with your whole heart. Do not think evil against them, for the Apostle Paul says,

> Every person must submit to the supreme authorities. There is no authority but by act of God, and the existing authorities are instituted by him; consequently anyone who rebels against authority is resisting a divine institution. [Romans 13:1–2]

The Lord will destroy all those speaking falsely, slanderously, or deceitfully to the tsar, a prince, or any boyar.[2] Rumormongers and slanderers are damned among men.

---

1. Even when not quoting directly, most of this chapter is paraphrased from the Pauline Epistles. See, for example, Romans 12:9–14:13, Ephesians 5:25–32, and 1 Thessalonians 5:12–23.

2. A reference to Psalm 12:2–3: "One man lies to another: they talk with smooth lip and double heart. May the Lord make an end of such smooth lips and the tongue that talks so boastfully!" Orthodox and Catholic Bibles do not always number chapter and verse in the same way as Protestant Bibles, especially in the Psalter. Numbers given here follow the *New English Bible*.

"Fine shirts, shifts, and robes . . . of brocade and taffeta, . . . cloth-of-gold, silk, white and red cloth, feathers, fur, ribbons . . . " (Chapter 31). Boyar dress was rich, elaborate, and liberally decorated, illustrating the boyars' position at the top of the social order. Here several styles of male and female dress are shown. Note the contrasting plainness of the priest's and servant's clothes. From Adam Olearius, *Vermehrte Moscowitische und Persianische Reisebeschreibung* (Schleszwig, 1656). Courtesy of the Princeton University Library, Department of Rare Books and Special Collections.

Give honor to those older than yourself and make obeisance to them. Honor those equal to yourself as brothers and greet the poor with love. Love those younger than yourself like children.[3]

Do not act falsely toward any part of God's creation. "Do not set your hearts on the godless world or anything in it" [1 John 2:15], but ask God for eternal blessings. Bear every sorrow and trial with gratitude.[4] Do not revenge yourself upon those who offend you. Pray for

3. This paragraph is an extension of 1 Timothy 5:1: "Never be harsh with an elder; appeal to him as if he were your father. Treat the younger men as brothers, the older women as mothers, and the younger as your sisters, in all purity."

4. A reference to James 1:2–3: "My brothers, whenever you have to face trials of many kinds, count yourselves supremely happy, in the knowledge that such testing of your faith breeds fortitude."

blasphemers. Do not render evil for evil.[5] Do not judge those who sin; remember your own sins, worry a lot about these.[6] Turn away from the advice of wicked men; associate with the righteous, write down their deeds in your heart and act as they do.

8. How One Should Decorate One's Home with Holy Icons and Keep a Clean House

Every Christian should put holy and venerable pictures, icons painted according to the church's rules,[1] on the walls of every room. These icons should be arranged and decorated beautifully. Place candles in candelabra before the holy images during every service.

When the service is done, extinguish the candles and cover all the icons with veils to ensure cleanliness, promote piety, and protect them from dust.

Always dust icons with a feather duster and wipe them with a soft sponge. Always keep the shrine clean.

When you go to touch the holy images make sure you are worthy— that is, pure in conscience.

While glorifying God, during the holy service and during prayers, light candles and burn sweet-smelling frankincense and incense. Set up the holy icons according to the Rule.[2]

5. This and the two preceding sentences refer to Romans 12:17–19. The concept of not rendering evil for evil, in particular, has a long biblical heritage. See, for example, Proverbs 20:22: "Do not think to repay evil for evil, wait for the Lord to deliver you."

6. A reference to Romans 14:10 (a concept repeatedly expressed by St. Paul): "You, sir, why do you pass judgement on your brother? And you, sir, why do you hold your brother in contempt? We shall all stand before God's tribunal." Jesus expressed similar sentiments in Matthew 7:1–6 and Luke 6:37–38, 41–42.

1. Orthodox Christians worship icons not for themselves but as symbols of the heavenly beings they represent. Because the images serve a divine purpose, the church strictly controls the forms and subjects considered suitable for depiction in icons. In this way, it seeks to limit the imposition of human individuality on the divine forms. Icons painted "not in accordance with the rules" are banned, and those who create or use them can be charged with heresy. The injunction is standard but had particular relevance at the time of the Domostroi's probable composition: see the references to the "Viskovatyi Affair" in the Introduction (note 32).

2. That is, according to the rank assigned each figure by the Orthodox church

The saints will feel honored when you treat their icons in this manner. You must always so revere them—during prayer, vigils, worship, and any other divine service, confessing, pleading with tears and a contrite heart, for the remission of your sins.

9. How One Should Make an Offering to Churches and Monasteries

You should always visit God's churches faithfully, bringing an offering, a candle, communion bread, incense and frankincense, commemorative beer, frumenty, and alms. When you need to pray for health or the repose of your soul, or on a holy day, visit monasteries also, bringing alms and an offering.

When you bring your gift to the altar, remember the words of the Gospel: If, when you are bringing your gift to the altar, you suddenly remember that your brother has a grievance against you, leave your gift where it is before the altar. First go and make your peace with your brother, and only then come back and offer your gift. [Matthew 5:23–24]

Bring your gift to God, as long as it is legitimately your property, for alms acquired through injustice are unacceptable. To the strong it was said, "If you give alms to the poor after you have despoiled them of their goods, it were better for you neither to have taken nor given."[1]

Give back to those who were wronged that which you took from them; that is better than alms. But alms from a righteous man, achieved with hard work and good deeds, are pleasing to God.

---

and used, for example, in arranging icons in an iconostasis. On the use and arrangement of icons during Orthodox services, see Ware, *Orthodox Church*, pp. 276–278.

1. St. Basil of Caesaria, "On Mercy and Justice," *Ascetical Works*, p. 509. Biblical precedents include Ecclesiasticus 34:18–20.

10. How One Should Invite Priests and Monks to One's House to Pray

On holy days, depending on who is present, let those in charge invite priests (as many as they can afford) into the home. The priests will complete the ritual appropriate to the occasion. They will pray for the tsar and grand prince N., autocrat of all the Russias, for his tsaritsa and grand princess N.,[1] for their royal children, for the boyars, and the whole army of Christians, for its victory over enemies and for the freedom of those imprisoned, for bishops, priests, and monks, for all Christians, and for all that is profitable for the man of the house, his wife, children, and servants.[2] If asked, they will sanctify water with the life-giving cross, with miracle-working icons, and with holy relics. For a sick person they will also consecrate oil to bring health and healing.[3]

When a sick person is in the house, let the homeowner invite seven or more priests and as many deacons as he can find. They will pray over commemorative beer for health and over frumenty to bring peace of mind. After someone departs this life, the priest or deacon will cense every room, sprinkling it with holy water and making the sign of the cross. Then those in the house, praising God according to the divine liturgy, should at once set up a table so that the priests and monks, along with the rest of the guests and the neighborhood poor, may eat and drink. Then all, contented and replete, will go to their homes praising God.

1. In one manuscript (GIM, Sobr. Zabelina, No. 446), the names "Ivan Vasil'-evich" and "Anastasia" appear in place of the "N." for tsar and tsaritsa. These names refer to Ivan IV the Terrible and his first wife, who were married from 1547 until her death in 1560, and may offer a clue to the date of the *Domostroi's* composition.

2. A reference to the Ecumenic Prayer and the Litany of Peace, spoken during the Divine Office (vespers, matins, and the canonical hours). See Raya and Vinck, comps. and trans., *Byzantine Daily Worship*, pp. 42, 50, 160, and 194–195, for a more contemporary version of this prayer.

3. In the Roman Catholic church, this sacrament became known as "extreme unction" and is limited to the dying. The more comprehensive Orthodox version, offered to any ill person, is described in Ware, *Orthodox Church*, pp. 302–303.

It is up to the master of the house or his representatives to offer someone food or drink or to send something to another's table according to the recipient's worth or rank or the quality of his counsel. All such decisions belong to the master and not to others. If, out of affection or in response to some service that has been rendered, someone who is not in charge feels he should give food and drink to another, he may do so if he later pleads his master's forgiveness for it. But to take food or drink secretly from the table or sideboard or to send it without the master's permission or blessing is blasphemy and self-worship; those who do it dishonor everything.

> When you are asked by someone to a wedding-feast, do not sit down in the place of honour. It may be that some person more distinguished than yourself has been invited; and the host will come and say to you, "Give this man your seat." Then you will look foolish as you begin to take the lowest place. No, when you receive an invitation, go and sit down in the lowest place, so that when your host comes he will say, "Come up higher, my friend." Then all your fellow-guests will see the respect in which you are held. For everyone who exalts himself will be humbled, and whoever humbles himself will be exalted. [Luke 14:8–11]

When many dishes are placed before you, do not immediately begin to eat, lest someone more honored than you has been invited. If you know your status is highest, you may begin, but you should take note of how much food is offered. At the homes of some devout people, food and drink are plentiful, and their guests can partake fully; with others you should eat only if they insist. If someone—insensitive, graceless, unlearned, and ignorant—begins to stuff himself without considering how much food is available, he will be cursed, mocked, and dishonored by God and man.[4]

4. Like much of the advice in the *Domostroi*, these recommendations on etiquette have a long history. See, for example, Ecclesiasticus 31:12–21 and 32:1–13.

11. How One Should Express Gratitude to God While Entertaining Guests

At the start of the meal, the priests should glorify the Father, the Son, and the Holy Ghost, then the Virgin Mother of God. If those present eat gratefully, in silence or while engaged in devout conversation, the angels will stand by invisibly and write down the diners' good deeds. Their food and drink will be sweet. But if those present utter blasphemy as they begin to eat, the food will turn to dung in their mouths. If they indulge in scurrilous conversation, dirty words, jesting, or any diversion—harps or dancing, clapping, galloping about, games, irreligious songs—then just as smoke drives away bees, so will the angels of God leave that table and that disgusting conversation. The demons will appear, rejoicing. Their desires will be loosed and all kinds of things that please Satan will happen.

Such people outrage God with dice and chess; they amuse themselves with the Devil's games. They throw God's gift of food and drink—the fruits of the earth—away in scorn, then tipple; they beat each other and pour a new round. They scorn God's gift; when the devils write down their deeds, the record is carried to Satan; the demons rejoice together at the destruction of Christians. All such deeds will stand on Judgment Day.

O, woe to the doers of such deeds! When the Jews sat in the desert to eat and drink, then, having stuffed themselves, got up to play and fornicate, the earth devoured twenty-three thousand of them.[1]

Tremble, o people! Do God's will just as it is written in the Law. From such wicked dishonor, Lord, protect every Christian.

Eat, then, and drink in praise of God. Do not overeat or get drunk or act frivolously. If you set food or drink before anyone, or they set any food before you, do not denigrate anything, or say, "This is rotten (sour, tasteless, too salty, bitter, moldy, raw, overcooked)." If you do,

---

1. A reference to 1 Corinthians 10:7–8, itself a reference to Exodus 32:1–29 (the story of the golden calf). In the Exodus story, God slew three thousand; the exaggeration is St. Paul's.

the evil you say will be laid upon you. Rather, praise God's gift of food and eat gratefully. Then God will smell fragrance in you and will make bad food sweet.

If any item of food or drink is not needed, rebuke the servant who made it so that in the future such a thing will not happen.

10. *How One Should Invite Priests and Monks to One's House to Pray*

On holy days, or if someone is sick, or to sanctify someone with oil, and depending on who is present, let those in charge invite priests (as many as they can afford) into the home. The priests will complete the ritual appropriate to the occasion. They will pray for the tsar and grand prince N., autocrat of all the Russias, for his tsaritsa and grand princess N., for their royal children, for the boyars, and the whole army of Christians, for its victory over enemies and for the freedom of those imprisoned, for bishops, priests, and monks, for requests of all sorts, for all Christians, and for all that is profitable for the man of the house, his wife, children, and servants. If asked, they will sanctify water with the life-giving cross, with miracle-working icons, and with holy relics. For a sick person they will also consecrate oil to bring health and healing.

When a sick person is in the house, let the homeowner invite seven or more priests and as many deacons as he can find. These will sanctify the oil and do everything required by the ritual. They will pray over commemorative beer for health and over frumenty to bring peace of mind. After someone has departed this life, the senior priest will cense every room, sprinkling it with holy water and making the sign of the cross. Then those in the house, praising God according to the divine liturgy, should at once set up a table, so that the priests and monks, along with the rest of the guests and the neighborhood poor, may eat and drink. Then all, contented and replete, will go to their homes praising God.

The organization of Chapters 10 and 11 is different in the Intermediate and later versions. In the later versions they appear as Chapters 14 and 15; see Appendix. This second set of Chapters 10 and 11 is from the Long Version.

You should do the same when you hold a memorial for your dead ancestors.[1] You should have memorial services sung in the holy churches and monasteries and should attend the divine liturgy. Afterward, you should feed the brotherhood at your table, for their peace of mind and their health. Invite them to your house: feed them, let them rest, and give them alms.

Water is blessed on January 6 and August 1, always with the life-giving cross.[2] The bishop or priest dips the cross into a cup three times, singing the troparion, "O Lord, save Thy people . . ." three times.[3] Then, after God enters into the water, he sings the troparion, "When Thou, O Lord, wast baptized in the Jordan . . ." three times. The holy crosses, icons, and miracle-working relics lie on a plate. When the priest takes the cross from the cup he holds it over the plate so that the water flows from the cross onto these holy objects. After the first cross is dipped and the water sanctified, the priest uses a sponge to anoint the holy crosses, icons, and miracle-working relics with that holy water, whether they rest in a church or in a house. He says the aforementioned prayers as he rubs each holy icon with the sponge and the holy water, and he treats the other holy objects in the same way. Then he sprinkles the altar with the holy water and makes the sign of the cross over the whole church. In a home, he sprinkles every room, and all the people, in the same way. Then those who are worthy and have faith will anoint themselves and will drink the water to heal

1. The custom of praying for forty days after a death and of honoring one's dead ancestors with a commemorative service became an important symbol of respect for the dead. It is tempting to see in it remnants of pre-Christian clan worship. Fedotov discusses the cult of the clan in *Russian Religious Mind*, 1:15–20.

2. According to Orthodox custom, January 6 (Epiphany, Theophany) commemorates Christ's baptism, whereas the Western churches celebrate on this date the arrival of the Magi. Baptism clears the celebrant's account of all previously committed sins, but because Christ is believed to have lived without sin, his baptism represents instead the unity of God and man and the sanctification of the water that baptized him. The "blessing of the waters" recalls this divine gift. For a sixteenth-century example of the ceremony, see Giles Fletcher's account in "Of the Russe Commonwealth," pp. 233–234. Paul of Aleppo attended a Summer Incensing of the Waters on August 1, 1655 (*Travels of Macarius, 1652–1660*, selected and arranged by Lady Laura Ridding [New York: Arno Press, 1971], p. 56). Both descriptions of this ceremony differ in details from that given in the *Domostroi*, and from each other as well.

3. This prayer, known as the Troparion of the Cross, is actually said only on August 1, which is also the Feast of the Procession of the Cross (Raya and Vinck, comps. and trans., *Byzantine Daily Worship*, p. 741).

themselves, as a purification unto their souls and bodies, for the remission of sins and that they may know eternal life.[4]

11. *How You and Your Servants Should Express Gratitude to God While Entertaining Guests*

As the start of the meal, the priests should glorify the Father, the
Son, and the Holy Ghost, then the Virgin Mother of God. They then
cut the sacred bread, and when the meal is done, they will exalt the
bread of the mass. When they have sung this service, those who are
worthy may eat the bread and drink the sacred cup. Let the priests
pray for health and for peace of mind, also.[1]

If those present eat gratefully, in silence or while engaged in devout
conversation, the angels will stand by invisibly and write down the
diners' good deeds. Their food and drink will be sweet. But if those
present utter blasphemy as they begin to eat, the food will turn to
dung in their mouths. If they indulge in filthy or scurrilous conversation, dirty words, jesting, or any diversion—harps, hooting or dancing, clapping, galloping about, games, irreligious songs—then just as
smoke drives away bees, so will the angels of God leave that table and
that disgusting conversation. The demons will appear, rejoicing. Their
desires will be loosed and all kinds of things that please Satan will
happen.

Such people outrage God with dice and chess; they amuse themselves with the Devil's games. They throw God's gift of food and
drink—the fruits of the earth—away in scorn, then tipple; they beat
each other and pour a new round. They scorn God's gift; when the
devils write down their deeds, the record is carried to Satan; the de-

4. This passage describes, not very accurately, a small portion of a long ceremony. For the whole, see *The Festal Menaion*, trans. Mother Mary and Archimandrite
Kallistos (Timothy) Ware (London: Faber and Faber, 1969), pp. 348–387. The second
of the two prayers mentioned here can be found on pp. 358–359 and 363. For the
first, see previous note to this chapter.
1. This and the two previous sentences, added to the earlier version of the
Domostroi, describe the communion ritual performed before supper in Orthodox
monasteries. See Raya and Vinck, comps. and trans., *Byzantine Daily Worship*,
pp. 76–77.

mons rejoice together at the destruction of Christians. All such deeds will stand on Judgment Day.

O, woe to the doers of such deeds! When the Jews sat in the desert to eat and drink, then, having stuffed themselves, got up to play and fornicate, the earth devoured twenty-three thousand of them.

Tremble, o people! Do God's will just as it is written in the Law. From such wicked dishonor, Lord, protect every Christian.

Eat, then, and drink in praise of God. Do not overeat or get drunk or act frivolously. If you set food or drink before anyone, or they set any food before you, do not denigrate anything, or say, "This is rotten (sour, tasteless, too salty, bitter, moldy, raw, overcooked)." If you do, the evil you say will be laid upon you. Rather, praise God's gift of food and eat gratefully. Then God will smell fragrance in you and will make the bad food sweet.

If any item of food or drink is not needed, rebuke the servant who made it so that in the future such a thing will not happen.

From the Gospel:

> When you are asked by someone to a wedding-feast, do not sit down in the place of honour. It may be that some person more distinguished than yourself has been invited; and the host will come and say to you, "Give this man your seat." Then you will look foolish as you begin to take the lowest place. No, when you receive an invitation, go and sit down in the lowest place, so that when your host comes he will say, "Come up higher, my friend." Then all your fellow-guests will see the respect in which you are held. For everyone who exalts himself will be humbled; and whoever humbles himself will be exalted. [Luke 14:8–11]

And to this you should add: When you are invited to a wedding, do not drink to the point of intoxication or stay late. For in drunkenness and late hours are bred quarrels, shouting matches, and fights, even bloodletting.[2] But if you are there, if you do not quarrel, or get into a scuffle, you will not be the loser, but the winner. If you stay late, waiting for a quarrel, your host will speak out against you. You will not sleep in your own house. Your servants will have no rest, and you will suffer reprisals from the other guests.

2. Again, this practical advice has roots in the Wisdom literature as well as experience. See Ecclesiasticus 31:25–31.

DRUNKENNESS

If you drink to the point of intoxication, and don't go home to sleep, but fall asleep in the place where you were drinking, not caring where you are, many others will be there—you won't be alone. In your drunkenness and carelessness, you will dirty your gown, you will lose your cap and your hat. If you have money in a pocket or a bag, others will take it; they will take your knives too.[3] The host with whom you drank will sue you, and you him. You will have lost your property and have been shamed before others. All those who had to protect a drunkard from himself will gossip about how you got drunk and fell asleep. So you see what shame, ridicule, and property loss lie in great intoxication.

Furthermore, if you get drunk and do set off for home, but fall asleep on the way, and do not reach your home, you will suffer even greater ills.[4] Thieves will take everything from you—all your clothes and everything you have on you—and will not leave you even your undergarments. If you don't sober up, you will be drunk for eternity, I say, you will cast your soul from your body. Many drunkards die from their liquor; they freeze to death on the road. I don't say, "Don't drink at all," but I do say, "Don't drink to the point of evil intoxication." I do not insult God's gift, but those who drink without restraint. As the apostle Paul wrote to Timothy:

Take a little wine for your digestion, for your frequent ailments. [1 Timothy 5:23]

To us, he wrote:

Wine puts life into a man, if he drinks it in moderation. . . . Was it not created to warm men's hearts? [Ecclesiasticus 31:27, here wrongly attributed to St. Paul]. [For] no . . . drunkards . . . will possess the kingdom of God. [1 Corinthians 6:10]

Many people dissipate their property through alcoholism. If you start to indulge yourself in unrestrained drinking, unthinking people

3. In the sixteenth century, people in the social groups addressed by the *Domostroi* generally went armed, carrying knives both for eating and for self-defense.
4. The threats that follow are not idle. Olearius, for example, mentions that drunks left lying in the Moscow streets were often found murdered and stripped of all they possessed (*Travels*, pp. 100–101).

will praise you. But later, when your property is lost because of this evil, these same people will curse you.[5] As the apostle says,

> Do not give way to drunkenness and the dissipation that goes with it, but let the Holy Spirit fill you. [Ephesians 5:18]

Get drunk in praising God, I say, with prayer and fasting, the giving of alms, and attendance at church with a clear conscience. Those who act thus are praised by God and will receive His reward in His Kingdom.

Intoxication with wine brings death to soul and body and loss of property. Drunkards waste both earthly goods and heavenly ones. For they do not live for God, but for alcohol. The Devil alone rejoices in them, and their fate lies with him unless they repent. You see, O man, what shame and rejection, from God and His saints, awaits. The apostle laments the drunkard, and all who commit sins, for they are not pleasing to God; their fate lies with the devils, unless they purify themselves with sincere repentance, as all Christians must, who live according to God's commandments in the Orthodox Christian faith, whose destiny lies with our Lord Jesus Christ and His saints, praising the Holy Trinity of the Father, the Son, and the Holy Ghost. Amen.

But now let us return to our former topic:

It is up to the master of the house or his representatives to offer someone food or drink or to send something to another's table according to the recipient's worth or rank or the quality of his counsel. All such decisions belong to the master and not to others. If, out of affection or in response to some service that has been rendered, someone who is not in charge feels he should give food and drink to another, he may do so if he later pleads his master's forgiveness for it. But to take food or drink secretly from the table or sideboard or to send it without the master's permission or blessing is blasphemy and self-worship; those who do it dishonor everything.

When many dishes are placed before you, do not immediately begin to eat, lest someone more honored than you is present. If you know your status is highest, you may begin, but you should take note of how much food is offered. At the homes of some devout people, food and drink are plentiful, and their guests can partake fully; with others

---

5. A reference to the parable of the prodigal son (Luke 15:11–32).

you should eat only if they insist. If someone—insensitive, graceless, unlearned, and ignorant—begins to stuff himself without considering how much food is available, he will be cursed, mocked, and dishonored by God and man.

Whenever there are guests to feed—merchants or foreigners, invited guests or those sent by God, rich or poor, priests or monks—the master and mistress of the house should be thoughtful and should give each person the honor due to one of that rank and dignity. Each should be received with love, gratitude, and an affectionate greeting. You should speak to each guest and greet each with a kind word, either offering food and drink with your own hands or sending it via another. Make each guest happy. Remember those sitting in the sleighs and the court-yards outside. Give them, too, food and drink. Do not forget those in the kitchen, either; send food to them as well.

If you have a son or a trustworthy servant, he can watch over every-thing, show respect to everyone, and greet each person with a kind word. Then no one will feel angry, dishonored, shamed, mocked, or neglected. Nor will the master and mistress of the house, their chil-dren, and servants feel bad.

If your male or female guests should quarrel, calm them by dem-onstrating good behavior yourself. If someone is rowdy, have him politely conveyed to his own estate. Always protect yourself from quarrels, showing the offender love and gratitude and (once you have offered your guests food and drink) letting them go with honor. By such means, God enters into the gift and brings honor to good people.

You should treat the poor in the same way as others, with com-passion and gratitude [for the opportunity to help them].[6] Then you will receive a reward from God and will be honored by others. When you distribute food in monasteries, or prepare a memorial banquet for your dead ancestors, act as described above. Offer food and drink and as much in alms as you can afford, for your health and your peace of mind. If the rich feed the poor, give drink and gifts, then dishonor, curse, censure, or mock them, talk behind their backs, or dishonor their place—or if the rich refuse to feed the poor, instead cursing or striking them and chasing them from the house, or if the rich people's servants mock them—only devils will be comforted. Ungenerous peo-

6. Classic Christian doctrine, the philosophy expressed here draws on Eccle-siasticus 4:1–8.

ple make God angry; others revile them, feeling anger and enmity. Such dishonorable people earn shame and humiliation. In their insanity, they sin before God. They deserve the ridicule and enmity of others, and the curses and malediction of the poor.

If you do not have enough to feed all those who come to visit you, then turn the unwanted guests away gently. Do not curse them, strike them, or treat them dishonorably. Refuse them politely. If, despite such courtesy, someone goes forth from your house grumbling, to the master or mistress's disrepute, a polite servant should speak courteously to the guest, saying, "Please don't go chatting to lots of people, lord, speculating about why our master had no food to give you." The grumblers will respect you in the future, if you don't speak against them now. If such an incident occurs, the servant should report to his master, after the feast, about that guest and how he departed. But if an important guest grumbles, the servant should tell his master right away, so he may deal with it as he wishes.

The mistress of the house should entertain her women friends of good standing, and any female guests who happen to visit her, in the manner described in this chapter. Her children and servants should act in the same way.[7]

Concerning people eating at one's table, see what is written in the *Prolog* by St. Niphont.[8] See also St. Antiochus on gluttony, chapter 3.[9]

12. How a Man Should Pray at Home with His Wife and His Servants

Every day in the evening, any man who can read should sing vespers,[1] compline, and the midnight service with his wife, children, and

---

7. This passage illustrates the sexual segregation characteristic of elite sixteenth-century Muscovite society. See the Introduction for a discussion of female seclusion in Russia.

8. The *Prolog* was a collection of spiritual writings very popular in the Russian Orthodox church. It is unclear which edition of the *Prolog* the author of this passage has in mind.

9. It is unclear which passage the author has in mind.

1. This and the two following terms refer to the Divine Office, celebrated in Orthodox and Catholic churches. The day began with matins (actually performed

servants—quietly, attentively, with gentle bearing, with prayer and with obeisances, carefully and in unison.[2] After the service do not eat or drink at all. These instructions apply to everyone.

Before lying down to sleep, every Christian must bow three times to the ground. At midnight, he should rise secretly and pray diligently to God, with tears, for his sins, as long as he can. In the morning, upon rising, all should do likewise, according to their strength and desire. Pregnant women should bow only from the waist.[3]

Every Christian should pray for his sins, for absolution, for the health of the tsar, the tsaritsa, their children and their brothers, for the boyars and the Christian army, for help against our enemies and for freedom for those captured in war, for bishops and priests, for the sick and the imprisoned, and for every Christian soul.[4] A woman should pray for remission of her sins, for her husband, children, servants, and relatives, and for her father-confessor. A man should pray similarly.

In the morning, after rising, pray to God. Sing morning song and the hours. On Sundays and holidays hold service, praying silently and with gentle demeanor. Sing in unison. Listen attentively. Burn incense before the saints. If no one knows how to sing the services, it is enough just to pray every evening and morning.

Men should not fail to attend church services every day—vespers, prime, and none [the noonday service]. {Women and servants should go when they are able,[5] when they can be spared [from their duties], on Sundays and on festivals and holy days.}

---

during the early hours of the morning), followed by prime (around sunrise), terce, sext, none, vespers, compline, and the midnight service (sometimes called nocturns). Usually the full regimen was observed only in monasteries, although the Russian court was known for being exceptionally devout. On the Divine Office, see Ware, *Orthodox Church*, p. 273.

2. *Edinoglasno*. In the sixteenth century, as exemplified (and condemned) by the 1551 *Stoglav* Church Council, it was the practice in some Russian churches to speed up long services by breaking the rite in parts, which were sung simultaneously. The results were incomprehensible to the listeners but not, they believed, to God. The church insisted that services be sung in unison, from beginning to end.

3. That is, a pregnant woman should not try to prostrate herself on the ground.

4. Another reference to the Ecumenic Prayer. See note 2 to first Chapter 10.

5. That is, when they are "clean." Women were not allowed to attend church while menstruating or until they had been cleansed ("churched") after childbirth. For more on this, see Levin, *Sex and Society*, pp. 169–172.

13. How Men and Women Should Pray in Church, Preserve Their Chastity, and Do No Evil

In church stand during every service. Pray with trepidation and silently. At home sing compline, midnight service, and the hours.[1] Anyone who adds more services for the sake of his salvation—as long as it is done freely—will receive a greater reward from God.

Women must go to God's churches as they are able, with the consent of and according to the advice of their husbands.

No one must talk in church; listen silently {and attentively to the divine service and readings.} Stand still, without looking around in all directions. Do not lean on a wall or pillar. Do not lean on a stick. Do not shuffle your feet. Do not step on one another's feet.[2] Fold your hands on your chest to form a cross; then pray firmly and without hesitation, with fear and trembling, with sighs and tears, {turning the eyes of your body toward the abyss and those of your heart to the hills.}[3]

Do not leave the church before the end of the service; always arrive in time for the beginning.[4]

On Sundays and the Lord's holy days, on Wednesdays and Fridays,

---

1. Even without the following sentence, observing this regimen would leave little time for anything else: it calls for eight services daily (vespers, compline, the midnight service, matins, prime, terce, sext, and none). Sixteenth- and seventeenth-century Russians did, however, often amaze (not to say horrify) foreigners with their religious devotion. See, for example, Paul of Aleppo, *Travels of Macarius*, pp. 26–27, 40, 46, 49, 51, 53, 68, and 70. Although himself an Orthodox cleric, Paul found himself alternately sympathetic, awed, and exhausted by the demands placed upon him.

2. Orthodox churches usually have no pews, requiring the faithful to stand through long services, hence these injunctions to stand still and pay attention.

3. Another use of this cliché, referenced in note 4 to Chapter 4.

4. Without pews to contain them, listeners found it much easier to blend into (and out of) the crowd without attracting notice. Because services often lasted a long time and because, especially among those of lower social standing, leisure time was scarce, people often attended only part of the service; in fact, they still do in Russia today.

during Lent and the Feast of the Virgin, live in chastity.[5] Prevent yourself from eating at prohibited times.[6] Avoid drunkenness, idle conversation, unseemly laughter, thieving, fornication, lies, swearing, jealousy, property acquired unjustly via usury, taverns or tolls from roads and from bridges. Do not love any kind of deceit. Do not get angry. {Do not remember evil. Do not rob, pillage, or commit violence, or render an unjust judgment.}[7] Do not make food or drink for anyone at all at an early hour, nor at a late one, after the service. Eat and drink praising God, at a proper time. However, the master and mistress should decide when to feed small children and laborers.

Or do you not know that unjust men will not inherit the Kingdom of God? For the apostle Paul said,

> . . . you must have nothing to do with any so-called Christian who leads a loose life, or is grasping, or idolatrous, a slanderer, a drunkard, or a swindler. You should not even eat with such a person. [1 Corinthians 5:11]

And he also said,

> {Make no mistake: no fornicator} or idolater, none who are guilty either of adultery or of homosexual perversion, no thieves or grabbers or drunkards or slanderers or swindlers, will possess the kingdom of God. [1 Corinthians 6:9–10]

But it behooves every Christian to guard himself from all evil.

{Every Christian should always have his rosary in his hands, and the Jesus prayer perpetually on his lips. In the church, at home, in the marketplace, walking, standing, or sitting, anywhere, as said the prophet David,

> . . . in every place where he has dominion, Bless the Lord, my soul. [Psalm 103:22]

---

5. Sexual intercourse was prohibited to devout Orthodox on fast days and holy days. For a full discussion of the implications of this and other restrictions, see Levin, *Sex and Society.*

6. That is, during a fast, early or late in the day, and between meals.

7. A restatement of ideas presented in Chapter 7, in both cases an amalgam of scriptural passages.

Also, say this:

Lord Jesus Christ, Son of God, have mercy on me, a sinner.[8]

Say this prayer six hundred times. For the seventh hundred, pray to the Immaculate Virgin:

My Lady, Most Holy Mother of God, intercede for me, a sinner.[9]

Then go back to the beginning, and repeat this continually.[10] If someone says these prayers, needing Her help, just as breath comes from the nostrils, so at the end of the first year Jesus, Son of God, will rejoice in him. After the second year, the Holy Ghost will enter into him. At the end of the third year, the Father will come to him, and having entered into him, will make the Holy Trinity. Prayer will devour his heart, and his heart will devour the prayer. If he says this prayer unceasingly, day and night, he will be free of all the Devil's snares, in Jesus Christ our Lord, may glory be unto Him forever, Amen. The Immaculate Mother of God, with all the heavenly hosts and all the saints, will protect those who pray with faith and live according to God's commandments from all the Devil's wiles in this age and the one to come.

The Proper Way to Make the Sign of the Cross and Obeisance

This is how bishops, priests, monks, tsars, princes, and all Christians must bow down to the image of the Savior, to the life-giving cross, to

8. This, known as the Jesus prayer, has become an important part of Orthodox spirituality. It is closely associated with the hesychastic movement of the fourteenth century, and its constant repetition, in conjunction with asceticism and physical exercises, is believed to prepare the believer for a mystical union with God, seen as Divine Light. On its use among laymen, see Ware, *Orthodox Church*, pp. 312–314. Ware also discusses hesychasm on pp. 72–80.

9. In the original, the wording exactly parallels that used in the Jesus prayer ("have mercy on me, a sinner"). Intercession is, however, Mary's primary role, as the shift in wording reflects. On images of Mary and the Holy Family as examples of domestic ideals in the society at large, see David Herlihy, *Medieval Households* (Cambridge, Mass.: Harvard University Press, 1985).

10. Archpriest Avvakum, leader of the Old Ritualists (see note 11) and admittedly an extreme case, once wrote that he repeated the Jesus prayer in this way every evening before retiring. Cited in Ware, *Orthodox Church*, p. 120.

the Immaculate Mother of God, to the holy heavenly hosts and to all the saints, to the holy vessels and relics. Hold the thumb of the right hand down and touch it to the last two fingers; these represent the Holy Trinity. Hold the middle and index fingers out straight, just slightly bent, so that the index finger is longer than the middle one; these represent the divinity and the humanity of Christ.[11] Then make the sign of the cross on your face. First touch your hand to your forehead, then to your chest, then to your right shoulder, and last to your left. Thus, in its essence, is depicted Christ's cross. Then bend your head to your waist, and after that make a grand obeisance, touching your head to the floor. You should have prayer and pleas on your lips, humility in your heart, distress at your sinfulness throughout, tears in your eyes, and longing in your soul. Sing to God with your lips and glorify Him. Sighing, pray with your mind and heart for useful things. Cross yourself with your hand, and with your body bow down to the earth, or to your waist. Repeat this throughout the service.[12]

Bishops and priests must make the sign of the cross with their hands in the same manner, when they say the blessing over any Christian.

The writings of the fathers on the subjects of Christ's cross and its representation, and of making obeisance, are well-known. By your respect for these you will understand the power of the cross.

From St. Theodoret:[13] This is how to bless someone with your hand and make the sign of the cross over them. Hold three fingers, as equals,

---

11. This two-fingered sign of the cross became a rallying point in the seventeenth century, when a group known as the Old Ritualists fought to prohibit changes introduced from Greece by Patriarch Nikon of Moscow. Here it is merely the generally accepted method for crossing oneself. As the passages attributed to Theodoret and Athanasius, below, suggest, the two-fingered sign was used throughout the early church and replaced by the three-fingered cross quite late in Byzantine history. The Russians were, therefore, right to regard their own custom as more ancient. See Ware, *Orthodox Church*, p. 122. (In the three-fingered sign, the rationale is the same, but reversed: the three raised fingers represent the Trinity, and the two bent ones the dual nature of Christ.)

12. The proceedings of the *Stoglav* Church Council (1551) offer similar instructions on signing the cross and its meaning. The *Stoglav* also refers the reader to an unspecified work by Theodoret. Otherwise, however, the two passages are quite distinct.

13. Although attributed to Theodoret, bishop of Cyrrhus during the Nestorian controversy of the fourth century and one of the foremost writers of the early church, this passage is probably Russian in origin. Following the Schism of 1666–1667, it was rewritten to support the three-fingered sign of the cross. E. Golubinskii discusses its history (*Istoriia russkoi tserkvi* [Moscow: 1911], t. II, pt. 2, pp. 477–478n.), without noting that the passage changed its philosophy.

together, to represent the Trinity: God the Father, God the Son, and God the Holy Ghost. These are not three gods, but one God in Trinity. The names are separate, but the divinity one. The Father was never incarnate; the Son incarnate, but not created; the Holy Ghost neither incarnate nor created, but issued from the Godhead: three in a single divinity. Divinity is one force and has one honor. They receive one obeisance from all creation, both angels and people. Thus the decree for these three fingers.

You should hold the other two fingers slightly bent, not completely straight. This is because these represent the dual nature of Christ, divine and human. God in His divinity, and human in His incarnation, yet perfect in both. The upper finger represents divinity, and the lower humanity; this way salvation goes from the higher finger to the lower. So is the bending of the fingers interpreted, for the worship of Heaven comes down for our salvation. This is how you must cross yourselves and give a blessing, as the holy fathers have commanded.

From SS. Athanasius and Peter the Damascene, on the same subject:[14] By the signing of the holy and life-giving cross, devils and various scourges are driven away. For it is without price and without cost and praises him who can say it. The holy fathers have, by their words, transmitted to us, and even to the unbelieving heretics, how the two raised fingers and the single hand reveal Christ our God in His dual nature but single substance. The right hand proclaims His immeasurable strength, His sitting on the right hand of the Father, and His coming down unto us from Heaven. Again, from the lands to our right the enemies of God will be driven out, as the Lord triumphs over the Devil with His inconquerable power, rendering him dismal and weak.}

14. Athanasius (298–373), bishop of Alexandria and opponent of Arianism. His works contain many references to the power of the sign of the cross and its ability to thwart demons, although the source of this particular quotation remains unidentified. See, for example, "Incarnation of the Word," in *The Nicene and Post-Nicene Fathers*, 2d ser., 4 (1952), pp. 51, 53, 56. Golubinskii (*Istoriia russkoi tserkvi*, t. II, pt. 2, p. 472n.) cites this passage from Peter the Damascene, attributing it to the fight against Monophysitism (the belief that Christ had a single, divine nature) but without listing its origins.

14. How Children Should Honor Their Spiritual Fathers and Submit to Them

This too you should know: how you, as spiritual children, must respect your father-confessors. Seek a confessor who is a good man, God-loving, wise and temperate, not one who is self-indulgent, a drunkard, a lover of money, or quick to anger.[1]

Respect a good priest and obey him in everything; bewail your sins before him; confess your sins without embarrassment or shame; fulfill his commands {and perform any penances he sets}. Invite him to your house often {and visit him also}. Reveal yourself to him in good conscience, accept his correction with love, and obey him in everything.[2] Revere him and bow down low before him. He is our teacher and our master: hold him in fear and come to him with love.

Make him an offering, as much as you can spare from the fruit of your own labors.

Consult with him often about how to live a useful life. Ask him how to restrain yourself from committing sin, how, if you are a man, to teach and love your wife and children, and how, if you are a woman, to obey your husband and consult with him every day.

Confess your sins frequently to your father-confessor and, when you do, reveal all of them to him. Obey priests in every way, for they watch over our souls and will give answer for us on Judgment Day. Do not upbraid, condemn, or revile them. If someone else causes a priest to suffer, then ally with the priest and, standing on the side of Him who judges, mourn the guilty one as he deserves.

---

1. Based on Titus 1: 7–9: "For as God's steward a bishop must be a man of unimpeachable character. He must not be overbearing or short-tempered; he must be no drinker, no brawler, no money-grubber, but hospitable, right-minded, temperate, just, devout, and self-controlled. He must adhere to the true doctrine, so that he may be well able both to move his hearers with wholesome teaching and to confute objectors."

2. Again, this passage echoes the Slavonic exhortation to confession. See note 3 to Chapter 5.

15. How to Raise Your Children
with All Learning and in Fear of God

If God sends anyone children, be they sons or daughters, then it is up to the father and mother to care for, to protect their children, to raise them to be learned in the good. The parents must teach them to fear God, must instruct them in wisdom and all forms of piety. According to the child's abilities and age, and to the time available, the mother should teach her daughters female crafts and the father should teach his sons whatever trade they can learn. God gives each person some capacity.

> Love your children. Protect them and save them with fear. While teaching them and considering their needs, lay stripes upon them. Correct your son, and he will be a comfort to you and bring you delights of every kind. [Proverbs 29:17]

Fathers must guard and protect their children, keeping them chaste and free from every sin, just as the eyelid guards the pupil and as though these were their own souls. For if children sin because of their father's and mother's carelessness, the parents must give answer for the sins on Judgment Day. If children are unprotected because of the failure of their fathers and mothers to instruct them, if they sin or do something bad, the fathers, the mothers, and the children will all have committed a sin before God and will be reproached and ridiculed by others. Then your house will be damaged and grief and loss will come to you, and you will be fined and shamed in the courts.

But if God-fearing, sensible, and intelligent parents raise their children in fear of God and educate them well, instructing them judiciously in knowledge and wisdom, trade and crafts, those children and their parents will be beloved of God and blessed by the priesthood and praised by good people. If you have such children, when they reach adulthood good people will wed their sons to your daughters with joy and thanksgiving, depending on your relative social positions and the

"If God sends anyone children, be they sons or daughters, then it is up to the father and mother to care for, to protect their children, to raise them to be learned in the good" (Chapter 15). The first task in protecting infants was to baptize them, within eight days after birth, as shown here. From Adam Olearius, *Vermehrte Moscowitische und Persianische Reisebeschreibung* (Schleszwig, 1656). Courtesy of the Princeton University Library, Department of Rare Books and Special Collections.

judgment of God. They will also give their daughters in marriage to your sons. Even if God takes a child from such parents in penance and for sharing, that child is a bloodless sacrifice from the parents. The child is carried to God, where it will rejoice in the eternal blood of Christ and will have the right to ask God for mercy and for the remission of its parents' sins.

16. *How to Amass a Dowry for a Daughter's Marriage*

If someone has a daughter, he would be wise to set aside for his daughter, in her name, a portion {of whatever goods come his way, whether he buys them in the town or across the sea, or tills fields in a village.} Or he should raise a little animal with its issue for her. {From her portion, whatever it is, he should buy,} year by year, linen, cloth, kerchiefs, and blouses for her and store them in a chest—dresses, too, and attire embroidered with precious stones, a necklace, religious objects, pewter, copper, and wood dishes. Add to this store little by little and you will not find it sudden or difficult; nevertheless, you will have plenty of everything.

As such wise parents raise their daughters and teach them the fear of God, wisdom, {and needlework,} the dowry grows along with the children. When they enter negotiations for the marriage contract, all is ready. {The father and mother will be carefree, for God will have given them all that they need, and they will have a joyous and happy wedding.} But if someone does not think at all about his children—and how he will marry them—beforehand, at the time of the marriage he must buy everything, and a sudden wedding is known to be work. {The parents' resources will be exhausted by such a wedding because they will have to buy everything at once and at great cost.}

If, by God's will, a dowered daughter should die, her parents should remember her, making provision for her soul by buying forty days' prayers and giving alms from her dowry. But if they have other daughters, they should consider these girls' needs also.

17. *How to Teach Children and Save Them with Fear*

Have you sons? Discipline them and break them in from their earliest years. [Ecclesiasticus 7:24]

Such a son will be a comfort in your old age and bring delight to your soul [variation on Proverbs 29:17].

> Do not withhold discipline from a boy; take the stick to him, and save him from death. If you take the stick to him yourself, you will preserve him from the jaws of death. [Proverbs 23:13–14]

> Have you daughters? See that they are chaste, and do not be too lenient with them. [Ecclesiasticus 7:24]

> Keep close watch over a headstrong daughter, or she may give your enemies cause to gloat, making you the talk of the town and a byword among the people, and shaming you in the eyes of the world. [Ecclesiasticus 42:11]

> Marry your daughter, and a great load will be off your hands. [Ecclesiasticus 7:25]

You will be praised before the congregation, and at the end of time you will not stand to answer for her.

> A man who loves his son will whip him often so that when he grows up he may be a joy to him. He who disciplines his son will find profit in him and take pride in him among his acquaintances. He who gives his son a good education will make his enemy jealous and will boast of him among his friends. [Ecclesiasticus 30:1–3]

> Correct your son, and he will be a comfort to you and bring you delights of every kind. [Proverbs 29:17]

> Pamper a boy and he will shock you; play with him and he will grieve you. [Ecclesiasticus 30:9]

> Do not give him freedom while he is young or overlook his errors. Break him in while he is young, beat him soundly while he is still a child, or he may grow stubborn and disobey you and cause you vexation. [Ecclesiasticus 30:11–12]

"Pamper a boy and he will shock you; play with him and he will grieve you" (Ecclesiasticus 30:9, quoted in Chapter 17). Despite such advice from the moralists, children in the sixteenth century played games much as they do now. Here, a mother or nurse watches indulgently as children enjoy the seesaw, swings, and Ferris wheel. From Adam Olearius, *Vermehrte Moscowitische und Persianische Reisebeschreibung* (Schleszwig, 1656). Courtesy of the Princeton University Library, Department of Rare Books and Special Collections.

Then will you receive insult and sickness of heart, your house be dishonored, your good name destroyed. You will be reproached by your neighbors, ridiculed by your enemies, fined by the government, and mocked by the evil ones. {But if you teach your children to fear God, instructing them in all they need to know, if you rear wise and chaste adults, if you achieve a lawful marriage for them with the priest's blessing, they will be the inheritors of your property, your house, all that you have. They will take care of you in your old age and, after your death, they will create an eternal memorial for you, their parents. They themselves will live a blessed life throughout the ages, receiving eternal reward from God, in this life and the one hereafter, living as they will within the Lord's commandments.

St. Basil of Caesaria's Admonition to the Young

Be pure in your soul and free from the passions of the body. Have a short stride, a quiet voice, and a pious word. Be moderate with food and drink, silent before your elders, obedient to those wiser than you. Be submissive to your superiors and genuinely loving to those equal to or below you. Separate yourself from all evil and carnal things. Say little, think much. Do not cut people down with words or indulge in idle conversation. Do not be impudent; blush with shame. Do not speak to wanton women. Keep your gaze in the valleys and your soul in the hills. Run from controversy, but learnedly pursue dignity. You need not change anything, if all respect you. If you can render any service to another, you can expect a reward from God and good things to enjoy for eternity.[1]}

18. *How Children Must Love Their Fathers and Mothers, Protect and Obey Them, and Make Their Lives Peaceful*

Children, obey the Lord's commandments:

Honour your father and your mother. [Exodus 20:12]

Obey your parents in everything: for that is pleasing to God. [Colossians 3:20]

1. St. Basil the Great, native of Caesaria (?330–379), was one of the great figures in the early church, a prolific writer who combined a lucid style with personal spirituality and tolerance for others' frailties. He had particular influence over the development of monasticism. The history of these excerpts from St. Basil's ascetical works began in Russia with the *Testament* (*Pouchenie*) of Vladimir Monomakh, Grand Prince of Kiev (1113–1125); Vladimir started the confusion between them and St. Basil's "Admonition to the Young." (For the text, see Cross, *Russian Primary Chronicle*, Appendix I, pp. 207–208; for more on its origins, see Fedotov, *Russian Religious Mind*, 1:254–255.) Thus strictures once directed at monks determined the conduct of young people in the secular world throughout the Kievan and Muscovite periods.

Look after your father in his old age; do nothing to vex him as long as he lives. [Ecclesiasticus 3:12]

Instead, bear his yoke on your own neck.

That it may be well with you, and that you may live long in the land. [Ephesians 6:3]

If you do this, you will cleanse your sins, be beloved of God, and glorified among men. Your house will be blessed unto the ages, and the sons of your sons will inherit, and you will achieve old age anointed with virtue; your days will pass in all prosperity.

If anyone speaks badly to his parents or causes them grief, curses them or rails at them, he has sinned before God and will be damned by the populace.[1]

If anyone beats his father or mother, let him be cut off from the church and from everything that is holy, and by a terrible death and by civil execution let him die,[2] for it is written: "A father's curse withers, and a mother's uproots."[3]

To leave your father in the lurch is like blasphemy, and to provoke your mother's anger is to call down the Lord's curse. [Ecclesiasticus 3:16]

Those who anger their fathers and insult their mothers think they do not sin against God, but they are worse than pagans, companions to the profligate. Of them the prophet Isaiah said: "The wicked are destroyed ... they do not regard the majesty of the Lord" [Isaiah 26:10]. Among those named wicked are those who dishonor their parents.[4]

1. Based on Exodus 21:17: "Whoever reviles his father or mother shall be put to death."
2. Based on Exodus 21:15: "Whoever strikes his father or mother shall be put to death."
3. A paraphrase of Ecclesiasticus 3:9: "For a father's blessing strengthens his children's houses, but a mother's curse uproots their foundations."
4. The passage from Isaiah contains no reference to people who dishonor their parents. The author has apparently made a mental leap between the preceding and the following quotations.

The eye that mocks a father or scorns a mother's old age will be plucked out by magpies or eaten by the vulture's young. [Proverbs 30:17][5]

But those doing honor to their fathers and mothers, obeying them in everything, as God has commanded, will rejoice in their own children. On Judgment Day the Lord will save them and will hear their prayers. "Ask, and you will receive." [Matthew 7:7, Luke 11:9].

He who honours his father will have a long life, and he who obeys the Lord comforts his mother. . . . Honour your father by word and deed, so that you may receive his blessing. For a father's blessing strengthens his children's houses. [Ecclesiasticus 3:6, 8–9]

And a mother's prayer saves from danger.

Even if his [your father's or mother's] mind fails, make allowances for him. . . . A son who respects his father will be made happy by his own children. [Ecclesiasticus 3:13, 5]
Honour your father with all your heart and do not forget your mother's birth-pangs; remember that your parents brought you into the world; how can you repay what they have done for you? [Ecclesiasticus 7:27–28]

Do not say, "I have done them much good, given them clothes and food, and filled their every need, but still we are not free." For by such material things you cannot give birth to your mother and thus suffer for her as she did for you.

He who obeys the Lord . . . obeys his parents as though he were their slave. [Ecclesiasticus 3:7]

Then you will receive a reward from God and will inherit eternal life as fulfillers of his commandment.

5. In older translations of the Bible, the birds are ravens and eagles, as in the *Domostroi.*

19. *How Every Person Must Begin His Craft or Any Work with a Blessing*

This is how everyone who lives in a well-ordered house (master and mistress, son and daughter, manservant and maidservant, {old master craftsman} and young {apprentice} must begin every endeavor: embroidery, eating, drinking, food preparation, baking, cooking, needlework, or crafts. Arrange your clothes, clean yourself of all filth, and wash your hands, then bow to the saints, three times to the ground (or, if appropriate, from the waist).[1] Anyone who knows how to pray properly should do so, blessing those present, saying the Jesus prayer, and crossing himself, saying, "Lord, Father, bless me."

Begin your work in this way and God's mercy will aid you. Angels will help you invisibly and demons flee from you. Such work honors God and profits your soul.

Eat and drink with gratitude. Then food will be sweet and anything that has been stored will be wholesome.

While working, engage in prayer or devout conversation or remain silent. If any work is begun with an idle or wicked word, with complaints or jokes, with blasphemy or filthy speech, from such work and from such conversations God's mercy departs. The angels go forth grieving and the profligate demons rejoice, seeing their will being done. Thoughtless Christians thus invite into their midst devils, who put into their minds evil, enmity, and hate. These demons arouse the Christians' thoughts to lust, anger, blasphemy, foul speech, and every sort of evil. The work, food, or drink becomes unprofitable; the crafts and needlework are not made for God. This makes God angry; such work is not blessed, needed, sweet, or solid. Food and drink will not be tasty; only the Enemy and his servants will find it pleasant, sweet, and full of joy.

God is displeased by anyone who contaminates food, defiles an artifact, steals something {while engaged in a craft, adulterates goods,

1. Appropriate: if one were pregnant, elderly, or infirm, for example. See note 3 to Chapter 12.

substitutes cheap items for good ones,} or lies to cover up such deeds. Devils write such acts down; the person will be called to account for them on Judgment Day. {His master will not trust him; other people will not want his service; no one will henceforth have any faith in him. If someone has acted crooked, has lied or been foresworn, or has traded deceitfully, his profits will not be blessed or enduring; alms from them will not be acceptable to God. In contrast, the fruit of righteous labor is both profitable to yourself and worthy to bring as a gift to God; God will accept alms from it. A righteous man is pleasing to God and honorable among men. Everyone will trust him. He will please God with his good deeds during this life and will reign in the life hereafter forever and ever.}

20. *In Praise of Women*[1]

Who can find a capable wife? Her worth is far beyond coral. Her husband's whole trust is in her, and children are not lacking. She repays him with good, not evil, all her life long. She chooses wool and flax and toils at her work. Like a ship laden with merchandise, she brings home food from far off. She rises while it is still night and sets meat before her household. After careful thought she buys a field and plants a vineyard out of her earnings. She sets about her duties with vigour and braces herself for the work. She sees that her business goes well, and never puts out her lamp at night. She holds the distaff in her hand, and her fingers grasp the spindle. She is open-handed to the wretched and generous to the poor. She has no fear for her household when it snows, for they are wrapped in two cloaks. She makes her own coverings, and clothing of fine linen and purple. Her husband is well known in the city gate when he takes his seat with the elders of the land. . . . When she opens her mouth, it is to speak wisely, and loyalty is the theme of her teaching. [Proverbs 31:10–23, 26]

1. In the Mediate and Long Versions, this title has been changed to emphasize the male role, becoming *A Paean for Men about Women,* or just *A Paean for Men.* On the versions, see the Introduction and Pouncy, "Origins of the *Domostroi,*" pp. 366–373.

Again, no athlete can win a prize unless he has kept the rules.[1] [2 Timothy 2:5]

A good wife makes a happy husband; she doubles the length of his life. A staunch wife is her husband's joy; he will live out his days in peace. A good wife means a good life; she is one of the Lord's gifts to those who fear him. [Ecclesiasticus 26:1–3]

For a good woman makes her husband more honorable: first, she will be blessed by having kept God's commandment; second, she will be praised by other people.[2]

"A capable," long-suffering, and silent "wife is her husband's crown" [Proverbs 12:4, combined with Ecclesiasticus 26:14].

If you, husband, find a good wife, she will bring blessings on your house. A man is blessed by such a wife, and his years will be filled in good repose. Praise and honor come to a man by means of a good woman. {A good wife, like the blessed Empress Theodora, saves [others] after the death of her husband.[3]}

21. Instruction to a Husband and Wife, Their Servants and Children, on How They Must Live Well

The master must himself learn and must teach his wife, children, and servants not to steal, live dissolutely, lie, slander, envy, offend, accuse falsely, quarrel with others, condemn, carouse, mock, remember evil, or be angry with anyone.

Be obedient and submissive to your superiors, loving to your equals,

1. "Win a prize": older versions of the Bible say "be crowned," as does the *Domostroi*, because the athlete's prize was a crown of laurel.
2. A reference to Proverbs 31:30–31: "It is the God-fearing woman who is honoured.... and let her labours bring her honour in the city gate."
3. In 842/843 St. Theodora, empress of Byzantium, ended the iconoclast controversy by permanently reinstating icons into Orthodox worship. See Ware, *Orthodox Church*, p. 39.

welcoming and kind to inferiors and the poor. Then everyone will meet your demands without delay.

Most of all, do not deny the laborer his wage.[1a] Suffer any insult, abuse, or reproach with gratitude for God's sake. Others may scorn and revile you because of your work, but eventually they will turn away from such madness and receive you with love. Do not seek revenge for their offenses against you; for your restraint, you will receive a reward from God.

Teach your servants the fear of God and all the virtues. Act well yourself; together, you and the servants will receive mercy from God.

If you yourself, from carelessness and neglect, or your wife, because she lacks a husband's correction, or any of your servants—men, women, and children—because of your failure to instruct them, engage in evil deeds (such as carousing, theft, or lechery), you will suffer eternal torment together. But if you act well and live in a manner pleasing to God, you will inherit eternal life in the Heavenly Kingdom.

22. What Kind of People to Hire and How to Instruct Them in God's Commandments and Domestic Management

People should keep servants of good character in their houses.[1b] The servants should be handy at that craft for which they are fitted and in which they have been trained. A manservant should not ever have been a robber, carouser, gambler, petty thief, brigand, lecher, sorcerer, drunkard, or swindler. One who serves a good master should be knowledgeable, God-fearing, wise, humble, given to good deeds, far-sighted, {and well-versed in domestic management}. He should not lie, rob, or offend anyone. {He should be diligent in performing good deeds, with humility and in accord with his master's instruction, as the Apostle Paul commanded when he wrote to Timothy:

1a. A reference to Luke 10:7, quoted in 1 Timothy 5:18: "The worker earns his pay."

1b. The domestic servants discussed in the *Domostroi* are full, hereditary slaves. In this translation, I use the more general term "servant" except where the discussion centers around the rights and responsibilities of ownership, then "slave."

All who wear the yoke of slavery must count their own masters worthy of all respect, so that the name of God and the Christian teaching are not brought into disrepute. If the masters are believers, the slaves must not respect them any less for being their Christian brothers. Quite the contrary; they must be all the better slaves because those who receive the benefit of their service are one with them in faith and love. This is what you are to teach and preach. [1 Timothy 6:1–2]

Teach them by imposing limits on them, using terror.[2] That apostle also wrote to Titus:

Tell slaves to respect their masters' authority in everything, and to comply with their demands without answering back; not to pilfer, but to show themselves strictly honest and trustworthy; for in all such ways they will add lustre to the doctrine of God our Saviour. [Titus 2:9–10]}

A slave should feed and clothe himself with funds awarded by his master or gained by his own efforts. He should be content with whatever his master gives him—a robe, a horse, clothes, a small field, an item to trade—and should supplement it with whatever he can acquire by his own labors.[3] He is responsible for its care {from then on}.

A good servant keeps his better clothes—outerwear and undergarments, shirt and boots—for holy days and to wear in the presence of his betters when the weather is good. Everything should always be clean. Such a servant will not wear clothes that have been thrown on the floor, muddied, stained, or crumpled. But if someone is stupid, crude, ignorant, and careless, whether his clothes form part of the wages he receives from his master or are made by his own hands, he will be unable to care for them. The master, or whoever he commands in his stead, must care for the best clothes of boors like these. When it is time for the servant to wear his good clothes, the master should

2. Terror: *groza*. See Preface, note 4.
3. A reference to the *peculium*: in most slave systems, masters grant slaves some property for their use (although legally the *peculium* remains the master's property and can be confiscated at any time). On the *peculium* in Russia, see Hellie, *Slavery*, pp. 132–133, 519. On the *peculium* in general, see Patterson, *Slavery*, pp. 182–186.

hand them out; when the servant has taken them off, the master cares for them again.

Here is an instruction for all domestic servants: When at work, wear old clothes; when you come before your master and his guests, wear clean everyday dress; but on holy days, or when appearing before important people, or when visiting somewhere with your master or mistress, wear your best clothes. But even on such occasions, protect your good clothes from mud, rain, and snow and, when you arrive home, take them off, dry them, iron out the wrinkles, and remove any bad odor, then put the clothes away neatly in their proper place. Such behavior brings lasting profit to both servants and master: honor from others and pleasure to themselves.

Servants must not, through intimidation or by banding together, steal from other servants, nor should they imperil others, anywhere, with such deeds. They should act as one to protect that which is their master's. They should not lie to their master and mistress, nor slander anyone in any way. Nor should their masters indulge tale-telling, but should investigate straightaway by confronting the accused. They should not let the wicked man escape {but should punish him, albeit with compassion, so that the other servants will fear to do evil}. They should reward the good servant, so that the others will envy him and seek a similar reward from their master; all will then serve righteously and well. By means of the master's admonition and good teaching, the servant will live long, save his soul, serve his master, and please God.

Most of all, instruct those in service always to go to church, and to listen to the services on holy days and in the household, and especially to pray together. They should preserve their bodies from all forms of lechery, drunkenness, and greed. They must keep themselves from drinking and eating at forbidden times, for this is gluttony and drunkenness. They should invite their father-confessors and the priests' wives to their homes. They should go to confession.

{When single youths and maidens reach full adulthood, arrange marriages for them. For the apostle says:

> Marriage is honorable; let us all keep it so, and the marriage-bond inviolate; for God's judgement will fall on fornicators and adulterers.
> [Hebrews 13:4]

If single people fornicate with one another because of your carelessness, even if it is kept secret from you, you will be tormented with many and great ordeals. You will be dishonored by such affairs. If you keep servants, but have no care for their souls; if you make them work overly long hours, whether in preparing food or making clothes or in any other form of service, you yourself will answer for their souls on Judgment Day. As the apostle wrote in his epistle:

Do not ruin the work of God for the sake of food. [Romans 14:20][4]

God's work is restraining the flesh, caring for the soul and things eternal. This, too, the apostle said:

If we have food and covering, we may rest content. [1 Timothy 6:8]}

Those who are married should live lawfully with their wives according to the teaching of their father-confessors.[5] Husbands should not lust after women other than their wives, nor wives after men other than their husbands.

A servant should teach his wife what he himself has learned from his master—that is, the fear of God and all forms of knowledge.[6]

A good female servant should heed her mistress and obey her in everything, serving with all the effort and skill that she possesses. She should not steal, lie, live dissolutely, or drink. {Nor should she listen to old women,[7] who tempt young women into evil—that is, they in-

4. Although it is accurately quoted, the original context of this passage gave it a very different meaning. St. Paul was arguing against traditional Jewish dietary laws, saying that Christians should not provoke conflicts by refusing to eat with people who did not keep kosher. Here, the author uses the passage to urge that servants not be kept from devotions so that their masters may eat on time.

5. This means not only that husbands and wives should refrain from adultery but that they should observe clerical prohibitions against intercourse on fast days and holy days, and should not adopt "unnatural positions." For more information, see Levin, *Sex and Society*, pp. 161–179.

6. In the Long Version, this reads: "Servants should teach their wives what they have learned from your [*tvoego*] correction and their father-confessors' instruction: the fear of God, knowledge, and humility" (*Domostroi OIDR*, p. 73).

7. Old women: *babki*. *Babka* is a pejorative term for a married woman or widow. Although such a woman is not necessarily old, the word in this context carries associations of "crone" or "witch." The power of postmenopausal women is much feared in preindustrial societies, as manifest in the numerous tales of Baba Yaga and other versions of the Great Mother Goddess in her devouring aspect. For a fuller discussion of the Divine Feminine in Russia, see Hubbs, *Mother Russia*.

troduce them to young men who are strangers to the area and who teach the young women to steal, to drink, and to indulge themselves in evil. Many women and girls keep company with these young men, listen to old crones, steal property from their master and mistress, and run away. Then they[8] take the property from your woman and kill her, or she commits suicide by drowning herself; either way your property is lost.

If you don't routinely think about these old women, an unknown man will someday come to your house, or your women and girls will go out for water, or to wash clothes, and will begin to speak to a man. Even if he is known to them, they shame and spoil themselves by speaking with this man who is not one of their own.[9]

But a crone [is even more dangerous, as she] can more easily spend time with them. Whenever she sees your women chatting, she will organize a little trading, questioning them about what you or your lady may need. Then they will ask her what she has, saying, "Give it to us. We'll show it to our mistress." The crone will reply, "I have sold this item to such and such a woman of good standing," and will even supply names, but it is all lies. "I will go to my child's godmother," she will say, "I will take it from her and bring it to you." Then your women will plead, "Bring it to us before supper, or how will they sing vespers?"[10] The crone will say, "From my child's godmother's house, I know how to get to your place. But beware of your master." Then she leaves them and does not return for a day or two. Through one day, and throughout another, she does not come to the house, but watches how they go to the river for water or to wash clothes. When the old woman finally approaches them, they cry out to her and ask why she did not visit them, why she did not bring the object that she wanted to bring. The old woman expresses great surprise, and tells them, "Yesterday and the day before I was visiting this and that woman of good standing," and she gives the other woman's husband's name. "They had a feast," she says, "and the lady fed me

8. Whether "they" refers to the crones or the young men is unclear. The runaway slave is also, of course, lost property as far as her master is concerned.

9. An example of the (by our standards) exaggerated Muscovite concern with female virtue. Even among slaves, a woman was dishonored if she spoke to a man who belonged to another household.

10. Again, this reference is unclear. Perhaps the author means to suggest that the object they are discussing is needed for vespers, but more likely the young women are indicating their excitement (as in, "how can we live without this?").

and would not let me go, so I spent the night there with her servants. I was there and could not leave, because many respectable women pleaded with me." Then your women reply, "Come to our house," despite your absolute prohibition and no matter how often you beat them.

By these means old crones get to know your serving women and girls. Once such an old woman has made their acquaintance, there is nothing to stop her standing and talking to them, meeting them at the river. Even if the master notices them, his women are talking to another woman, not to a man. But then she will start to visit them at your house, and they will make her known to their mistress. Woe is me, all are enthralled by our common enemy, the Devil; we are conquered by our own weaponry. As blessed Theodora of Alexandria bravely said,

> Do not be charmed by women. Do not protect your husband's bed, but make yourself worthy, by means of repentance and great patience, to be a chosen vessel of God.[11]

We must keep quiet about others, because otherwise we will displease our listeners.

> Let those who have ears to hear, hear and ponder the words in the depths of their hearts.[12]

But now let us go back to these servants.}

A good servant should not come to her mistress bringing wicked tales, or wizards with roots or herbs. If anyone else contemplates such a thing, a good servant will refuse even to recognize her. Nor should

11. Theodora of Alexandria reportedly lived during the reign of Emperor Zeno (474–491). She was the wife of Paphnutius, a nobleman known for his piety, but was seduced into adultery through the Devil's wiles. In penance, she took monastic vows, as a man, under the name of Theodore, living a holy and ascetic life (Raya and Vinck, *Byzantine Daily Worship*, p. 445).

12. This is a concatenation of and variation on two biblical passages. The first, "If you have ears to hear, then hear," appears frequently in the synoptic Gospels as an introduction to or conclusion of Christ's parables. See Matthew 11:15, 13:9, 13:21; Mark 4:9, 4:23, 7:16; Luke 8:8, 14:35. The second phrase, "and ponder the words in the depths of their hearts," seems to be a reference to Luke 2:19: "But Mary treasured up all these things and pondered over them [in older Bibles, 'pondered them in her heart']."

servants discuss their masters around such people, for these are servants of the Devil. Good servants serve their masters faithfully and justly, with good deeds and righteous works.

The master and mistress should bestow goods on their people (men, women, and children); they should also feed them, clothe them, and let them live in warmth, peace, and prosperity forever. Then the master—with his soul and his house well-ordered, his servants free of sorrow, and the poor, the stranger, the widow, and the orphan likewise cared for—may rest from his righteous labor and bring alms to the churches, the parishioners, and the monasteries.[13] {If you have nothing to give, at least say a comforting word; if that is not enough, do not become embittered, nor grieve because of your poverty, because you have nothing to give to the poor. Remember the words of the Lord:

> Where a man has been given much, much will be expected of him.
> [Luke 12:48]

That is to say, if you have much, you must give a lot.

> Where a man has been given little, less will be expected. [extrapolated from above]

By less is meant a little cup of water, or a comforting word. For the least shall be first.[14] Also,} the good man will invite to his home those who are pleasing to God and useful to his soul. Nothing will be found within his house that was procured by coercion, pillage, vengeance, pledges, calumny, sharp practices, tale-telling, or false judgment. If God guards its owners from such evil, this house will be blessed now and forever.

{The master and mistress of the house, with their children and their

13. This sentence reads somewhat differently in the later versions: "The master and mistress, if they live according to this admonition, as written here, will save their souls and manage their household, and their servants likewise. Both spiritually and physically, they will live painlessly. The master and mistress should also have care for the poor and the stranger, the destitute, the widows and orphans, and should ameliorate their lot—that is, their lack of spiritual and worldly goods—from the givers' own righteous labors. Think about their spiritual health, and watch over their bodily health. Also, take and send alms to God's churches, to the parishioners, to monasteries and prisons—as much as you can afford."
14. A slightly garbled reference to Matthew 19:30: "But many who are first will be last, and the last first."

domestic servants—men and women, young and old—should, every year during Lent, visit their father-confessors and make confession. Those who are worthy should take communion also. If they go more often than once a year, they will receive an even greater reward from God.[15] The father-confessors should explain this to the master of the house and his dependents. The master, especially, should take great care to do this for the sake of his own soul and those of his dependents.

Give nothing in alms to a slave, for the sake of his soul. Instead, give to the master, for all who are in his household and all who will demand alms of him. To do otherwise is evil.

Throughout the year, on Sundays, Wednesdays, Fridays, the Lord's holy days, and during all the holy fasts, abstain from sexual intercourse. Occupy yourself with good deeds of all kinds. Do not get drunk. Go to God's churches with an offering, to pray for your health and peace of mind, and—if you are ready spiritually and are following your father-confessor's advice—touch the holy objects. You will find more on these subjects in Chapters 38 and 32 [in this edition, 35 and 28].}

23. How Christians Should Heal Themselves of Illness and Every Affliction.
{This Applies to Tsars, Princes, Chancery Personnel, Bishops, Priests, Monks, and All Other Christians}

If God sends someone illness or affliction, that person should seek a cure in God's mercy, in tears and prayer, by giving alms to the poor, in sincere repentance and gratitude, in forgiveness of others, in his own goodness of heart, and by expressing genuine love toward everyone.[1]

---

15. This advice reflects the standards of most sixteenth-century Orthodox more accurately than the recommendations given in Chapters 12 and 13.

1. This standard Christian doctrine finds biblical expression in James 5:13–16: "Is anyone among you in trouble? He should turn to prayer. Is anyone in good heart? He should sing praises. Is one of you ill? He should send for the elders of the congregation to pray over him and anoint him with oil in the name of the Lord. The prayer offered in faith will save the sick man, the Lord will raise him from his bed, and any sins he may have committed will be forgiven. Therefore confess your sins to one another, and pray for one another, and then you will be healed. A good

Have your father-confessors pray to God, sing services, and consecrate both water and oil using their revered crosses, holy relics, and miracle-working icons. Visit the holy places where miracles are worked; on arriving, pray with a pure conscience. Through these means, you will find healing for any sicknesses you receive from God.

Distance yourself, too, from all sins. Above all, commit no evil; instead, keep the commandments of your father-confessors and fulfill the penances they set. Thus you will cleanse yourself from sin, healing illnesses both of the spirit and of the body and meriting God's mercy. Every Christian must heal himself of both spiritual and physical ills and from soul-destroying and unhealthy passions. He must live according to the Lord's commandments, the teaching of the church fathers, and Christian law, just as has been recommended in the first fifteen chapters of this book (see also Chapter 25). He who acts in this way will please God, save his soul, rid himself of sin, achieve spiritual and physical health, and inherit eternal good.

But someone who is indifferent and dishonorable has no fear of God and does not do God's will, observes neither Christian law nor the traditions of the church fathers, does not rejoice in God's church, church services, the monastic rule, prayer, or singing praise to God. He eats and drinks without restraint and at improper times. He does not maintain a lawful life: he has intercourse on Sundays, Wednesdays, and Fridays, on holy days, during Lent, on the Virgin's Day, and at other times when it is forbidden.[2] Contrary both to nature and to law, such men lust after women who are not their wives, commit Sodom's sin or any abomination detested by God. This includes lechery, unchastity, disgusting speech, the singing of Devil-inspired songs accompanied by bells and trumpets, all Devil-pleasing acts, and all forms of dishonor deserving of God's wrath. Here belong sorcery and witchcraft as propounded in *Rafli* and almanacs,[3] censured books, *The Rav-*

---

man's prayer is powerful and effective." The *Domostroi* here endorses an unusually strict interpretation of the apostles; in general, both Orthodox and Catholic churches were somewhat more tolerant of the medical profession, although both emphasized the importance of prayer.

2. The word literally used in the *Domostroi* is the more condemnatory "fornicates." In English, "fornication" usually implies premarital sex, but this author applies it to any illicit sexual practice.

3. That is, in astrological/numerological literature translated from western European sources. The Church's opposition to almanacs and similar literature stems from their astrological associations. *Rafli*: a Byzantine astrological work, incorpo-

en's Croak,[4] *The Seraph,*[5] and as manifest by those who interpret arrows of destruction, little axes, internal pains, entrails, pebbles, magic bones, or by means of any other Devil-inspired art. Here, too, are included anyone who tries to defeat death with sorcery, herbs, roots, or grasses; anyone who is too indulgent to insist that others fast at the appropriate time;[6] anyone who, by interpreting dreams or through soothsaying, makes magic, praises the Devil, or promotes evil and adultery; anyone who swears falsely in God's name or who slanders another (on this, see Chapter 24). From all such deeds, customs, and mores grow pride, hatred, wicked grudges, anger, enmity, offense, lying, theft, swearing, wicked speech, sorcery, witchcraft, ridicule, blasphemy, gluttony, drunkenness, eating early and late in the day, evil deeds of all sorts, lechery, and impurity. The good man who loves people but does not hold God in his heart will be counted with those who hold to these wicked customs and who indulge themselves in any way.

Just as a father who loves his children saves them with sorrow and leads them to salvation by chastening them, God punishes us for our multitude of sins.[7] He will not suddenly bring us death. He does not want sinful deaths, but awaits our repentance. He who turns back to God will live. But if we do not turn back and regret our wicked deeds, for the sake of our sins, He will send hunger, plague, fire, or flood. We will be captured or slaughtered by pagans, our towns and churches sacked, every holy object destroyed, our every possession plundered. He may cause the tsar to seize our property in anger, so that we will be mercilessly punished with a shameful death while our property is carried off by robbers and thieves, or confiscated through judges' fines while we suffer torture. At other times He may cause drought, excessive rain, unseasonably cool summers, cruel winters, fierce frosts, or unproductive fields. Then cattle, wild beasts, birds, and fish will grow scarce, bringing inescapable, sudden death to our parents, wives, and

---

rating western and Arabic elements, translated in Pskov during the sixteenth century.

4. This book has never been identified. Perhaps it is not a book at all but belongs with the following section, as an omen interpreted by magicians.

5. A fourteenth-century Spanish-Jewish work on predicting eclipses.

6. Not observing church rules is here equated with occult practice.

7. On this, see Proverbs 3:11–12: "My son, do not spurn the Lord's correction or take offense at his reproof; for those whom he loves the Lord reproves, and he punishes a favourite son."

children. These loved ones will contract serious diseases and come to a most evil end.

If from all these ills I have just described we do not become wise, do not learn, and do not achieve repentance, insight, and fear, seeing therein the just wrath of God, more punishment will come. The Lord, punishing us to turn us to repentance just as he tested the long-suffering Job, will send more afflictions and diseases—torment by evil spirits, twisted limbs, arthritis, tumors and cancers throughout our bodies, constipation, kidney stones, deafness, blindness, diarrhea, racking coughs, vomiting, bleeding and infection in our lower orifices, consumption, coughs, headache, toothache, rheumatism, syphilis, general weakness, and the shakes. All serious diseases are punishment caused by God's wrath.

Still, we neglect all these our sins and do not repent, gain wisdom, or learn fear. Even seeing how God punishes us, we cling to the diseases He has sent. We think we do not need mercy or forgiveness of our sins. We commit evil and throw ourselves before impure demons. We renounce holy baptism and embrace devilish deeds. We invite sorcerers, soothsayers, magicians, visionaries, and herbalists to our homes. With their plants we place our hopes in earthly aids that destroy our souls and prepare us for the Devil, to suffer in the pit of Hell forever.

What foolish people we are! How thoughtless are we! We do not ponder our sins or wonder why God is punishing us. We do not repent of our sins and cease from our evil deeds and improper acts. We do not ponder the eternal, but wish for the perishable and temporary. Stop committing evil and soul-destroying acts! Let us purify ourselves through sincere repentance, for the merciful Lord will pardon our sins and grant us physical health and salvation for our souls. He will not deprive of eternal good anyone who labors in the present for the sake of the Heavenly Kingdom, for it is written in the holy Acts of the Apostles:

To enter the Kingdom of God we must pass through many hardships. [Acts 14:22]

In the Holy Gospel it was said:

The gate is wide that leads to perdition...but the gate that leads to life is small and the road is narrow. [Matthew 7:13–14]

Again the Lord said,

The Kingdom of Heaven has been subjected to violence and violent men are seizing it. [Matthew 11:12]

{Let us remember the holy men who suffered for the sake of God, their many pains and illnesses, and how they bore them with gratitude, not summoning sorcerers, wizards, magicians, herbalists, or diabolical physicians. Rather they placed all hope in God, bearing their purification gratefully for the sake of their sins and the delights of eternal goodness. So did act the long-suffering righteous Job and poor Lazarus, who lay suppurating at the gates of the rich man, gnawed by the worms of Hell, but who now lies in the bosom of Abraham.[8] So did St. Simeon Stylite[9] suffer from the suppuration of his body, teeming with worms. Throughout the ages, many other righteous ones, pleasing to God, suffered all sorts of aches and many and varied diseases, which they bore patiently, for their souls' salvation and the life eternal. Through such afflictions many Christians, rich and poor, entered the Heavenly Kingdom. They came from all ranks—princes and boyars, priests and monks. They suffered many and various injuries and illnesses, and all these afflictions were defeated and these wrongs borne for God. They prayed for God's mercy and expected his help. In return, God the merciful poured kindness on his servants, granting them healing and remitting their sins. He also saved from affliction any who placed their hopes in the life-giving cross and the miraculous icons— the holy images of Christ and the Virgin, the archangels and all the saints—and the holy relics, in the sanctification of water and oil, in the singing of the cathedral service and the divine liturgy, in all-night vigils in His holy churches, in honorable monasteries and miracle-

8. Job's trials and tribulations are related throughout the Book of Job. For the story of Lazarus, see Luke 16:19–25.
9. Stylite: one who achieved sainthood by living for years on the top of a pillar in the desert. An ascetic movement in early monasticism (fourth century), "pillar sitting" produced several church heroes before it lost popularity. St. Simeon was the best-loved of these in the Russian church. A seventeenth-century church dedicated to St. Simeon still stands on Kalinin Avenue in Moscow, surrounded by modern shops and office buildings.

working shrines, as well as those who (while at home, on the road, on the waters, or anywhere else) called on their faith in the Lord our God, His Immaculate Mother, and the saints. All these received mercy, physical health, and salvation for their souls. Even those who perished from their afflictions were by this means cleansed of sin so that they could receive eternal life.

Let us watch ourselves carefully and model ourselves on those whom I have just described, mirroring their patience. Let us imitate the lives of the holy fathers, prophets,[10] apostles, bishops, martyrs, righteous ones, fools for Christ's sake,[11] holy female saints, Orthodox tsars and princes, priests, monks, and all the Christians who from time immemorial have lived lives pleasing to God. How these did suffer afflictions in this life for Christ's sake!

Others, through fasting, prayer, and endurance, bore for Christ's sake hunger, nakedness, severe cold, the sun's burning heat, curses, spitting, other forms of mockery, beatings, torments, and torture inflicted by impious emperors.[12] Many died, cut up or burned with fire, eaten by wild beasts, beaten with stones, drowned in the waters, confined in thieves' dens, exiled to wildernesses, buried in the depths of the earth, imprisoned in fortresses, or held in captivity. Still they endured these ills and scourges, their various tortures. "He confesses," as the holy writings say. No eye saw nor ear heard that they, as a

10. This list is taken from the Troparion of All-Saints (Raya and Vinck, comps. and trans., *Byzantine Daily Worship*, p. 409).

11. *Iurodivy*. Russians paid special respect to those who became "fools for Christ's sake": ascetics who originally sought, through their erratic behavior, to bring public ridicule on themselves. "Fools for Christ" subjected themselves to extreme privation—going naked during the Russian winter, for example—and so earned a veneration great enough to confer, at times, the right to criticize the tsar with impunity. Basil the Blessed, from whose chapel comes the popular name of St. Basil's Cathedral, was one such "holy fool." On the holy fools, see Ewa M. Thompson, *Understanding Russia: The Holy Fool in Russian Culture* (Lanham, Md.: University Press of America, 1987).

12. Emperors: literally, tsars. From the context the author probably has Roman and Byzantine emperors in mind (the word "tsar" comes from Caesar and was applied first to the Roman emperors). The Russian grand princes began to assume the title in the fifteenth century as a gesture of self- and national aggrandizement, but at the time of the *Domostroi* this usage was still new and unfamiliar; Ivan IV, the first crowned tsar, had taken the throne only in 1547 (ten to thirty years previously). The list of tortures comes from those inflicted on early Christian martyrs but may have seemed particularly relevant to the *Domostroi*'s readers: Ivan the Terrible inflicted similar torments on his enemies. (This passage became attached to the text during the first set of revisions, probably added during the *oprichnina* or shortly after.)

result of this suffering and these torments, received a reward from God and now delight in eternal goodness. Nor did it enter any man's heart that God was pleased with those who loved Him. Yet how God's churches sing their praises now! For we pray to these saints and call on their help, asking them to pray to God for us, and we are healed by their miraculous images and holy relics. Let us imitate these saintly lives and the way in which they suffered, with gratitude and patience, that we too may receive God's grace.

Ruling No. 61 of the Sixth Ecumenical Council, on wizards and sorcerers:[13] If you encounter sorcerers, so-called wise men, magi,[14] or others of this ilk or those who frequent them, punish them according to the commandment of the holy fathers, the ruling in the canon, by banishing them from church for six years. You should punish in the same way those who drag bears, or any other kind of animal, around to amuse simple folk and those who offer others lustrations, interpretations of their birth or heritage, or advice based on astrology or other forms of folk magic. If you have any of those they call cloud-dispatchers,[15] spell-casters, makers of talismans, or sorcerers living among you, who do not abjure their destructive pagan deeds,[16] throw them out of the church altogether, as the holy commandments enjoin. As the apostle [Paul] said,

> Can light consort with darkness? Can Christ agree with Belial, or a believer join hands with an unbeliever? Can there be a compact between the temple of God and the idols of the heathen? [2 Corinthians 6:14–16][17]

13. The Sixth Ecumenical Council, also known as the Third Council of Constantinople, met in A.D. 680 to condemn the Monothelites, who held that Christ, although both human and divine, had but a single will.

14. *Sotniki*, an old word for wizards. See *Kniga pravil sviatykh apostol, sviatykh soborov vselenskikh, i pomestnykh, i sviatykh otets* (Montreal: Izdanie Bratstva prep. Iova Pochaevskogo, 1971), pt. 1, p. 150.

15. Presumably, people who cast spells to forestall or to bring rain. The ability to control the weather was often attributed to witches. On this myth and its context in Russian folklore, see Hubbs, *Mother Russia*, p. 40.

16. Literally, "Hellenistic." In modern versions of the canon, "pagan" is used. (See, for example, *Kniga sviatykh apostol*, pt. 1, p. 150.) The earlier phrasing illustrates the hostility that pre-Petrine Russians felt for secular Greek culture, despite their reverence for Greek Orthodoxy.

17. In the *Domostroi*, the sentences in this passage are out of order, thus: "Can light consort with darkness? Can there be a compact between the temple of God

To repeat: People who use destructive charms, who frequent sorcerers and wizards, who invite such to their houses—wanting to use them to see something unspeakable—who feed and keep bears,[18] dogs, or hawks, for hunting or for the amusement and delight of simple folk, those who believe in lustrations, in the power of birth or heritage, as said above, or in horoscopes and forecasts based on the stars, those who say they can drive the clouds away—all such must be ordered banished from the church for six years, then to stand for four years among those who must prostrate themselves, and for two years more among the faithful. Only then can they receive communion. If they are unrepentant, and do not give up these cunning pagan ways even after their banishment, then they must be cut off completely from the church. The hallowed fathers and teachers of the church spoke on sorcerers and wizards, including, among others, St. John Chrysostom. He said,

> As for sorcerers and those who cast spells: if you wish to call on the name of the Holy Trinity, if you are one who makes the sign of Christ's holy cross, you must utterly forsake such people.[19]

Ruling No. 24 by the Synod of Ancyra:[20] He who works magic or follows pagan customs, or who allows anyone who does so to enter

---

and the idols of the heathen? Can a believer join hands with an unbeliever? Can Christ agree with Belial?" See *Domostroi OIDR*, p. 29.

18. Bears, in Russia, were associated with the *skomorokhi*, entertainers who wandered among the rural villages through the seventeenth century. The church virulently opposed the *skomorokhi*, perhaps, as Russell Zguta (*Russian Minstrels* [Philadelphia: University of Pennsylvania Press, 1978]) has argued, because they were descended from the pagan priests of preconversion Kiev. More generally, bears had pagan connotations; some scholars have theorized a pre-Christian bear cult. See Fedotov, *Russian Religious Mind*, 1:9. In this case, however, the reference to bears comes from the Sixth Church Council itself, so its relevance to Russian practice is coincidental.

19. Chrysostom expressed these and related concerns on numerous occasions. See, for example, his *Baptismal Instructions*, trans. Paul W. Harkins, *Ancient Christian Writers*, vol. 31 (Westminster, Md.: Newman Press, 1963) and *Discourses against Judaizing Christians* (1.7.5–11 and 8.5.1–8.8.9), trans. Paul W. Harkins, *The Fathers of the Church*, vol. 68 (Washington, D.C.: Catholic University of America Press, 1977).

20. The Synod of Ancyra met in A.D. 315. Its eighteen bishops considered under what conditions converts who had lapsed into paganism could be readmitted to the church. For its rulings, see *The Definitions of Faith, and Canons of Discipline of the Six Oecumenical Councils, with the Remaining Canons of the Code of the Universal Church,*

his house, whether just as an experiment or because he intends to use their services, according to the canon shall be banished from communion for five years. In the commandments, this is broken into steps: three years prostration; two years in prayer, without the oblation.

To repeat: You must expose anyone who gives himself over to sorcerers, herbalists, or other practitioners of magic and who invites them to his house, for these wicked ones will execute their desires through him. If someone has been healed through sorcery, find and exorcise him, for by evil he was more evilly healed. All such people should be cast out of the church for three years; for two years more they should stand and pray, yet remain excommunicate. At the end of five years, they may again partake of communion.

Ruling No. 61 of the Sixth Council, the one in the Trullus Palace:[21] Such people shall be commanded not to partake of communion for six years.

Ruling No. 11 of the Sixth Ecumenical Council, held in Constantinople, in the Trullus Palace: No Christian may have contact with Jews. If a cleric is found eating unleavened bread, or summoning a Jewish doctor to heal himself, or mixing with Jews at a bathhouse, or having any other contact with them, he shall be defrocked; if a layman does so, he will be excommunicated for nineteen years.[22]

Ruling No. 82 of St. Basil the Great:[23] Those who invite sorcerers into their lives, or bring such to their children, are murderers, and must be banned.

To repeat: Anyone who places himself in the hands of sorcerers, wizards, or shamans in order to learn their evil ways shall be consid-

---

Together with the Apostolical Canons, trans. William Andrew Hammond (New York: James A. Sparks, 1844), pp. 150–157. Despite the title, Hammond includes few canons from the ecumenical councils, but those of the local councils appear in full.

21. Presumably by mistake, the compiler of this addition is repeating the ruling given above. (The Sixth Church Council, held in Constantinople, *was* the one that met in the Trullus Palace.)

22. Jewish doctors enjoyed a good reputation for healing; presumably the connection between religion and medicine accounts for the inclusion of this nasty little piece of anti-Semitism, even though Muscovite Russia allowed few Jews to cross its borders. For an early example of similar views, see St. John Chrysostom, *Discourses*, pp. 222–223.

23. This is usually numbered 72, not 82, among the canons of Basil the Great, also called Basil of Caesaria. The canons were extracted by clerics from various letters, not written as a single document. Ruling number 65 (presumably the no. 93 mentioned here) is a longer version of the same. See *Kniga pravil sviatykh apostolov*, pt. 2, pp. 214, 216.

ered as having the will to murder and be excommunicated. Those who believe in wizards and enter their homes, to be purged from poison or for elucidation of some unspeakable rite, shall be excommunicated for six years, as was commanded by the sixty-first ruling of the Sixth Ecumenical Council, the one that met in Constantinople in the Trullus Palace. This ruling is also number 93 in St. Basil the Great's epistle.[24]

24. *On the Unrighteous Life*

A person who lives in an ungodly way, not according to Christian law, causes injustice, oppression, and offense. He takes things by force; he does not pay for the objects he seizes; he causes death by creating undue delay; he harms young men in every way. Such a man treats his neighbors badly, as well as his peasants in the village, those he serves in a chancery, and those over whom he wields power. He imposes harsh taxes and unlawful punishments. He farms others' fields, cuts their forests, plows their lands, mows their meadows, raids their fishing places, beehives, covers [for birds], and any other catch. He violently grabs everything pleasant, as he robs, steals, and marauds. He accuses people of crimes they did not commit and wrongfully convicts them. He forces people into slavery against their will, using deceit or force against the innocent.[1] He judges crookedly, investigates unjustly, bears false witness, and shows no mercy to those who repent. He seizes, by force, horses, villages, vineyards, homesteads, property of all sorts. He pays too low a price for a debt-slavery contract or extracts payments in the form of alcohol, interest on a loan, excessive taxes, or increased tolls.

If the master or any member of his household commit any of these improper deeds—lechery, unchastity, foul speech, oath-breaking, irrational fury, bearing grudges—and those in charge neither prevent

24. Which of St. Basil's many letters the author has in mind is unclear.
1. In the second half of the sixteenth century, Russians could be converted into limited service contract slaves (to borrow Richard Hellie's term) against their wills, if they had spent more than six months as someone's domestic servant or if they defaulted on certain kinds of loans. See Hellie, *Slavery*, pp. 46–56. The *Domostroi's* author condemns this practice.

the deeds nor punish them strictly, all will go to Hell together and will be damned in this world as well. For such unblessed fruits earn no pardon from God and merit other people's condemnation. Those who have been wronged cry out to God! The sinner brings his soul to destruction and his house to disgrace; he will attract only damned and unblessed things. Such people eat and drink anything they can grab—not God's, but the Devil's fruit. In the end, they descend to Hell. Although the souls of such evildoers are alive, they produce only injury. Alms from the fruits of such deeds do not please God whether one is dead or alive. If you wish to escape eternal torment, give back your ill-gotten gains to the one you wronged. Repent; henceforth, neither you nor yours must act so. For it is written,

The Lord is swift to offer mercy, to receive those who truly repent.
He will grant remission even from great sin.[2]

25. On the Righteous Life

A good person lives according to God's will, the Lord's commandments, the patristic tradition, and Christian law. Such a man, if he is a ruler, judges all justly and without arbitrariness regardless of whether they are rich or poor, close to him or not. He is content with the payment to which he is entitled and the knowledge that he is doing right.

Anyone who is good, whether he lives in a village or a town, is neighborly. He exacts reasonable rents and dues from his peasants, whether for the government or his own chancery, at the proper time; he does not use force, robbery, or torture. If someone's crops do not grow, leaving him with no means with which to pay, a good lord will make no demands upon him. If his neighbors or his peasants lack the wherewithal to sow, have no horse or cow, have nothing with which to pay their dues, a good lord will lend to or help those in need. If the lord himself has little, he must keep what he has, but a good

2. The source of this quotation has not been identified.

master still suffers with his whole heart for those he cannot help. He protects his people faithfully, too, from any who would hurt them.

Neither the lord nor his people should hurt anyone in the fields, on the land, in the home, in the storerooms, or while working with animals.

A good lord desires no ill-gotten gains; it behooves every Christian to live with the blessed fruits of his labor and with justly acquired property.

God will behold your good deeds, your mercy, your unfeigned love toward everyone, your justice in matters great and small. God will shower you with mercy and with abundant rewards; He will multiply your prosperity in every way.

Alms from such righteous labors please God. He will hear the givers' prayers, remitting their sins and conferring on them eternal life.

{Merchants, master-craftsmen, and small landowners should likewise be straightforward and devout as they pursue trade, engage in crafts, or till the soil. They should not steal, rob, pillage, slander others, tell lies, curse, engage in duplicity or sharp trading practices. They should trade, work their crafts, or raise grain by means of their own honest strength, their innate talents, and righteous labors. As they perform each good deed and amass their property according to Christian law and the Lord's commandments, they please those in this life and merit the life eternal.}

26. How a Person Should Live by Gathering His Resources Together

In regards to all your household objects, the tools used in your shops, your commercial goods, the contents of your treasury, living chambers, courtyard, and supply rooms, your villages, the objects used in crafts, your accounts (both income and expenses), your credits, and your debts: gather all unto yourself. These are the resources by which you live.

Hold your purchases in line with your income and expenses.

27. *If Someone Lives without Considering His Means*

Every person—rich or poor, great or small—must consider his means and govern his life by balancing his expenses with his income. A chancery official should govern his life according to his salary from the tsar, his other income, and his *pomest'e*.[1] He must hold household at a level he can afford, by thinking ahead and controlling his expenses. By doing this he will have food, drink, and clothes for himself and his household; he can associate with respectable people.

In contrast, someone who does not consider his means, manage his property and provisions, and control his expenses, who imitates other people, living beyond his means by borrowing or acquiring ill-gotten gains, will find his honor turn to great dishonor. Such a person will find himself subject to ridicule and scorn; in bad times no one will help him. His behavior is a sin before God and deserves the reproaches of others. For every person must flee vainglory, flattery, and ill-gotten gains and live according to his means, thinking ahead, acquiring and spending according to his own true income. Such a life is most pleasant—pleasing to God, praised by others, secure for oneself and one's children.

28. *If Someone Keeps More Slaves Than He Can Afford*

If you keep in your household slaves you cannot afford or who produce little, if you do not satisfy your people's needs for food and

1. *Pomest'e*: originally, land granted to military servitors on conditional tenure, to be returned to the crown on the holder's death. Because it gave the tsar greater control over his servitors, *pomest'e* gradually replaced the older form of landholding, *votchina* (patrimonial property, owned absolutely and in perpetuity by a particular clan). Over time, however, holders of service estates acquired privileges that brought their estates closer to *votchina* holdings. By the late seventeenth century, the two were virtually indistinguishable. For more information, see Blum, *Lord and Peasant*, pp. 180–188.

clothing, if you keep someone who is unhandy or does not know how to think for himself, these slaves (whether men, women, or girls), chafing at their servitude, will lie, steal, and live dissolutely.[1] The men will rob and steal, will drink in the tavern and commit evil. Because they own such foolish slaves, the master and mistress will be considered to have sinned before God and will be reproached by others. Their neighbors will show no friendliness to them, but instead will fine them. Disgrace will come to their house; their stupidity will have harmed themselves.

{Each person should acquire additional slaves only after thinking about how he will feed, clothe, and maintain them so that they will live in peace of mind, fearing God and knowing good governance. If you keep your slaves in this way, you yourself will find God's grace and will save their souls. But do not keep more slaves than you can afford. Do not sell those you do not need into slavery elsewhere, either; let them go free. Whenever possible, give them property as well. You will receive a reward from God; it will profit your soul.}

29. A Husband Must Teach His Wife How to Please God and Her Husband, Arrange Her Home Well, and Know All That Is Necessary for Domestic Order and Every Kind of Handicraft, So She May Teach and Supervise Servants

Husbands should instruct their wives lovingly and with due consideration. A wife should ask her husband every day about matters of piety, so she will know how to save her soul, please her husband, and structure her house well. She must obey her husband in everything. Whatever her husband orders, she must accept with love; she must fulfill his every command. Above all, she must fear God and keep her chastity as decreed above.

When she rises from her bed, she should first wash herself, then complete her prayers. Then she should order the daily work for her

---

1. Slaves often did steal from need, as mentioned by Olearius (*Travels*, pp. 149–150).

women and maids: telling each which embroidery to work, which food to cook that day, which breads to bake of finely sifted wheat flour.

She herself should know how to sift the flour, prepare the kneading trough, mix and roll the loaves. She should know how to bake sourdough breads and sweet rolls and, when they are cooked, buns and filled pies also. She should know how much flour the servants take, how much they bake, how much grain is in a *chetvert'*,[1] an *osmina*,[2] and a sieve, how much remains in the sieve, and how much can be cooked. If the mistress herself can cook and bake everything—meat, fish dishes, pies, pancakes, kasha, jellies, and fritters—she can teach her servants what she knows herself.

If, when the women bake bread, they wash the clothes at the same time, they will use but a single fire and will not waste wood.

The mistress must watch the servants as they wash fine shirts and good robes, checking how much soap and ashes are used. Wash and steam all clothes well; rinse them clean, dry them, and roll them up. Treat tablecloths, napkins, cloths, and towels the same way. The mistress should know the count of everything herself; she should give everything out to the servants and take all back in full measure, making sure it is bleached and clean. Old clothes should be washed; they can be given to orphans.[3]

When the servants bake bread, order them to set some of the dough aside, to be stuffed for pies. When they bake wheat bread, have pies made for the family from the coarse flour left in the sieve. For meat days stuff them with whichever meat is to hand. For fast days use kasha, peas, broth, turnips, mushrooms,[4] cabbage, or whatever God provides; this will please your family.

The wife should know how to cook every dish, meat and fish, for feast and fast, and should teach these techniques to her servants. Similarly, she should know how they make beer, mead, vodka, weak

1. *Chetvert'*: here, one-quarter of a *desiatina*, about half an acre.
2. *Osmina*: half a *chetvert'*; here, about one-quarter of an acre.
3. The Russian term for "orphan" (*sirota*) referred to unfortunates, including peasants and the poor. See, for example: R. E. F. Smith, *The Enserfment of the Russian Peasantry* (Cambridge: Cambridge University Press, 1968), pp. 15, 38–41, 57, 156; R. E. F. Smith and David Christian, *Bread and Salt: A Social and Economic History of Food and Drink in Russia* (Cambridge: Cambridge University Press, 1984), p. 69.
4. Throughout, the *Domostroi* uses the names of two specific mushrooms instead of the general Russian word *griby*: *gvozdi* (saffron milk-caps) and *ryzhiki* (milk agarics). Both words are of Polish origin. See Helmi Poukka, "O vozmozhnom pol'skom istochnike *Domostroia*," *Scando-Slavica* 12 (1966): 119–122.

beer, kvass, vinegar, and sour cabbage—every liquid normally used in cooking and breadmaking.[5] She should know which crops grow in which fields and how much of a harvest can be expected. Because of her husband's instruction, her dread of him, and her own good understanding, all her enterprises will be successful; her household will have plenty of everything.

The mistress must supervise any seamstress whom she has ordered to make a shirt or a kerchief, to weave, to work gold or silk embroidery; the same holds for any artisan who is learning a new skill.[6] She must weigh and measure spun thread, taffeta, brocade, gold, and silver thread before she hands it out, and must gather it up again when the day's work is finished. She is the one who must decide how much material is necessary: she should give out only that much, cutting and measuring the amount herself. She should know all about needlework so that she can teach her women what they need to know.

Some servants do wrong, heating their houses, baking their bread, or washing their clothes at their master's expense. They get flax and spin it for themselves and their families. Some spin flax for the mistress but keep the tow and more for themselves. The mistress can prevent this by keeping a tight rein on her household. A good housewife monitors the work of every servant, giving out only those supplies that are needed and checking how much is used and how much returned. Such a woman knows who works hard or little each day. She herself is a fund of knowledge, and she records everything in the account books.[7]

The mistress of the household should absolutely never commit any evil deeds. Unless she is ill, she should never be found idle, for the servants must habitually look to her as an example. If her husband invites guests or his friends, they should always find her sitting over

5. This contradicts advice given in later chapters (36, 46, 47) that women should have nothing to do with producing or drinking alcohol.

6. The Russian word indicates that both male and female artisans are meant. Women were allowed to interact with men subordinate to them but not with men who were their social equals. The purposes of seclusion, therefore, were not to prevent male-female contact but to deter undesirable marriage alliances and to deny women a public role. (On female seclusion, see the Introduction and Nancy Shields Kollmann, "The Seclusion of Elite Muscovite Women," *Russian History* 10 (1983): 170–187.)

7. This assumes the lady of the house could both read and write; how many sixteenth-century Russian women actually could is questionable.

her embroidery. Thus she will earn honor and glory, and her husband praise.

The servants should never wake the mistress; the mistress should wake the servant. She should even fall asleep over her embroidery (after she has first said her prayers).

30. *How a Good Woman Supervises Her Domestics' Needlework. What to Cut Out and How You Should Keep the Scraps and Snippets*

A good housewife uses her intelligence, follows her husband's instruction, and works hard. She allots to her maidservants fine or coarse linen, or another cloth, as her purpose requires. She sees that stuff is dyed for bodices, caftans, and jumpers.[1] She will have material cut and sewn for household needs. If her family has more than it needs, the mistress of the house should sell the extra tablecloths, napkins, cloths, etc. and use the money for whatever she lacks. Then she need not ask her husband for money she could have found by herself.[2]

Fine shirts, shifts, and robes should be cut when the mistress is present. All scraps and snippets—of brocade and taffeta, expensive fabrics and cheap ones, cloth-of-gold, silk, white and red cloth, feathers, fur, ribbons, worn sheepskins, new fabrics and old—should be saved and put away. Place small pieces in bags; roll large remnants up and tie them. All should be sorted by quantity and stored.

Thus you will make something new out of the old and will not need

The original Short Version title for this chapter is more poetic but hard to translate: *Dobrye zheny rukodel'nye plody i berezhen'e vsemu* (literally, "The Embroidered Fruits of a Good Woman['s Labor] and Her Supervision of All [Domestic Matters]). Despite the rest of the title, this chapter includes no instructions on cutting out robes; the duplication between this and the following chapter may indicate that they were originally a single segment.

1. Jumper: sarafan, a loose, sleeveless, high-waisted robe, usually worn with a blouse. See, for example, the picture of nineteenth-century peasant women in Clements, Engel, and Worobec, eds., *Russia's Women*, plate 4, following p. 132.

2. This contradicts the advice given in the previous chapter (that a woman should not make any decisions without consulting her husband), but it is more practical.

new material. All you require will be in your warehouse; you need not search for it in the marketplace. God granting good foresight and a clear understanding, all will be done at home.

31. How to Cut Out a Robe.
How You Should Keep the Scraps and Snippets

When you, your wife, your children, or your servants need new clothes, follow these instructions whatever material you use: brocade, taffeta, wool, the cloth used to make belts, silk, broadcloth, camel's hair, Persian or other leather. Have the servants cut a quiver (saddle, shoulder cape, pouches, leather boots, fur coat, caftan, undercaftan, overtunic, fur bodice, cloth bodice, hat, trousers, or any other kind of clothing) in the presence of their master or mistress. They should pick up the scraps and the snippets. These can be used by anyone engaged in domestic work—to patch up an old robe, to trim a new one, or in other ways.

Store the scraps and the snippets as you accumulate them. If you have to stop in the marketplace to buy scraps, you must pay three times the price; even then, you may not find anything you like.

When you cut out good clothes for a young son, a daughter, or a young bride:[1] a bodice, a fur bodice, a fur coat, a hooded cape, or a tunic of wool, brocade, damask, satin, or velvet, add two or three inches at the hem, the edges of the seams, and the sleeves. Then, as the young person grows, you can enlarge the size of the robe for two, three, even four, years and it will still fit. Cut robes that are worn infrequently this way.

1. Young bride: that is, a new daughter-in-law, probably still in her teens, come to live with her husband's family. The legal age of marriage in the Orthodox church was twelve for girls and fourteen for boys. Actual ages at marriage are not known, but the scattered evidence available for the elite suggests that youth in the upper service classes married early (before twenty) and usually lived with the groom's parents. See, for example, the "Life of Yuliana Lazarevsky," in Zenkovsky, trans. and ed., Medieval Russia's Epics, pp. 391–399, and Levin, Sex and Society, pp. 96–98.

32. *How to Maintain Domestic Order*

You should establish an orderly workroom for each craft, whether men's or women's. You should have the appropriate tools in the household for carpentry, tailoring, ironmongering, and bootmaking. Each women's craft with its associated tools should also be given a place of its own. Each workshop should be carefully maintained in a suitable room.

You should not talk to anyone about any subject unless it comes from your own knowledge. People do not go uninvited into a stranger's house for any reason, yet they enter their own without so much as a "by-your-leave."

You should also set up a place for cooking and bread-making utensils.

You should have all crafts performed at your own house—the working of copper, tin, iron, wood, or whatever you may need.[1]

If you ever need a loan from someone, or if you choose to lend out your jewel-encrusted silk, your necklaces, your wife's jewel box, your silver, copper, or pewter dishes, clothing of any kind, or other supplies, examine the item (whether new or old) for places where it may be crumpled, dented, moldy, cracked, or torn. Both he who borrows it and he who owns it must write down any defects, so that the details will be known to both parties. Anything that can be weighed should be weighed and the price established for each object.[2]

If this has been done, and an accident occurs which is the borrower's fault, conflict will not then arise between the parties. They can establish damages for the item.

Be honorable in your lending and borrowing. Care for a borrowed

---

1. This suggests a very large household, although not all the artisans employed by the family lived with them.
2. Even this very practical advice has biblical precedents. See, for example, Ecclesiasticus 42:7 ("When you make a deposit, see that it is counted and weighed, and when you give or receive, have it all in writing.") and 29:2 ("Lend to your neighbour in his time of need; repay your neighbour punctually.").

"If you choose to lend out your jewel-encrusted silk, your necklaces, your wife's jewel-box, your silver, copper, or pewter dishes . . . " (Chapter 32). This exquisite ivory casket, probably a jewel-box, comes from Archangel and dates from the early eighteenth century, but the techniques used in its creation had won renown for Russian artisans even before the fall of Constantinople in 1453. Courtesy of the Walters Art Gallery, Baltimore.

item more even than your own, and take it back on time, so your lenders need not ask for it themselves or send someone for it. If you do, they will continue to offer you friendship and opportunities for profit.[3]

If you do not protect another's goods, if you keep them too long or return them damaged, you will suffer future disgrace and present loss. You will have to sell your possessions and you will lose your credit.

33. [How] the Mistress Must Oversee Her Servants' Domestic Work and Crafts Every Day. How She Must Watch Her Own Behavior

Every day the mistress should oversee her servants, those who bake, cook, and engage in any kind of craft. If a certain maidservant works well, according to the orders given her (whether in cooking food, baking bread, making rolls, pies, or fritters, or embroidering well), the mistress should reward her by giving her money and food, as recommended in "How the Master, Meeting with His Servants, Should Reward Them as They Deserve" [Chapter 59].

But if someone works badly, disobeys orders, is lazy, incompetent, unsanitary, or a thief, the mistress of the house (just like the master) must correct her. For more information on punishment, see: "How to Reward or Punish Someone" [second part of Chapter 38].

The family living quarters, bedchambers, storerooms, porch, and stairway should always be kept clean. Wash tables and dishes well. The tablecloth should also be clean.

The mistress herself should be morally strong in every situation, for then her servants will be polite, as written above [Chapter 29]. With her servants the mistress should never engage in idle talk or mocking speech. She should not invite market women, idle wenches,

3. This and the preceding two paragraphs seem to be aimed at wealthy merchants (like Sil'vestr's son Anfim): wealthy because the goods described are valuable and merchants because they make loans.

or sorcerers of any sort to the house. {Such practices spawn many evils and make the housewife indulgent toward her servants. If such people start coming to the house, and the mistress of the house does not reproach those who invited them, but instead greets the sorcerers herself, the magicians will first make her servants thieves, then dissolute. If the mistress is unwise and does not separate her servants from such people, punish her as well as them, as written elsewhere [Chapter 38].

Now let us stop talking about such wicked people, and move on.} Bedding and robes hung along the beams and kept in chests and boxes, kerchiefs, shirts, and all-purpose cloths should be in good repair, clean, bleached, arranged, and packed away. They should not be wrinkled or all bundled together. Jeweled silk, necklaces, and fine clothes should be kept under lock and key. The mistress should keep the keys in a small box and should control access to the storerooms.

34. [How] a Wife Must Consult Her Husband and Ask His Advice Every Day. How a Woman Should Act While Visiting and What She Should Talk about with Guests

Every day a wife should consult with her husband and should ask his advice on every matter. She should remember what he requires of her. When she visits or invites people to her house, she must still obey her husband's commands. While entertaining guests or visiting, she should wear her best clothes. During meals, she should not drink alcohol. A drunk man is bad, but a drunk woman is not fit to be on the earth.

With her guests she should discuss needlework and household management, discipline and embroidery. If she does not know something, she may ask the advice of a good woman, speaking politely and sweetly. Whenever anyone asks her to do something, she should bow low in submission and comply. Whether she is in her own household or is the guest of someone else, she will heed the good proverb, which tells how good women live, how they impose discipline, manage their households, teach their children and servants, obey their husbands and ask their advice.[1a]

A good woman monitors herself. She asks politely about good things she does not know. She refuses to listen to or to indulge in bad, mocking, or lecherous speech. Instead she looks for evidence of good management: well-prepared food; unusual dishes or needlework; a good, thoughtful, and intelligent hostess; intelligent, polite, orderly, handy, and thoughtful servants. She asks politely and demurely about those things that are new to her; she must be submissive in that way. Then, having returned to her own home, she tells her husband all she has learned, to bring repose to his soul.

Such good women make suitable friends, not because of the food they offer, but because of the benefits of their conversation and their knowledge. Each woman should take stock of her own behavior and should not mock. She should not gossip about anyone. If others ask questions about someone, even if they sometimes torment her, she should answer, "I do not know anything about that. I didn't hear about it and don't know about it. I do not talk about inconsequential things, or pass judgment on princesses or boyars' wives,[2] or on my neighbors, either."

35. How to Teach Your Servants to Run Errands {without Gossiping}

Order your servants not to gossip about people, about where they have been visiting or what they saw there. Nor should your servants speak badly about your house or say, when visiting others, what is done in your house.

[To the servant:][1b] When your master sends you on an errand, bear

---

1a. The reference here is presumably to Proverbs 31:10–31 ("Who can find a capable wife?").

2. The author means, "I don't talk about my social betters," supporting the idea that the intended reader of the *Domostroi* probably came from a slightly lower social stratum, although still one influential enough to be party to court gossip.

1b. This chapter shifts abruptly from addressing the servant to addressing the

this in mind: If others ask about the item you carry or about anything else, do not reply. Claim not to know the answers to their questions. Instead, leave quickly, go home, and tell your master what happened. But do not bring back news other than that for which you were sent. Thus you may prevent quarreling between masters, unbecoming or lewd speech; these things are not at all good.

{Do not chatter about rude deeds, words you have overheard, or things you have seen. If someone's servant comes to your own master or mistress, do not ask probing questions about what he has brought; take the item from him and let him go quickly. If a stranger's servant starts to gossip, do not listen to him. Instead, scold him, asking him the purpose of his errand. Word will get around,[2] and others will not bother you.} Your master and mistress will be well-regarded if you are polite in this way.

[To the master:] If you send your servant or son anywhere, with instructions to do something, tell him exactly what to do or what to buy. Then go back and ask him to repeat what you told him. All is not well until he can repeat your orders verbatim.

If you send food, drink, or anything else to someone by means of a servant, ask the servant when he returns where he carried it. If his answer matches your instructions, all is well. Send drink in a sealed container and food in whole pieces, so he cannot deceive you.

If you send items for trade, gather and measure them, count any money, weigh anything that can be weighed, and seal up anything valuable. Then no one will be tempted to sin.

Instruct your servant whether, if the master of the house to which he is sent is out, he should leave what you have sent or should bring it home. If your servant is intelligent and polite, even if you forget to go back and check with him, he will come to you. He will take off his hat, most politely, ask your permission, and report as he was instructed. If he does do this, it is good.

[To the servant:] Wherever you are sent, knock softly at the gates. If you enter the courtyard and someone asks you your business, tell him nothing. Answer, "I was not sent to you. I will speak with the person to whom I was sent."

---

master, and back again. The words in brackets have been added to help readers identify the "you."

2. Literally, "he will remember," but the point seems to be that he will also tell others, who then will not bother to gossip in this particular household.

At the door of a storeroom, a cottage, or a monk's cell, wipe your muddy feet, blow your nose, and cough. Say a prayer as a test. If no one replies with an "Amen," say another prayer, even a third, louder than the first. If you still get no answer, knock lightly.

If they admit you, {enter, bow to the icons,[3] present your master's petition, and proffer your gifts.} Do not, while you are there, pick your nose with your finger, cough, or sneeze. {Do not clear your throat or spit. If you must do these things, go outside to do them, standing politely by the side of the house.} Do not look from side to side. Do what you were instructed to do, and do not talk about anything else. When you are done, go straight back to your own house and tell your master what happened.

When you find yourself in another's house, even if the master is not there, do not wander about or pick up objects (whether good or bad, expensive or cheap) without permission. Do not move things from place to place or take anything away with you. Do not carry off anything without the owner's blessing. The same is true for food and drink. Do not eat anything unless ordered to do so. This is sacrilege and gluttony. Do not trust anyone who dares to do such things. Because of his roving eyes, he should take no more messages, in accord with the words of the Gospel:

> You have proved trustworthy in a small way; I will now put you in charge of something big. [Matthew 25:21 and 25:23]

If your master sends you to deliver food, do not eat it. Take only and exactly what is sent. Make sure your master sends something whole; then no one will doubt you.

[To the master:] {A sensible son, male or female servant who hears rumors or sees evidence of anger or rudeness at home or in the world outside will say nothing, not even that which he or she has been ordered to say, until all has been set to rights. Those in full possession of their faculties will bring peace where they hear quarrels, and love where they find enmity. Where others curse and howl, the sensible convey compliments and goodwill. Such intelligent, polite, and

---

3. Before the 1917 revolution, every Russian home had a "beautiful corner" where icons of the family's favorite saints hung. Custom demanded that on entering a room, one greet the saints first, by bowing in the direction of the icons, and one's hosts second.

thoughtful servants bring love and eternal peace. If you have intelligent servants such as these, care for them and reward them as though they were your own children; consult them in everything.

From the elders:[4] Remember the story of the wise disciple of a certain hermit who lived in the desert. A man who was going away gave a second hermit his cell to rest in for a while. But the Devil caused the first hermit to be eaten up with envy, so the first hermit sent his disciple to say wicked things to the one who lived in the cell, to make him leave. The sensible disciple went to the stranger bearing peace and good wishes from his master instead of evil.

Sometime later, the first hermit, in his Devil-induced arrogance, went to see the stranger, wanting to beat him and throw him out of his cell. The good disciple raced to tell the stranger of his master's visit and his wishes for peace and goodwill. The stranger immediately ran out to meet the other hermit, bowing low before him, lauding the other, and denigrating himself. Thus affection grew between them, and they praised the disciple.

[To the master:] If you have untutored, thoughtless male or female servants,[5] they will not be respected anywhere you send them. For they will stand in the courtyard saying all sorts of unpleasant things. If the people in the household are sly, if they sing the praises of this stupid servant, if they unwisely ask questions about the servant's master and mistress, the foolish one will tell everything he knows, despite his instructions. His master and mistress will suffer while he goes among the populace spreading gossip. Mindless servants such as these cause enmity, ridicule, mockery, and shame. Because of this, a farsighted man and woman must teach their children and servants, their male and female slaves, the fear of God and courtesy, as written above [Chapter 22].

This is how you can recognize the stupid servant: when he comes back from visiting others, he will chatter about everything, just as he tells others about your domestic affairs. If the master and mistress themselves like to gossip with their servants, engaging in slander,

---

4. The source of this little story is unknown, but it belongs to the genre of *exempla* tales (stories used to teach moral lessons). *Exempla* were very popular throughout medieval Europe.

5. *Rab i rabynia*, the Old Russian words for male and female slaves. The word used elsewhere in the *Domostroi* is *domochadtsy* (literally, "house children"), except in biblical passages. This passage has, however, been added from a different source.

censure, mockery, and lies, that master and mistress bring trouble on themselves, their house, their children, and their servants. They encourage all that is sly, hateful, lying, and venomous. In pursuit of their passions they lose all sense. By their actions, they turn good deeds and love into eternal hatred, injuring both their bodies and their souls. Both now and in the future they will suffer evil at God's hand.

A wise master and mistress, on the other hand, do not like and will not engage in idle chitchat, mockery, ridicule, lies, and slander. They do not pass along nasty tales about other people, censure them, listen to gossip, or make jokes at another's expense. If someone rebukes, ridicules, or mocks them or speaks badly about them (to their faces or behind their backs), they will evaluate it from the perspective of their own wisdom.If someone begins to abuse us during business, we must turn away and make amends as though we were the one heaping reproach.[6] If we are reproached or annoyed at some other time, we should bear it patiently and accept it with gratitude. According to the apostle [Luke],

How blest you are when men hate you, when they outlaw you and insult you. [Luke 6:22]

We should not seek vengeance for this or express enmity. We should have love toward those who give it. The apostle Paul, in his teachings, said:

"If your enemy is hungry, feed him; if he is thirsty, give him a drink; by doing this you will heap live coals on his head." Do not let evil conquer you, but use good to defeat evil. [Romans 12:20–21, quoting Proverbs 25:21–22][7]

Teach your servants in this manner. If you see your brother's sin, and do not take note of it, if you do not remonstrate with him privately about it, but mock him and heap reproach upon him, you will be a pagan and a tormentor, you will share his sin. If you find your brother guilty of some sin, or learn of his committing some unworthy act, and

---

6. This parallels Sil'vestr's self-description in Chapter 64: "If an agent caused trouble for us with other people, by arguing, we took the fault on ourselves."

7. In the *Domostroi*, the third phrase is moved to the end.

you speak to him alone and privately, and with affection, if he listens to you and stops his unworthy deeds, you will save your brother's soul. You will receive a reward from God. If he does not accept your words, even if he comes to hate you, you are free of his sin. He will have to answer for himself before God. Meanwhile, God, seeing your good deeds and wise humility, your thoughtful admonition and your patiently enduring abuse for His sake, will bless you with His great compassion, with remission of your sins and the life everlasting.

Chapters 26 and 32 [in this edition, 22 and 28] discuss these subjects also.}

36. *Instruction to Women and Servants on Drunkenness.*
And on Secrets, Which You Should Never Keep.
How You Should Not Listen to Servants' Lies or Calumnies
without Correcting Them.
How to Correct Them with Fear, and Your Wife Also.
And How to Be a Guest and
How to Manage Your Household in Every Way

A woman should never under any circumstances drink alcohol—wine, mead, or beer—nor should she receive it as a present. Liquor should be kept in the cellar or the icehouse. A woman should drink weak beer or kvass, both at home and in public.[1]

If women come visiting, therefore, do not give them alcohol. Nor should your own women and maids drink to the point of drunkenness, in public or at home.

A wife should not eat or drink without her husband's knowledge, nor conceal food or drink from him. Nor should she have secrets from her husband.

At the houses of her women friends, she should not ask for drink or food, or for scraps or tidbits without her husband's knowledge, nor should she allow such behavior in others. She should not keep a

1. That is, presumably, if she chooses to drink any alcoholic beverage. The *Domostroi* offers a fairly wide selection of fruit juices and other nonalcoholic drinks in later chapters.

stranger in her house without her husband's knowledge.[2] She should consult with her husband, not her manservant or maidservant.

A woman should guard herself from evil and should protect her male and female servants also. She should not gossip with her husband, telling him falsehoods. She should not hold grudges. If someone errs, she should tell her husband about it directly, without embellishment.

The husband and wife should never listen to gossip or believe a tale without direct evidence. A wife should not lightly inform upon her domestics to her husband.[3] She should report, truthfully, only that which she cannot correct herself or a truly wicked deed. If a maid heeds neither scolding nor punishment, the mistress must not keep her, or she will commit some new evil. In these instances, the wife should discuss with her husband what kind of punishment to mete out.

When the mistress entertains guests and drinking is appropriate,[4] she herself must not touch alcohol. A single adult man should bring the drink, the food, and all the utensils. He should be the only man present, whatever the time of day. Then any dishonor or ignorance can be laid to his account.

Men and women should not breakfast unless they are ill; eat and drink at appropriate times.[5]

2. This prohibition illustrates how difficult it can be to supervise someone kept in a strictly separate world, as well as men's fear that women would escape their control, expressed in the repeated admonitions to wives to share all information with their husbands.

3. Again, this contradicts earlier advice to tell her husband everything. Throughout this chapter, the role confusion between housewife as authority and wife as subordinate is particularly strong.

4. Another apparent contradiction. Perhaps these guests are male and the wife acting on her husband's behalf.

5. Throughout most of the Middle Ages, the church considered two meals a day (dinner, served around noon, and supper, served in the evening) sufficient for good Christians; more was gluttony. Breakfast appeared quite early but only gradually gained acceptance. The *Domostroi* preserves the older ethos. For more on the acceptance of breakfast, see Barbara Henisch, *Fast and Feast: Food in Medieval Society* (University Park: Pennsylvania State University Press, 1976), pp. 16–25.

37. *How a Woman Should Care for Clothing*

Take care of the dresses, shifts, and kerchiefs you wear every day. Do not scatter your clothes about; do not let them smell musty; do not wrinkle them or drop them in dirt or water. Do not throw them down just anywhere. Gather them together, store them carefully, and guard them well. Teach your servants to do this too.

The master, the mistress, their children, and their servants should work in old clothes. When the work is done, they should change into clean everyday clothes and boots. But in good weather, on a holy day, to go out in public, to go to church or to visit, put on your best clothes. Throughout the day, guard yourself from mud and rain and snow. Do not spill drink on your clothes or spatter them with food or fat. Do not let your clothes get musty; do not sit in dust or moisture.

When you come back from a festival, from church, or from visiting, take off your best clothes, examine them, dry them, remove the wrinkles, brush them, and clean them most thoroughly. Put them away in a closet.

All old and everyday clothes (outer and inner robes, linen and boots) should be washed frequently. Old clothes should be patched and darned. Then they remain fit for others to see as well as pleasant for you. You can also give them to the poor for your salvation.

All clothes and cloths should be packed away and folded carefully. Put them somewhere in a chest or box. {Always keep them under lock and key, so you need not fear scandal.}

38. How to Keep {Dishes in Good Order and} Arrange the Domestic Utensils. {How to Keep Rooms} Neat and Clean. {How the Housewife Should Punish Her Servants. How Her Husband Should Supervise Her, Punish Her, and Save Her with Fear}

Warm water in the morning. Wash the table, dishes, jars, spoons, ladles, and goblets. Rinse them off and dry them. Do the same after dinner and in the evening. Wash the pails, trays, kneading troughs, sieves, colanders, clay pots, pitchers, and metal saucepans as well. Rinse them, dry them, and put them in a clean and suitable place. Every dish and every utensil should always be clean and accounted for.

Dishes should not be carried about the shop, the courtyard, or the house. Dishes, goblets, ladles, and spoons should not be scattered about the shop. They should be arranged somewhere in a clean place. They should be turned upside down. Any dish that contains food or drink should be covered for reasons of hygiene. Dishes containing food or liquid and kneading troughs in which you are working should always be covered, even inside the house. Tie the cover down to protect the contents from cockroaches and other unclean things.

{Jars, dishes, spoons, goblets, ladles, and all the best dishes—silver, pewter, and wood—should be kept under lock and key in a safe place. When you have guests or a celebration with respectable people, bring them out to the table. After the feast, look them over, have them washed and counted. Then lock them up again. Treat the everyday dishes as described above.

Inside the house,} wash the walls, benches, floors, windows, doors, storerooms, and porches. Rinse them, sweep them, and scrape off the dirt. A house should always be clean; so should the staircases and the entranceway. Everything should be washed, raked out, rinsed, and swept.

Put straw in front of the entranceway for wiping muddy feet, so the staircase will not be muddied. Before the doors of the warehouses and

"Jars, dishes, spoons, goblets, ladles, and all the best dishes—silver, pewter, and wood—should be kept under lock and key in a safe place. When
you have guests or a celebration with respectable people, bring them out
to the table" (Chapter 38). The *Domostroi*'s author was concerned to prevent theft; looking at this seventeenth-century goblet, made large so that
guests could pass it around at drinking parties, one can see why. Some
goblets, like this one, had spouts to direct the flow of liquor (in the sixteenth century, still predominantly mead or wine); others, such as those
used during wedding rituals (see Chapter 67), lacked them. Courtesy of
the Walters Art Gallery, Baltimore.

granaries, put a bast mat, an old piece of felt, or a towel for wiping
muddy feet so they will not dirty the pavement. In muddy weather
change the hay or straw in the entranceway and change the bast mat
or the piece of felt at the doors. Either put down a clean mat or rinse
the dirty mat and dry it; then it will be ready to put down under
people's feet again.

By doing these things, an orderly woman will always have a clean
and well-arranged house.

{Your servants should always sweep in the courtyard, and in the
street before your gates, and should rake when it is muddy. They
should shovel snow in the winter as well. They should pile up the

kindling, the wood, and the lumber.[1] Then everything will be neat and clean.}

In the stables, the bakery, and all the workrooms, all should be in order, everything put away in some appropriate place, clean, and swept. To enter such order is like entering Paradise.

The wife should supervise all this and should teach her servants and children in goodly and valiant fashion. If someone fails to heed her scoldings, she must strike him. If the husband sees something amiss for which his wife or her servants are responsible, or notices that all is not in accord with what is written in this document, he should reason with his wife and correct her. If she heeds him and does everything according to this book, he should love her and reward her.

But if your wife does not live according to this teaching and instruction, does not do all that is recommended here, if she does not teach her servants, then the husband should punish his wife. Beat her when you are alone together; then forgive her and remonstrate with her. But when you beat her, do not do it in hatred, do not lose control. A husband must never get angry with his wife; a wife must live with her husband in love and purity of heart.

You should discipline servants and children the same way. Punish them according to the extent of their guilt and the severity of their deed. Lay stripes upon them but, when you have punished them, forgive them.

The housewife must grieve over her servants' punishment, insofar as that is reasonable, for that gives the servants hope.[2]

Only if his wife or son or daughter will not pay attention to scoldings, if they show no respect and refuse to do what they were told to do, should a husband or father bring understanding with the lash. But do not beat the culprit before others; punish him alone, then talk to him, and grant him forgiveness.

A wife should not get angry at her husband about anything, nor a husband at his wife.

Do not box anyone's ears for any fault. Do not hit them about the eyes or with your fist below the heart. Do not strike anyone with a stick or staff or beat anyone with anything made of iron or wood.[3]

1. *Rupos*, a Polonism.
2. This emphasizes mother as intercessor, the domestic equivalent of the Virgin Mary. See note 9 to Chapter 13.
3. Ivan IV should have heeded this advice. In 1581, in the midst of a dispute,

From such a beating, administered in passion or anguish, many misfortunes can result: blindness or deafness, dislocation of an arm, leg, or finger, head injury, or injury to a tooth. With pregnant women or children, damage to the stomach could result, so beat them only with the lash, in a careful and controlled way, albeit painfully and fearsomely. Do not endanger anyone's health; beat someone only for a grave fault.[4]

When you must whip someone, take off the culprit's shirt. Beat him in a controlled way with the lash, holding him by the hands while you think of his fault. When you have punished him, you must talk with him; there should be no anger between you. Your people should know nothing of it.

There should be no fights among your people that stem from past quarrels or rumors unsupported by direct investigation. Whenever you discover signs of bad feeling or unkind words, question the offender alone, kindly. If he sincerely repents, punish him lightly and forgive him. If the person is innocent, do not connive with the slanderer. To prevent enmity henceforth, punish appropriately and only after personal investigation. If an offender does not repent, punish him severely. Otherwise the guilty remain guilty and only the righteous learn righteousness. "A sword will not strike bent heads, but a humble word will break bones."[5]

Ivan struck his eldest son, also called Ivan, over the head with an iron-tipped staff. The younger Ivan died, leaving Russia without a mentally or physically capable heir. After Ivan's younger son Fedor died childless, the country collapsed in a fifteen-year interregnum (1598–1613) known as the Time of Troubles.

4. By sixteenth-century standards, this is the voice of reason. Nonetheless, the psychological effects of systemic corporal punishment are severe and long-lasting. For effects on the individual, with comments on how such individuals produce a violent society, see Alice Miller, *For Your Own Good: Hidden Cruelty in Child-Rearing and the Roots of Violence*, trans. Hildegarde Hannum and Hunter Hannum (New York: Farrar, Straus and Giroux, 1983). For the effects of physical punishment on early modern European society, see David Hunt, *Parents and Children in History* (New York: Basic Books, 1970).

5. This has the ring of a proverb, but, if so, it seems not to be a biblical one. Perhaps it is a variation on "The lash of a whip raises weals, but the lash of a tongue breaks bones. Many have been killed by the sword, but not so many as by the tongue" (Ecclesiasticus 28:17–18).

39. *If a Man Does Not Teach His Household Himself, He Will Receive Judgment from God. If He Acts Well Himself and Teaches His Wife and Servants, He Will Receive Mercy from God*

If a man does not himself follow the recommendations in this document, if he does not teach his wife to do likewise, does not structure
his household in accordance with God's will, does not care for his soul
or teach his people, he will be destroyed now and forever. His house
will also be destroyed. If a good man cares about his salvation, instructs
his wife, and teaches his domestics the fear of God and the art of
lawful Christian living, just as is written here, he, together with all
his household, will pass his life in prosperity, as God has promised,
and will receive divine mercy.

40. *How the Master or His Deputy Should Buy Supplies to Last the Year*

The chancery official, majordomo, steward,[1] or merchant in whom
trust has been placed, or the master himself, should regularly check
the marketplace for household supplies—grain, hops, butter, meat,
and fish (both fresh and salted). When the *gosti*[2] or peasants[3] have

1. Chancery official (*prikaznyi chelovek*): the great magnates had their own private chanceries which resembled the state chanceries in function and operation (in
fact, the state administration grew out of the Muscovite tsars' private chanceries).
Majordomo (*dvoretskii*) and steward (*kliuchnik*) are here interchangeable: names for
men who might be in overall charge of a large household (as officers in charge of
the royal household, these could be prestigious positions, but households of lesser
standing employed them also). In private households, these offices were occupied
by elite slaves, another indication that the author of the *Domostroi* has a select
audience in mind.

2. *Gosti* (sing. *gost'*): state-appointed merchants who traded internationally on

imported goods or supplies of wood, buy enough to last the whole year. Then you will not spend a ruble, or even ten rubles, for something worth a quarter of that.

It is more expensive to buy from a middleman: it will cost you twice as much, so do not buy from them unless you must.

With those items that do not spoil, buy more than you need when prices are low. You can sell the extra when prices rise.

Sometimes your own household will produce a surplus, earning you renown among your peers.

When the servants of a capable and intelligent master buy anything from a *gost'*, a peasant, or a local trader, they trade amicably and pay for their goods on the spot.

Above all, keep an eye on the trader during the sale.[4] Treat him with honor. First offer him bread, salt, and something to drink;[5] you lose nothing by this. It creates friendship; from then on this merchant will recognize you. He will not offer good items to someone else, charge more than he should, or sell you a bad product.

If he wants good service, the master should entertain visiting merchants himself, plying them with liquor and food, greeting them kindly and affectionately. All gain from such good fellowship.

Bestow a gift on the merchant, suitable to the size of the deal and the merchant's status. Then he will double his efforts on your behalf.

Anyone who follows these recommendations escapes sin and shame. He will be praised by merchants in all lands and will have prosperity in his home.

Do not curse the responsibilities that come with such prosperity: feed and clothe your household, give alms to the poor. For this pleases God and profits your soul.

---

behalf of the crown. Usually no more than thirty *gosti* were appointed at a time. There is no exact English equivalent.

3. These would be peasants who came into the city to trade their surplus, often to the great disgust of the local merchantry who wanted higher prices.

4. An example of Russian trade practices at their worst, or at least the measures necessary to protect oneself from a merchant's abuse. For more on this, see the Introduction.

5. Bread and salt are traditional Russian symbols of hospitality. The Russian term for hospitality is *khleb-sol'* (bread-salt).

41. *What to Do with Goods from Faraway Lands*

If you buy a whole beaver from a merchant (or two or three or as many as you like), do not throw away the skin. Work it; you can give it to someone at home, or it can be sold for half again as much as you paid for it.

Store bolts of taffeta and other valuable items: silk, gold, silver, squirrel skins, etc. Buy what you need for your household, your trading, and your crafts, when items are plentiful and cheap in the market, for this will profit you. If you have your own artisans—tailors, bootmakers, or carpenters—you can use the remnants to trim a new garment or to patch an old one. Either way, you save on new material.

Whenever you find wood (timber, firewood, boxes, dowels, oak, bast, linden wood, boards, laths, gutters, or troughs), brought on carts in the winter or on rafts or boats in the summer, stock up for the year. Do not let anything pass you by. If you do not buy when goods are cheap, later you will get stuck with something you do not like and pay extra for it into the bargain. Buy whatever is available, if the price is right, even if you do not need it right then. If you buy too much, you can sell it at a profit later.

42. *On the Same Subject. How Someone Who Has No Villages Should Buy Supplies for Summer and Winter. How to Raise Animals at Home and Always Have Enough Food for Them*

To stock up for a year, the man or woman in charge, if he or she has no *pomest'e*, *votchina*, field, or village,[1] must buy the following: a

1. Members of the military service classes (*boiarstvo* and *dvorianstvo*) would have landed property of some kind. Even those who lived in Moscow relied on their rural estates for provisions. (For accounts of the various goods supplied, see Crummey, *Aristocrats and Servitors*, p. 127.) "Those without villages" yet still within the

year's supply of grain (brought on carts in winter), half-carcasses of aged red meat and fish—fresh sturgeon, hung in long pieces or preserved in boxes, salmon, salmon caviar, and black caviar.[2]

Salt fish and cabbage in the summer; store these dishes in ice in the winter. Store drinks in winter, too; cover the jars and pack them with ice. Cover the jars with bast, and in the summer the contents will still be fresh.

In the summer, you can eat fresh meat;[3] the person responsible for domestic supplies should buy it.

Buy a young ram and skin it at home. The sheepskin can be used for a coat, and the ram's entrails will make a pleasant addition to your table.

A good housewife or cook knows many ways to cook mutton. From the breast she makes soup. She stuffs the kidneys, roasts the rib, stuffs the shoulders with eggs, boils the feet. She cuts up the liver and wraps it, with an onion, in its membrane, then fries it in a frying pan. She stuffs the lung with a little milk mixed with flour and egg, and the sweetbreads with eggs. She makes soup from the ram's head, brain, and entrails. She stuffs the tripe with kasha. She boils pieces of kidney, or stuffs them for grilling. Such a woman can make many pleasant dishes from just one ram.

Pack jellied broth on ice to keep it fresh.

Buy fresh meat in the summer. Buy for a week at a time when you shop on Monday, Wednesday, or Friday;[4] by buying larger amounts, you will pay less. You can keep the meat fresh for two or three days, even a week, by salting it or packing it in ice.[5]

---

economic and social circles addressed by the *Domostroi* included state secretaries and other influential chancery personnel, rich merchants, and the (rare) well-to-do clergyman.

2. The variety of goods mentioned in this and other chapters of the *Domostroi* suggest a thriving market economy (although one with a limited clientele). For more on this, see the Introduction.

3. The appearance of fresh meat on the table was more noteworthy when people ate salt meat for most of the year than it is today. For more on the impact of fresh versus salted food, see Henisch, *Fast and Feast*, pp. 28–58.

4. Traditionally, these were market days.

5. Although Russian winters are very cold, Russian summers are quite hot (similar to the continental climate that prevails in the American Midwest). It is hard to imagine that sixteenth-century Muscovites had ready access to ice in the middle of summer (Russia has no mountain ranges to speak of). Perhaps people stored it underground in winter and were able to keep it from melting; or perhaps this anomaly indicates foreign origin.

In September, buy a milkless cow—one or as many as you need.[6] Do not rush to make a purchase; when prices go down, you can buy more.

Salt the meat so it will last the year and hang it in the storeroom. Your family can eat the entrails throughout the autumn. If you process the hide and the tallow, you can sell them and recoup half your money. Render the suet, too, to meet your needs for the year.

Good housewives stew the cow's entrails, head, ears, lips, jawbones, brain, intestines, tripe, stomach, fatty flesh, feet, liver, and kidneys. They stuff the entrails with kasha cooked with suet and simmered (the kasha can be made from oatmeal, buckwheat, barley, or whatever is available). If these [sausages] are not eaten up in the autumn, they make a pleasant Christmas feast.

You can make the cow's tripe, lips, ears, and feet into broth that will last all year. Such broth is especially good with sour cabbage.

Raise a pig at home and kill it in the autumn. Salt this meat, too, to last you through the year. Render the lard and eat the head, feet, stomach, intestines, and spine during autumn and winter.

It is pleasant to visit the house of a farsighted man or woman. Where good order reigns, all appears prosperous and the family content. They never suffer loss. When others go to the market and pay high prices, they go to their cellar.

If you raise geese, ducks, and hens at home, make sure you have a pond for them. Let them find their own food in summer; during the rest of the year, feed them with whatever is to hand.

If you keep a milch cow, you can find food for it in the fields in summer.[7]

In a well-ordered home you can find feed in either summer or winter: dregs of beer, vinegar, kvass, and sour cabbage soup; husks of oats, rye, wheat, and barley; leftovers from making groats and oat flour.

In autumn people salt cabbage, serve beets, store turnips and carrots. You can collect all the rubbish—leaves, roots, peelings, crumbs

---

6. Cows that lost their milk were sold in September, before the onset of winter, so the owner did not have to provide forage for them. As winter got closer, the owners became more desperate to sell, and prices went down.

7. Russian urban homesteads were large and sprawling, as many contemporary visitors observed. Still, a cow requires a considerable amount of space. The "fields" mentioned in the text were outside the city walls.

from the table and from breadmaking, all the pieces of food left lying around the house—and put them in a jar to feed animals (work horses, cows, geese, ducks, pigs, hens, and dogs). This costs you nothing, yet brings profit and pleasure. You will always have abundant food for yourself and your guests.[8]

If you produce everything at home—hens and eggs, cheese and milk—you will celebrate your good fortune every day. You will never have to go to market. You will have pies, kasha, pancakes, horn-shaped rolls, jellies, and milk dishes whenever you desire them, all prepared at home.

The housewife should know how to make everything herself and should teach her servants what she knows. Such servants enrich a man.

If a man is farsighted and interested in domestic management, and his wife capable, God will increase their stock of pigs, geese, hens, ducks, milk, sour cream, butter, cheese, and eggs. Such people eat well; they have enough to entertain others and can give alms from the blessed fruits of their righteous labors. They can sell anything they do not need, gaining in return a little blessed money to use for their own needs or to give in alms pleasing to God.[9]

If a young person or a widow cannot create enough waste to feed his or her milch cows, as recommended in this chapter, such people should feed their animals with hay or oats.

If you have chaff from grain, mix it with boiling water or with oil to feed your animals.

Feed and milk your cows yourself. Wash each cow with your own hands. Put on an old, clean robe; bring warm water and with a clean rag wash the cow's udder. Milk the cow in a clean place and with every care; treat it gently.

Put out the food, whatever it may be. Feed the horses feathergrass[10] as well. Be like the peasant in his cottage, who feeds his animals himself. In this way you establish a relationship with them.

Feed young calves, lambs, hens, geese, pigs, and ducks in the same way, with whatever food is appropriate.

8. Because you waste nothing, even using your trash to feed animals, which you can then eat.

9. The author is distinguishing between "blessed" money, gained through moral means, and ill-gotten gains. See Chapters 9 and 24 for other instances of this distinction.

10. Feathergrass: a kind of prairie grass.

43. How Order Depends on Storing Supplies Needed throughout the Year, and for Fasts as Well

The master must stock everything his household needs throughout the year: rye, wheat, oats, buckwheat, oat flour, barley, malt, peas, and hemp. Only then can his wife and servants provide good food during a fast, changing it every day so they satisfy the family and honor their guests at low cost. Under these circumstances, the wife can make any food that is wanted during a fast. (Hempseed oil and groats should also be kept in the house.) She prepares pies, pancakes, cookies, horn-shaped rolls, kasha, noodles made from peas, strained peas, soup, dumplings, boiled kasha, stew, turnovers, and blintzes (filled with mushrooms, poppy seeds, kasha, turnips, cabbage, or whatever else she can find),[1] sops in broth, and round wheaten loaves. A good man and a woman well-versed in domestic management store all the ingredients for such dishes in their home, to cook when the time is right.

When she buys fresh fish, a good housewife separates them for salting, smoking, cooking, and drying. She rolls the small ones in flour and fries them. During a fast she adds fish to the cabbage soup from time to time. She can serve this on fast days to family and guests.[2]

When there is no fresh fish, people put out radishes, horseradish, cabbage, pickles, and any other vegetables they may have.[3] They serve caviar, dry-cured fish (smoked or boiled), fish soup, shredded cooked fish, fish giblets, ruff [a small perch], Baltic herring[4] in barrels (pickled, in pies, in kasha or barley groats), and smelt.

1. The actual phrase is "whatever else God sends," which means the same thing but emphasizes divine Providence.
2. This means not to the servants, who receive plainer fare (see Chapter 51).
3. Again, in the original, "whatever other vegetables God sends."
4. Literally, German herring. The Order of Livonian Knights still had strong ties to the German principalities in the sixteenth century, and the capitals of the Baltic states belonged to the Hanseatic League. Herring, culled in the North and Baltic seas, quickly salted and often smoked as well to preserve it, supported most of northern Europe through the Lenten season. The Hanse was the main supplier of Baltic herring and was preferred because it had the best quality control. For more on "King Herring," see Henisch, *Fast and Feast*, pp. 33–43. Russians were luckier

A well-ordered house has plenty of food for fast days; you need buy nothing in the marketplace. You have bilberry wine, cherries in syrup, raspberry juice, and desserts (apples and pears in kvass and syrup, pastilles,[5] doughnuts) for yourself, for guests, and for those who are ill. All these should be stored at the right time.

He who gives food to the needy, to the sick, to new mothers, and to visitors will receive a great reward from God.

If you cannot use a whole case of fish yourself, go in with one or two friends to buy a case of sturgeon, beluga, herring, or whatever kind of fish you like. If you buy sturgeon or caviar by the case, you will save money. If, on the other hand, you have to buy something later because it is not in your storeroom, either you will not find it in the market or you will pay three times the usual price because it is out of season, and even that will not net you a tasty fish.

44. *How One Should Lay in Supplies in Advance*

A house run by a sensible, God-fearing master and mistress should contain everything the household will use during the year. This includes lumber, drink, food, grain, fat, meat (aged half-carcasses of red meat, ham, corned beef, dry-cured meat), winnowed grain, fresh and salt fish, biscuits, flour, oat flour, poppy seeds, wheat, peas, butter, hempseed, salt, malt, hops, soap, and ashes—anything that can be stored in advance without perishing. If the husbandman gathers some of each every year, during times of scarcity he can live on his stores as though they were a gift. He may lend to the needy and the sick,

than most northerners because ample rivers made herring but one of the many fish available; elsewhere, herring attracted such extreme dislike that people devised special ceremonies to celebrate its departure at Easter.

5. Pastilles (*pastila*), a type of fruit candy. For a recipe, see Darra Goldstein, *A la Russe: A Cookbook of Russian Hospitality* (New York: Random House, 1983), p. 292. Goldstein gives recipes for numerous other dishes mentioned here and elsewhere in the *Domostroi*—for example, turnovers, pancakes, kasha, frumenty, and various soups. Many of the dishes considered "classics" of Russian cuisine by Westerners, like beef Stroganoff and chicken Kiev, were invented in the nineteenth century under the influence of French haute cuisine; their history, too, can be found in Goldstein's entertaining vignettes.

helping those who deserve help. Or, if you store items in quantity when they are cheap, you can sell them when prices rise. Then you may consider the original item a gift, for the money you spent for it has been returned to your house.

The house of a good man and a good woman will never know scarcity. You can keep supplies for many years, unless they rot.

45. *How to Cultivate a Kitchen Garden and Orchard*

If you have a kitchen garden, whether you tend it on your own or are supervised by your master, your mistress, or their deputy, you should first construct a wall about it, to prevent entry by dogs, pigs, hens, geese, ducks, and other animals. Then your fruit will go unharmed and you will not quarrel with your neighbors. Your animals will stay in your garden, and your neighbor's in theirs, only if your fences are strong. For this reason your household should be walled or fenced all about, its gates always shut. Toward nightfall the gates should be locked and guarded by dogs. The servants should keep watch, and the master and mistress listen at night. The kitchen garden should always be locked; let him who does this be ever mindful of his responsibility, both day and night.

You must keep watch while the beds are dug in spring and the manure added, when the manure is stored in winter, and while the fallow beds are prepared for planting melons. All seeds should come from your own stores.

Once all the seeds and grains are sown, water them, shelter them, and protect them from frost. Keep the soil clear under the apple trees, sweep up dry leaves, transplant seedlings, graft twigs and buds. Weed the beds and the patches of grain, protect the cabbage from caterpillars and fleas (pick or shake them off).

Sow beets all around the garden near the fence, where the stinging-nettle grows. Beginning in the spring, you can cook your own beet greens; you need not buy them in the marketplace. Instead, you can give them to the needy, doing God's work. If you are young, you may sell this product for something else.

When one of the cabbages or root vegetables you have planted ripens, cook the leaves. When the cabbage begins to form into a ball, cut it from time to time and cook it. Tear up the outer leaves and feed them to the animals. At the same time, and again before autumn, cut the beet greens and dry them. They are always good, both when first picked and later.

Cook cabbages and root vegetables all summer. Pickle cabbages, beets, and cucumbers in the fall.

In summer melons, beans, carrots, cucumbers, and other fresh vegetables make a nice change. If you have more than you can eat, sell the extra.[1]

You must cultivate your orchard yourself. Space the trees at least twenty feet apart, so they will grow tall and bear abundant fruit. Vegetables may grow undisturbed among the trees (unless the branches are thick; then nothing will grow under them).

Sow beets and gather fruit—fallen apples, cucumbers, melons, and the like—at the right time. Eat some immediately and preserve the rest. Preserve apples or pears in kvass or syrup and make berry or cranberry juice. When they are cheap, dry mushrooms and pickle them. You should preserve or sell all your vegetables; waste nothing.

Save the seeds in your house, so you need not buy seeds in the marketplace next year. If you have extra, you can sell them.

{Whenever you pick vegetables from your garden, take the first fruits to the church.[2] There the priests will bless them. Later, when the priests eat what you have grown, they will again bless you who made the vineyard.[3] Send some to your father-confessor's home as well. If you have enough, send vegetables to the church servitors, the poor, and the needy. These are alms from your righteous labors and blessed fruits. Invite priests to your vineyard also, to eat and to bless it.[4]

When God sends crops to the villagers, they bring the first fruits of their labor to the church and to the priests, to the places where they go to pray. Those who love God give part of their surplus to orphans, to the poor, and to those who beg at the monastery gates. The houses

---

1. Again, the literal phrasing is "if God sends more than you can eat."
2. Based on Exodus 22:29: "You shall not hold back the first of your harvest, whether corn or wine."
3. The boundaries of the sixteenth-century Russian state encompassed no known vineyards (although grapes were grown in neighboring Poland). But this may be another reference to the passage from Exodus quoted above and not meant literally.
4. Another possibly metaphorical reference.

of those who act in this way are blessed, as are their vineyards,[5] their villages, their fields, their pastures, their cattle, and all their animals. The Lord will multiply the fruitful seed; the Lord will fill their home with goodness and remit their sins. They receive God's mercy now and will inherit eternal life.}

46. How a Man Must Keep Liquor Stored for Himself and His Guests. How to Present This Liquor to Company

When a bachelor, of moderate means and thrifty, wishes to keep beer in stock for his guests, he fills the casks in March, after the barley malt has been brewed. For special occasions, he adds a little honey to ordinary beer, keeping it on ice and calling it mead or March beer. To celebrate holy days, name-days,[1] weddings, births, christenings, memorials to the ancestors, or the visit of a merchant, invited guest, or respected abbot, the host should decant mead from a vat into five pewter jugs or (depending on the number of people being served) small casks. He should put nutmeg in one little bag, cloves in a second, beneficial herbs in a third. He will warm these on the stove and mix them with the mead. He should mix cherry juice with warmed wine and put it in a jug, combine raspberry juice and wine in a second jug, and add wine to prepared syrup in a third. Then he can offer his guests six kinds of mead,[2] two kinds of wine and cherry juice,[3] in either casks or pewter jugs, and two kinds of beer as well.[4]

Anyone who keeps his house stocked and has an orderly wife will

5. Unlike the earlier references, this one seems literal, which suggests a Byzantine or a Western source for the entire passage.

1. As in the Catholic church, Orthodox Russians usually celebrated their name-days, the feast of the saint after whom they were named, rather than their actual birth date. This list of celebrations corresponds to the legal definition of days on which restrictions against producing alcohol at home were relaxed. See Smith and Christian, *Bread and Salt*, pp. 85, 91.

2. To get six kinds of mead, one would have to combine the herbs and spices in all possible permutations.

3. A mistake: the directions produce three varieties of wine mixed with juice or syrup, not two.

4. That is, ordinary beer and beer mixed with honey (but not spices).

never be shamed before his guests.[5] Except for the occasional rare item, God has provided everything they need at home.

47. A Brewing Lesson for That Same Young Man. How to Brew Beer, Make Mead, and Distill Vodka

For brewing beer, ale,[1] or sour cabbage soup, take malt or meal and hops. These supplies should be measured or counted and the amounts recorded.

When beer is brewed from barley, oats, or rye, or when hops are steamed, you must supervise the fermentation and siphoning off yourself. All should be done carefully and cleanly, so nothing is stolen or wasted.

Do not drink just for something to do.[2]

Once the beer is boiled, even after it is boiled if the malt is strong, a cask or more of a second beer may be prepared. When all the beer is made, pour water on the lees. Add thirty or forty pails to barley lees, or fifty, even sixty, to a good, strong mash. This mixture ferments well and is good enough for the family.

Beer from the first grade makes good sour cabbage soup. You can make vinegar, too, from a good mash; be careful to keep it in a warm place.

You must wash before you approach the brewery.

Store beer hops for making honeyed wine [hippocras]; keep them, along with the mash, on ice in the summer, so they do not spoil. Keep yeast in stock for making hippocras also.

When you transfer these drinks to casks, watch your servants carefully. Old vessels are best for storage, since they are readily available and have already been tested.

You must distill mead yourself. While it ferments, seal the room.

---

5. At the beginning of the chapter, the host had no wife. Another contradiction.

1. Ale: *braga*. Sixteenth-century English had a comparable word, bragget (beer mixed with honey and spices), but both the word and the drink have passed out of use.

2. This comment has no connection to what goes before or after it, as though the author were jotting down notes of whatever came to mind.

Only you may oversee the process. No one else must taste the brew while you blend it.

Distill vodka yourself, as well.[3] Never leave it unguarded. If you are otherwise occupied, have someone trustworthy take your place. At bottling time, estimate the end results from the amount in the caldron and distill three separate grades.

Let no one into the cellar, icehouse, smokehouse, or granaries without you. Mete out all the supplies yourself, measuring and weighing, recording what each person receives.

48. How a Steward Must Supervise Cooks and Bakers

Cooks, bakers, and pastry cooks should keep their utensils in order. Caldrons, frying pans, copper and iron pots, trivets, sieves, cooking spoons, ladles, and containers should be clean, wholesome, and sterilized (by boiling).[1] Each utensil should be entered in the accounts and in an inventory; record the weight of copper and pewter items.

Part of the steward's job is to check the premises every day, seeing that everything is present in the right quantity, in good repair, clean, dry, in its place, and locked up. Casks and dishes should be washed, too, in good condition, and neatly stacked.

3. The terminology here is somewhat vague. "*Goriachoe vino*" [lit. "hot," i.e. fortified, wine] can mean either vodka or brandy. To make things worse, both are often abbreviated "*vino*" (wine). Here a distilled beverage is clearly indicated: vodka, brewed from grain, seems more likely than brandy, distilled from wine, but the author may have intended either. For more on the introduction of spirits into Muscovy, which seems to have occurred around the time the *Domostroi* was produced, see Smith and Christian, *Bread and Salt*, pp. 87–91.

1. Despite our (often justified) perception of the Middle Ages as an unsanitary age, advice like this is standard in medieval cookbooks. (See, for example, Henisch, *Fast and Feast*, pp. 90–93.) How well Russians observed such standards is more debatable; Olearius, among others, comments that Russian dishes and linen were both dirty and meager (*Travels*, p. 155).

49. *How a Man Must Consult His Wife Before Giving Orders to the Steward concerning the Dining Area, Cooking, and Breadmaking*

Every day in the evening, when they have said their prayers, and again in the morning, after rising at the bell and attending morning service, the husband and wife should discuss how to assign work to their household.

In planning meals, the steward should, in accordance with his master's instructions, tell the other servants what to buy for the household. When they bring home what they have bought, the steward should collect and verify it.

{You should give anyone who buys items for the household—fish or meat to eat, liquid to drink—money sufficient for a week or a month. When the buyer returns, he should bring the change and an account to his master. Then the servant can take the money back again. That way you will learn all you need to know about the resources available to you and about the quality of that man's service as well.}

The steward should give ingredients to the cook and supplies to the baker for his pastries. Since people easily remember that which they distribute themselves, he can then make a full report to his master.

He must give to the kitchen both meat and fish, in the quantities ordered by the master. When the food is baked and boiled, he must take it from the cook and place it on the table. He should follow his master's instructions but keep in mind how many guests are present.

Similarly, he must hand out ingredients for desserts and collect the results.

As food is cleared from the table, the steward must check whether the meats are whole or broken.[1] He should set aside untouched food. He ought to separate leftovers of meat and fish and put each dish in a clean strong jar. He should cover the jars and set them in ice. If only

---

1. Medieval people of this social level had large households and entertained on a grand scale so food would usually be prepared as whole joints, large pies, and so on, and served repeatedly until finished.

a small amount is left, he may give leftover food and scraps to the servants, but whole meats should be kept for the master, the mistress, and their guests.

Bring drinks to the table according to the master's order, keeping in mind the number of guests. For the mistress bring ale or kvass.

Tableware and cookware should be washed in hot water after the meal, rinsed, wiped, and dried. The person responsible should then gather them together, count them, put them away, and lock the cabinets.

You must maintain the tableware in good condition. Pewter jugs, goblets, ladles, small items—cruets for vinegar, pepper mills, tureens, saltcellars, spoons, plates, jars—tablecloths, and veils [for covering dishes, presumably] should always be clean and ready to set out. The table itself should be clean, as should the chairs, the benches, and the rooms. The icons should be arranged on one wall, the room neat and orderly.

Strain vinegar and pickled cucumbers, lemons,[2] and plums through a fine sieve. Wash the cucumbers, lemons, and plums and pick them over. When placed on the table, all should be clean and skillfully arranged.

Clean smoked and dried fish before serving. Aspic—meatless or with meat, caviar, or cabbage—must be clarified. Lay these out on platters, arranged attractively for the table. All beverages should be strained through a fine sieve.

Stewards, cooks, bakers, all those who handle food, and especially waiters, who appear in public, should be clean and neat. {Feed them a little and give them something to drink before the meal so they will not suffer as they wait on tables.} They should wash their hands before they prepare food. The serving platters and the steward's tools, even those of the undercooks, must be washed and in good condition; so should those belonging to the mistress and her servants.[3]

When you bring food or drink to the table, see that the vessel you

2. Pickled lemons: lemons preserved in salt to survive transport (they had to be imported). The word for lemons is taken from Polish, so they may have come from Italy via Poland, but Astrakhan would be a closer and more convenient source. In any event, they were probably expensive; their mention underlines the wealth of the *Domostroi* household. Pickled plums sound horrible, but probably honey, not salt, was used for preservation.

3. More evidence of sex segregation: the mistress in essence maintains a separate household.

carry is spotless. Both food and drink should be pure, without dust, unburned. Check carefully as you put it down. As you do, do not cough or sneeze. If you must, turn aside first. This is polite. {If you go outside to sneeze or spit, remember to wipe your feet before returning inside. Everyone should do this.}

50. *Order to a Steward: How to Arrange a Feast*

When your master holds a great feast, supervise the kitchen and the bakery yourself. Assign a good man to serve the food and another to stand beside him, to handle the drinks and the serving platters.

Distribute beverages according to your master's instructions. Do not offer drinks on the side, without an order from your master.

When the feast is over, check the silver, the pewter, and the dishes; count the pieces. Check cooking and breadmaking supplies. Examine the stores of liquor. Refill casks that have been opened.

During the feast, you will need to station a conscientious man in the courtyard. He should watch the road and all the household belongings so that nothing is stolen.

Take care of a drunken guest so he will not destroy anything or cause a fight.

{The people stationed in the courtyard to watch the guests' horses, sleighs, and carriages should guard them carefully so that none of the servants can steal or fight. They should not pick quarrels among the guests, nor steal or spoil any of the household's supplies. They should pay attention to what goes on. If someone does not do this, tell the master.

Those who are stationed about the yard should not drink while they are there or leave their posts. Whether they are in the courtyard, the cellars, the bakery, the kitchen, or the stables, they should keep everything safe.}

When the table empties, you must gather all the dishes and have them washed. You must go over all the food—meat, fish, chilled aspic, and soups—and take care of them as written above.

On the evening following a feast, or even sooner, the master should check that all is in order. He should question the steward at length on what was eaten and drunk, on who received what. The steward should be able to account for every expense and every item. The steward should answer the master straightforwardly in every particular.

If, God willing, all is in order, if nothing is broken or spoiled, the master may reward the steward. The same applies to the other servants: if the cooks and bakers have worked courteously and carefully and have not gotten drunk, then the master will feed them and give them drink. {Then they will be happy and will keep up the good work.}

51. Instruction from a Master to His Steward on How to Feed the Family in Feast and Fast

Let all things be just as was written in the previous instruction from a master to his steward. Hand out to the kitchen whatever food is to be served to the master, his household, and their guests during meat days and on fast days also. The same rules apply for beverages, too: the master should tell the steward which drinks to bring for the master and the mistress, for the family, and for guests. Again, as in the previous instruction, you must do everything according to your master's orders.

The steward should ask the master for his orders every morning. As the master commands, so shall he do. The master in turn must consult his wife about domestic matters; then he can instruct the steward how to feed the servants.

As everyday food servants receive rye bread, cabbage soup, and thin kasha with ham.[1] Sometimes they may have thick kasha with lard. This is what most people give their servants for dinner, although they vary the menu according to which meat is available. On Sundays and holy days servants sometimes get turnovers,[2] jellies, pancakes, or other, similar food. At supper they eat cabbage soup and milk or kasha.[3]

---

1. Kasha: porridge made from grain, usually buckwheat groats, simmered in broth. Kasha is now an adopted English word so I have not translated it.
2. Turnovers: *pirozhki*—literally, small pies.
3. There is an old Russian peasant proverb: "*Shchi da kasha, pishche nashe*" (Cab-

On fast days the servants have cabbage soup with thin kasha, sometimes with broth, peas, or turnip soup. At supper on these days you may offer cabbage soup, cabbage, oatmeal, pickles, or fish and vegetable soup. On Sundays and holy days, for dinner, give them various kinds of pies, barley-pease porridge, barley groats, or kasha mixed with herring (or whatever else you have available).[4] For supper, serve cabbage, pickles, fish and vegetable soup, and oatmeal.

The serving women, maids, children, other kinfolk, and dependents[5] should get the same food, but with the addition of leftovers from the master's and guests' tables. As for the better class of merchants, the master should seat these at his own table.

Those who cook and wait at table eat after the meal; they also get leftovers from the table.

The mistress honors seamstresses and embroiderers as the master does merchants: she feeds them at her own table and sends them food from her own dish.[6]

The servants' drink is second-grade beer; on Sundays and holy days, ale. Trading people always drink ale, and the master may give them any drink he wishes, or order it given. If they drink merely to quench their thirst, merchants should be served weak beer.

Instruction from the Master or Mistress to the Cook or Steward, on Cooking Food for Meat or Fast Days for the Family, the Servants, and the Poor

Chop cabbage, greens, or a mixture of both very fine, then wash them well. Boil or steam them for a long time. On meat days, put in red meat, ham, or a little pork fat; add cream or egg whites and warm the mixture. During a fast, saturate the greens with a little broth, or

---

bage soup and gruel are our food). One certainly could not prove otherwise from the *Domostroi*.

4. "Whatever God provides."

5. *Blizhnye*, a word that literally means "those who are close to you"—i.e., neighbors, relatives, friends, or those near in rank. The author probably includes here various dependent members of the household, as well as nonresident poor people who regularly received support.

6. This gives a clue to the social stratum held by the intended reader of the *Domostroi*: seamstresses and merchants are considered, if not his social equals, at least near equivalents.

add some fat and steam it well. Add some groats, salt, and sour cabbage soup; then heat it. Cook kasha the same way: steam it well with lard,[7] oil, or herring in a broth. {You can also wash, chop and clean dried, fresh, or salt meat, or dried, smoked, or pickled fish. Boil these well, too.}

Cook all food thoroughly. Knead bread, make kvass, and dry-cure meat well; bake turnovers well, too. Cook food under conditions of the utmost cleanliness, as you love your soul. The mistress or majordomo[8] should personally taste any food intended for the family. If something is poorly prepared, the mistress should rebuke those who prepared it. If the majordomo neglects this duty, the mistress must rebuke him as well. If the mistress neglects this chore, then her husband must censure *her*.

As you love your soul, feed your servants and the poor;[9] thus you honor God and redeem yourself. Toward this end, the master and mistress must constantly look for ways to help their servants and the poor. The master and mistress must think, all the time, about food, drink, and clothing. They must watch for evidence of anything lacking, of injury or neediness. They must care for as many of the poor as they can, as many as God's assistance allows, and do it from their whole hearts, as though these were their own children or relatives. If someone does not rejoice in his good fortune and does not suffer with these unfortunates, let him be anathema.[10] But he who protects and cares for the needy with his whole heart will receive mercy from God, remission of his sins, and everlasting life.

7. The lard was for meat days, presumably. "Oil" may also mean butter but again only on meat days.

8. *Dvoretskii*, as opposed to *kliuchnik* (steward), used above. Why the shift in terms is unclear.

9. To judge from contemporary accounts, slaves resident in the city were often fed inadequately or not at all. Instead, they were required to provide their own food, clothing, and housing from meager allowances. As a result, many turned to robbery and murder. See, for example, Olearius, *Travels*, pp. 149–150, and *Domostroi*, Chapter 28.

10. *Anaféma*: a Polonism (in Russian, as in English, the stress falls on the second syllable).

52. Concerning the Care of Goods
Stored in Granaries and in Corn Bins

In the granaries it is the steward's responsibility to see that all supplies and cereals (malt, rye, oats, and wheat) are not spoiled, spilled, withered, nibbled by mice, caked, or moldy. Anything in casks or boxes (meal, other supplies, peas, hempseed, buckwheat, oat flour, dry biscuits made of rye or wheat) should be covered and packed tightly. Nothing should get wet, spoiled, or musty.

Everything must be measured and counted; you should know how much was brought from the village or the marketplace. All the amounts should be written down.[1] If something can be weighed, it should be weighed. The steward should also record what and how much goes to meet expenses, which supplies are used by each part of the household, and the names of those who receive goods on the master's orders. If all this is written down, nothing can be done in secret. The steward should measure and record amounts of bread, rolls, beer, vodka, ale, kvass, sour cabbage, vinegar, siftings,[2] bran, dregs of any kind, yeast, and hops. Hops, mead, butter, and salt should also be weighed.

53. How You Should Manage the Drying Room in the
Same Way. {Preserving Fish, Meat, Tongue,
Smoked, Layered, and Dried Fish}

In the drying room are kept half-carcasses of meat; air-cured corned beef; joints; tongue; smoked fish; fish preserved in thin layers; dry-

---

1. Again, this was standard advice, and often standard practice, in the medieval West. (See Henisch, *Fast and Feast*, pp. 93–94.) No such account books survive from Russia, however, before the late seventeenth century; the *Domostroi* is either ahead of its time, a lone extant source, or reflecting a different ethos here.
2. I.e., grain left in the sieve.

cured fish, wrapped in bast matting and in baskets; barrels of herring and ruff.

Whatever you have should be recorded in an inventory. The account should state how much of each item was bought, weighed, dried, and stored. All food should be kept carefully, not allowed to spoil, be gnawed, or crushed. It should be protected from harm and locked away.

{Look over everything, put it away, and keep it dry. Keep the best food in a pit. If something has spoiled, take it out to use as is fitting: to feed the family well or to give to the poor, wherein lies salvation. But if it has rotted, throw it out the gates.}

54. *How to Preserve Food in the Cellar and the Icehouse*

In the cellar, in the icehouses, and in the small storerooms are kept bread, rolls, cheese, eggs, dairy goods, onions, garlic, fresh and salt meat, fresh and salt fish, fresh honey, and such cooked foods as meat and fish dishes in aspic. There you should also store cucumbers, pickled and fresh cabbage, turnips, other vegetables, mushrooms, caviar, pickles, fruit juice, {cherries in syrup, raspberry brandy, apples, pears, melons, watermelons in syrup, plums, lemons, fritters, pastilles,} apple kvass, bilberry juice, Rhenish wine,[1] vodka, mead, fermented and unfermented beer, and ale.

The steward must know how much is stored in all these areas. Everything should be counted and marked as to what it contains and whether it is full or not. A written record should be kept of how much of what is to be distributed and where, according to the master's order, and how much is actually handed over. Then the steward can consult his account, will know what to say to the master, and can give a satisfactory answer to any question.

All items should be clean and covered, not moldy, mildewed, or sour.

Rhenish wine and other alcoholic drinks should be kept in a separate cellar under lock and key; only the master should have access there.

1. Rhenish wine: white wine from the Rhine Valley in Germany.

55. *How the Steward Must Arrange Items in the Storerooms and Barns according to the Master's Instructions*

The steward, in obedience to his master's orders, must arrange the following items in an orderly manner in the storerooms, cellar, and barns: old clothes; expensive clothes; servants' dress; girdles, mantles, cloaks, hats, and sleeves;[1] bearskins, hides, horse blankets, felt; saddles; quivers for both spears and arrows; sabers, hatchets, boar spears, arquebuses; bridles, halters, tassels, frontlets and horse ornaments; harpoons; leather whips and knouts; reins, walrus tusks, and leather; saddle straps, horse collars; bows and arrows; pillows; dark-colored furs;[2] pouches, saddle bags; light-colored furs; hides; tents; bed curtains; linen, hemp, rope, and twine; soap and ashes.[3] Used goods should be there too, such as scraps of fabric and leather, nails, chains, locks, axes, spades, anything else made of iron, and luxury items.

Sort these things out. Put whatever you can in boxes or in crates. Place the rest in bins, hang them on spokes, or put them in boxes— whichever is most suitable. Keep them in a dry place and under cover. Protect them from mice, damp, snow, and anything that might harm them. Count and record everything, including how much is new and how much old. If something spoils, repair it. Everything should be as ready for use as you can make it.

You should set up sections in the warehouse for these items: sleighs, sleds, wagons, wheels, damaged beds, bows, horse collars, arrows, bast mats, hempen reins, bast fibers, bast rope, halters, weights, saddle straps, and horse blankets.

1. In the Middle Ages, sleeves were typically separate from the rest of the garment. The wearer tied them on as part of dressing.
2. Why the *Domostroi* distinguishes dark- from light-colored furs is unclear.
3. This list has a distinctly military tone to it (arquebuses, bows and arrows, etc.). Although these implements were used for hunting as well, this is one of the few indications that the author may have included the military service classes in his intended audience.

Arrange any other items used for riding or driving standing against the wall, lying flat, or hanging up—whichever is most suitable. Cover the interiors of the high-quality sleighs, carts, sledges, and heavy carriages. These too should be kept in a dry place under lock and key.

In yet another barn keep boxes, measures, small chains, distillery casks, troughs, chutes, gutters, vats, wooden troughs for kitchen use, fine sieves and coarse sieves, flagons, and items used in cooking and storage.

If a cask or jar rots, or the hoops on the casks molder, command that that cask or jar be strengthened, the notches recut, the base repaired, and new hoops put on. Then all will be ready, parboiled, washed, and dried, untouched by rot, mold, must, or odor. Yeast and hops should be allowed neither to dry out nor to rot. Whatever you need will be available for your use.

Keep oak casks among your supplies, either repaired or recently made. You should store old casks, vats, tuns, slats for casks, boxes for food, and jars of all sorts. You can use these in times of need; then you will not spoil good ones.

56. How You Should Arrange Hay in the Haylofts and Horses in the Stables, Stack Firewood in the Courtyard, and Care for Animals

The hay should be arranged in haylofts, not strewn all over the staircase and porch or trampled in the courtyard. The servants should sweep it into piles so it does not get trampled underfoot in the mud. Lock it up so it cannot get spilled, blown about, or spoiled.

Treat straw in the same way. Keep it in the rafters, in an enclosed space. If any starts to fly about, sweep it up.

Check the stables every day. The servants should put hay in the mangers for the horses to eat; make sure no hay lies around the horses' feet. Each horse should have a bed of straw, raked and shaken every day.

Servants should be careful when they lead the horses to water. Do not let children drive them out, drag them in, or comb them.

Outside, horses should be fed from a trough placed in front of them, full of oats. Then servants should wipe them down and cover them with horse blankets. In summer, keep them cool; they will like that.

See that the servants feed your cows, geese, ducks, and hens. Have them put straw down in the sheds and rake it. They should also bring water for the animals. Keep certain dishes just for the cattle, the dogs, and the hens so you will not defile clean ones.

Go around each evening, night, and morning to check that the work has been done. At night, have a lit candle in your lantern. While you visit the stables, do not take the light out of the lantern if you are anywhere near the hay or the straw, or you may cause an accident.

Logs, kindling, boards, shingles, short pieces of wood, cut sections of boards, or logs must be arranged in their proper place, at the side of the courtyard, not in the road. Logs, boards, and shingles should be under cover, if only under a roof, for in a dry place they cannot blow about or get wet. Only dry logs burn well. It is better, too, for the servant who must go out and bring them in; he does not get muddy.

57. What to Do with Waste Produced in Kitchens, Bakeries, and Workrooms

In the kitchens and bakeries, do not throw out scraps, husks, cabbage roots, peelings, beet leaves, turnip tops, dregs from the caldrons of ale or vodka, sediment from sour dishes, parts cleaned from meat or fish in the kitchen, or the remains of sour cabbage soup or sourdough. Gather all these things and put them in old dishes. (Such jars are not fit for kitchen or cellar[1] so put them in a separate room.)

With this mixture you can feed sick horses. If you mix it with oatmeal, cut hay, or such, you can give it to the cows, pigs, geese, ducks, hens, and dogs. You should mix the food separately for each type of animal so it will meet their needs.

People sprinkle with meal scraps from the table, the pots, and the caldrons. They do the same with any food that is burned. They feed

---

1. Because of the smell, presumably.

this mixture to their animals, even in the villages; the animals are quite content to eat it.

58. How the Master Should Often Check the Cellars, Icehouses, Granaries, Drying Rooms, Barns, and Stables

Every day in the evening, no matter what, the master should personally check the cellars, icehouses, granaries, drying rooms, storerooms, barns, and stables. He should examine every item in storage: drinks, food, utensils, supplies, and lumber.

As you go through the stable, the bakery, the kitchen, or any other domestic department, check for yourself that the steward, the head cook, the baker, or the head groom has arranged everything as described in this memo.[1] Ask how much of each item there is and if the measure and the amount of everything is written down. Assess the total yourself, and find out how much has gone out and to whom it was given. The servants should be able to answer all your questions exactly. Visit the steward, the baker, the cook, the brewer, and the head groom in turn.[2] If the steward is present, reward him for his service only if all is in order according to this book, if all is well-maintained, if the count comes out correctly and all is arranged well, if he gives the account at length, from memory, and honestly. If anyone, through carelessness, has omitted or damaged anything, lied, or stolen, punish him in a way appropriate to his crime and fine him.

The master, mistress, steward, or housekeeper,[3] first thing every morning, should make the rounds of all the courtyards, checking the locks on every room. Where whole seals remain, all is well. But if a room is badly locked, a lock broken or unfastened, a seal broken or badly sealed, then the person in charge must enter that room and examine everything. If thieves have been there, you will know. But if it was your own servants who stole, or if something was poorly locked

---

1. Memo: *pamiat'*, a chancery word.
2. This would prevent "cooking the books," except by conspiracy, as well as providing a more detailed account of household operations.
3. Housekeeper: *kliuchnitsa*, the feminine form of steward.

through carelessness, then reproach and punish those responsible in a way appropriate to their crime. You should investigate where everyone spent the night and how the deed [i.e., the break-in] was accomplished; by this means you will establish the truth.

In the evening you should again go all around the house, to look it over and to sniff out where the fires have not been banked.[4] In the cellar and the icehouse, both in the evening and in the morning, you should see that everything is nailed shut, that nothing leaks through knotholes or from the jars.

During the day, you must see that nothing drips, that nothing is moldy or rotten, but covered, clean, and sorted. Everything must be whole and carefully kept. If this is not so, again, punish those responsible as seems appropriate.

Examine everything in the kitchens, bakeries, rooms, stables, and haylofts, among the animals, artisans, seamstresses, apprentices, traders, and chancery personnel.[5] Everything should be in accordance with your orders. If it is not, punish each in a way appropriate to his crime, as written above. But love and reward those who show evidence of good management and care. The good should acquire honor and the wicked know fear.

59. How the Master, Meeting with His Servants, Should Reward Them as They Deserve

You should reward your servant if he carries out your orders carefully, lives as you have instructed him, serves you honestly, does not betray your confidence to get a laugh, and fulfills his duties (if supplies are covered and in good condition, surroundings swept and wiped, dishes washed and put away in their places, if leftovers have been separated into whole pieces kept for the master and the guests to eat later and scraps put aside for dispersal, if he brings appropriate food

4. Here, as in Chapter 61, we are reminded of the dangers of fire, which ravaged Moscow at least once a generation. Where almost all buildings, and even the sidewalks, were made of wood, fire posed an omnipresent danger.
5. Chancery official: *prikazchik*, an alternate term for *prikaznyi chelovek*. See Chapter 40, note 1.

to the table in accord with his master's orders). Greet such a servant with kind words and let him eat and drink, to satisfy his needs.

If, on the other hand, one of your servants failed, out of stupidity or ignorance, to complete a task, punish him for that by scolding him in front of everyone. Then the others will be careful to obey you in future.[1a] If the same thing happens again, if he is lazy and his fault severe, beat him and strike him (within reason).

The good man should acquire honor and the wicked know punishment; then all will learn.

The mistress of the house should treat the women and maids of her household in the same way, gathering them together and correcting them just as written here.

60. Concerning Traders and Shopkeepers: Check Their Accounts Often

The master must personally meet with those who trade in the shops and those who buy supplies for the household in the evening, at bedtime, once a week. The master should review their purchases and sales with them one evening; his son should alternate with him in performing this task.[1b]

Praise the servant who is careful, has a good memory, enjoys his work, keeps full accounts, has no guile, and does not pad his bill. Reward such a one with food and drink; meet his needs. If he shows foresight, reward him by giving him a robe.

If, on the other hand, a servant is lazy, coming late to the shop because of oversleeping, if he fails to take your goods to the *gosti*, if

---

1a. There is some confusion here. The Short Version has "viny otdati," which means "to excuse a fault." The Long Version has the more plausible "ino otdati," "then surrender" or "then submit."

1b. This seems to be one of the few occasions on which the *Domostroi* recommends a form of (very practical) education, by ensuring that the heirs would be fully cognizant of how the household was run. Under the actual conditions of sixteenth-century Russian life, where written records were rarely kept, this apprenticeship would have been vital to the family's economic survival, even more so than in a household that conformed to the author's repeated exhortations to keep written accounts and inventories.

"The master must personally meet with those who trade in the shops and those who buy supplies for the household . . . once a week" (Chapter 60). This appears to be a cloth-merchant's or tailor's shop; note the bales of cloth piled on the shelf. Apparently there has been a dispute of some sort; one man, clearly of lower status, bows before an icon held by one boyar while a second noble grasps his robe. In the background, children, oblivious to their elders, run and play outside. From Adam Olearius, *Vermehrte Moscowitische und Persianische Reisebeschreibung* (Schleszwig, 1656). Courtesy of the Princeton University Library, Department of Rare Books and Special Collections.

he manifests any carelessness or discontent, rebuke him, and, if appropriate, impose a fine on him.

Seat those responsible for good service by your side at the table. Give them food and drink from your own dishes. Reward and protect them in every way.

If you acquire a servant (domestic servant or trader) who is lazy, somnolent, thievish, or drunken, yet will not respond to correction or beatings, give that work to another. If you encounter such a servant, feed him, then send him away from your house so that others will not be affected by such a blockhead.

61. *How to Maintain a Homestead, Shop, Barn, or Village*

A good person who is domestically inclined and endowed by God with a homestead, village, market stall, barn, stone house,[1] still, or mill should, as written above, buy supplies when they are cheap. {In a village, store things at a time when there is no agricultural work to be done.} The steward or other person in charge should constantly check the fence around the courtyard to see whether a paling has rotted. He should also check the fences in field and garden, the gates, and their locks. He should note whether a roof has molded or aged and whether the gutters have clogged. He should wash and sweep out all of these, clean the gutters, and reinforce anything old, broken, damp, or torn to pieces by the wind.

The same is true inside the house; check tables, stalls, benches, and chains. Replace or repair anything in poor condition in the cellar, icehouse, or mill, on a bridge, in the courtyard, kitchen, stables, or cellars. Even old clothes and boots should be patched. All should be strong, covered, and dry. Such a homestead is constantly renewed.

Check the stoves regularly: inside, on top, and around the sides. Seal the flue with clay. Fix any old[2] brickwork that has fallen out. Keep the top of the stove swept. Then you have no reason to fear fire. You can sleep on such a stove[3] or dry things on it. Every stove should have on the front something to catch sparks, made of clay or iron, and a floor beneath, to prevent fire.

All the rooms, as well as the courtyard and the area in front of the

1. These were very rare in Russia before the late sixteenth century and unusual outside court circles even in the seventeenth century. See, for example, Anthony Jenkinson's account of Moscow in 1557 (in Berry and Crummey, eds., *Rude and Barbarous Kingdom*, p. 55), Giles Fletcher's visit in 1588–1589 (ibid., pp. 125–126), and Adam Olearius's description of the trip he made in 1636 (*Travels*, p. 89). Another curious reference in the *Domostroi*, although the author may mention them simply because they *were* so unusual.

2. The Short Version has "new" here, but the context clearly requires the Long Version's "old."

3. A time-honored Russian custom, attested in numerous sources, including fairy tales. Flat-topped stoves, however, came into use only in the mid- to late sixteenth century, another indication that the *Domostroi* dates from that period.

gates, should, {as written above,} be clean, swept, and dry, not muddied or littered. Brooms, shovels, and other household objects should not be scattered about; gather them and put them away.

You should have wells in the courtyard and the kitchen garden, or if you have no well, you should always have water handy. In the summer, keep water in the house as well, in case of fire.

{Get water from the river early in the morning; gather firewood then too. Say a blessing when you draw the water from the river or from a well.[4] Make sure that wherever you put the water is covered.[5]}

62. How the Homestead Tax Should Be Paid, and the Taxes on a Shop or Village, and How Debtors Should Pay All Their Debts

Everyone should take care not to accrue taxes or dues on his homestead,[1] shop, village, or forests. Accumulate the money gradually and pay in advance of the due date. Then you need not work too hard or lose money in interest or surety.[2] You will not suffer from reminders or drag yourself down [financially].

Anyone who does not pay his dues and taxes on time and in full must pay double. Such irrational people live in slavery, in fear of rightering,[3] and in debt. In the end they impoverish themselves.

Anyone who lives within his budget does not burden himself with unpaid taxes or take upon himself mounds of debt. He will live free,

4. A pagan survival, although doubtless not recognized as such by this author. The blessing propitiates the *rusalki* (dangerous water spirits, reputed to be the ghosts of young girls who died before their wedding day) for their loss. For a modern survival of this myth, see the ballet *Giselle*, based on a Slavic folktale.

5. To keep it pure and, in summer, free of insects.

1. Homestead tax: *dvorovoe tiaglo*. People in the military service classes and the chanceries were exempt from the *tiaglo* (burden), as were the clergy. Of the various social groups addressed by the *Domostroi*, therefore, only merchants would be affected by these strictures. On the meaning of the *tiaglo* at different times, see Blum, *Lord and Peasant*, pp. 104–105, 512–514.

2. Surety: *poruka*. In this case, a bond given to ensure payment of future taxes. For another, more political, use of surety, see Sil'vestr's "Epistle."

3. Rightering: *na pravezhe*, being beaten on the shins with rods, publicly. For a contemporary description, see Fletcher, "Of the Russe Commonwealth," p. 175.

without toil. He will enjoy his life, and after his death his children will receive an inheritance. His household will not be short of supplies, his shops of goods to trade, or his villages of animals. None of his property will be pledged in written debt contracts,[4] notes of hand, or surety bonds or seized in payment of taxes or dues.

If you have borrowed money, with or without a written contract, whether the loan is secured with a pledge or carries no interest, pay it on time; in the future people will have faith in you. If you do not pay on time, or do not pay the interest in advance, you must pay a penalty. This will bring you loss and shame, and no one will lend to you again.

63. Instruction to a Steward, How to Store Preserved Food in the Cellar: Food in Tubs, Boxes, Measures, Vats, and Pails; Meat, Fish, Cabbage, Cucumbers, Plums, Lemons, Caviar, and Mushrooms

Store all food unopened or in brine, covered with a board or heavy stone. Pickle cucumbers, plums, and lemons in brine.[1] Cover cucumbers with a sieve under a mat of woven reeds. Clean the mold off regularly and top up the brine. If food is dry-cured, the top of it will mold and, if this is not removed, the food will spoil. So pack all such items in ice. Hang meat up after a while. Store fish only in fresh air. When hanging food, wash it first.

Hang any fish or salted meat after spring comes. When it is well-aired and ready to eat, bring it in from the line and carry it to the drying room. Hang up what you can and put the rest in a pile. Roll dried fish in bast matting. Put layers of fish on slats and pieces of fish under cover, arranging them so the wind can blow through. Keep each item in the way best for it. How to do this is explained above.

Routinely check provisions stored in the granaries, storage bins, and

4. Literally, *kabaly* (sing. *kabala*), a written contract formalizing a loan; here, presumably, one in which the property acted as collateral.

1. Here the lemons seem to be fresh when the steward acquires them and pickled later, which is even less likely in Russia than lemons transported in brine. See Chapter 49, note 2.

drying rooms to see if anything has spilled, dried out, or become damp, musty, moldy, or caked. If anything has, break it apart and put it in the sun or on a stove to dry out. If anything starts to spoil, eat that first or give it on credit, as alms, or to the poor. Sell only if you have a lot of something. Keep anything that is fresh and dry carefully so you preserve what you take in.

Treat all drinks the same way (mead, beer, fruit juice, cherries in syrup, apples and pears in syrup and in kvass, cranberry juice). Keep the jars full and buried in ice. When you drink from one, refill it and return it to the ice. If you suspect that a jar has spoiled, soured, or become moldy, bore a hole in it with a small utensil to find out.

Preserve apples, pears, cherries, and berries in brine.[2] If mold forms on the jars, clean it off, filter the brine, and pour it out. To prevent spoilage, keep full containers of food and drink on ice in the icehouse.

All clothing and fabric that are kept in storage should be looked over once a year, shaken, hung out, and dried thoroughly. Repair anything that has rotted, whether the garment is new or old. Then put it away properly as before, and keep it dry, under cover, and locked up.

If hay has spilled, blown about, spoiled, molded, or grown musty, carry it out from the hayloft on a sunny, windy day and dry it in the wind. Shake it and return it to the hayloft. If any is irretrievably spoiled, sell it or feed it to the horses. If you have too much, sell the extra as well. But keep the good hay longer; put it in a dry place and cover the haystack.[3]

64. A Father's Epistle Instructing His Son

A blessing from Annunciation Cathedral priest Sil'vestr to my beloved only son, Anfim.

2. Brine can mean either a salt or a sugar solution. Here, probably a mixture of honey and water would be used.
3. In the Intermediate and later versions, this chapter ends with text moved from Chapter 58 ("The master, mistress, steward, or housekeeper" through "the wicked know fear.").

My dear sweet child,[1] obey the teaching of the father who gave you life and raised you, educating you well and teaching you the Lord's commandments. I taught you to fear God, to follow the Holy Scriptures, and to keep all Christian laws. I gave you a good living, teaching you the principles of commerce and which commodities to trade. You have been blessed by the bishop and favored by the tsar, the tsaritsa, the tsar's brothers, and all the boyars.[2] You associate with respectable people; you have both commercial ties and friendship with foreigners.[3] You received many worldly goods and have augmented them as God commanded.[4] You lived this way while in our care and should continue to do so after our death, when you live only under the eye of God.[5]

I contracted a lawful marriage for you with a worthy daughter of good ancestry. At your union, we blessed you with holy objects: crosses, holy icons, property acquired through righteous labor. If we committed any sin in ignorance, God will rectify it. For now, son Anfim, I commit you to our creator, our good guardian, Jesus Christ, and to His mother, the Immaculate Theotokos,[6] our intercessor and helper, and to all the saints.[7] As it says in Scripture:

1. By my reckoning, Anfim was about forty when this was written. Even in the Middle Ages, some parents found it hard to accept that their children grew up.

2. The Russian terms here have historical significance. Tsar and tsaritsa came into formal use only with the coronation of Ivan IV (1547), although they were used informally as early as the reign of Ivan III (1462–1505). The full titles here are *tsar gosudar'* and *tsaritsa gosudarynia* (sovereign tsar and sovereign tsaritsa), which both emphasize Russia's independence from outside (i.e., Mongol) domination and the extent of royal power (*gosudar'* means slave owner). The "tsar's brothers," in Russian usage, include his cousins. Boyars occupied a place immediately below the royal family. In other words, Anfim enjoys patronage of the most influential sort. (He was, in fact, state secretary of the Treasury.) For more on these social distinctions, see the Introduction.

3. This is true. Anfim traded with Livonia and was friendly with, among others, the Hanseatic merchant Joachim Krumhausen. For more information, see Pouncy, "*Domostroi* as a Source," pp. 220–226.

4. In the parable of the ten talents (Matthew 25:14–30).

5. Throughout, Sil'vestr alternates between "we" (presumably referring to his wife and himself) and "I."

6. Theotokos (Greek: Slavonic, *bogoroditsa*): "God-bearer," that is, the one who carried God in her womb. The Orthodox church emphasizes Mary's role as the Mother of God, even above her virginity (although references to her purity abound, as this text illustrates); throughout the *Domostroi*, the phrase usually translated as Mother of God is *bogoroditsa*, but here the Greek form is given to avoid "His mother . . . the Mother of God."

7. Sil'vestr retired to a monastery some time between 1556 and 1560, but did not die until at least 1575, so he probably refers here to his retirement from active

When you die, leave your children instructed in the Lord's commandments; it is better than leaving them ill-gotten gains.[8] Better is
the little which the righteous has than the great wealth of the wicked.
[Psalms 37:16]

I say to you, child, resist the temptation to acquire unlawful property;
do good deeds.

My child, have faith in God. Place all your hope in the Lord, for no
one who puts his trust in Christ will perish.[9]

As an expression of your faith, willingly visit God's holy churches.
Do not sleep through matins, stroll during sext, sin at vespers, or drink
your way through compline. Sing the midnight service and the hours
in your own home every day. Such is the duty of every Christian.[10]

If you have time, attend additional services. Your self-discipline will
earn you a great reward from God.

Whenever you pray, whether in God's house or your own, stand
worshipfully, in awe of God, listening attentively. Except under extreme circumstances, never talk to anyone or look about you.

Say the monastic rule and the ecclesiastical rite purely and in unison,
not in groups.[11]

---

participation in the world rather than his actual death. If, however, rumors of his
fall from favor after the death of Tsaritsa Anastasia in 1560 are correct, he may have
feared death, Ivan IV's temper being notoriously unpredictable. In either case, his
motive in writing the epistle is to provide Anfim with a moral guide to substitute
for his own personal involvement.

8. The Bible is full of similar quotations, but I could not find this exact phrasing.
The closest is Proverbs 10:2: "Ill-gotten wealth brings no profit; uprightness is a
safeguard against death." See also Proverbs 11:4–7, 19:1 and 20:7; Ecclesiasticus 5:8.

9. A reference to John 3:16: "God loved the world so much that he gave his
only Son, that everyone who has faith in him may not die but have eternal life."

10. Much of the "Epistle" echoes, in shorthand, advice given in the *Domostroi*,
although the parallel passages are fragmentary and out of sequence. Whether
Sil'vestr's work inspired the longer text, came out of the same moral tradition, or,
most likely, deliberately drew on it (as a "cover letter" for a copy he had made for
Anfim) remains unknown. For reasons explained in the Introduction, however, it
is unlikely that Sil'vestr himself wrote both.

11. Another reference to the ruling by the 1551 *Stoglav* Church Council (see note
2 to Chapter 12). The liturgy used in monasteries (the monastic rule) differs from
that sung among the laity primarily in its length and the frequency of services
(daily, as opposed to weekly, performance of the entire liturgical cycle). In the
sixteenth century, Russian monasteries generally used the *typicon* (rule book) of the
Monastery of St. Sabbas in Jerusalem, which had replaced the older Studion rule.
A layman like Anfim might encounter the monastic rule while on pilgrimage or
otherwise visiting a monastic community (for example, to see his father). For more

Honor priests and monks, for they are God's servants.[12] By their offices we are purified of sin. By praying to the Lord for forgiveness of our sins, they make Him merciful.

Submit yourself, my child, to your father-confessor, indeed to any priest, when it comes to spiritual matters. Your wife should do likewise.

Invite priests to your house to pray for the health of the tsar and tsaritsa, their children and brothers, for priests and monks, for all Christians.[13] Request a service to ameliorate your and your servants' sins.

Have the priests sanctify water with the life-giving Cross and the miracle-working icons. If, in addition, they sanctify oil to bring health to one who is sick, be as beneficent toward them: bring alms and offerings for the health of Holy Church.

When your parents die, hold a memorial service for them (when you do, make sure you are pure in heart); then you yourself will be remembered by God.[14]

Invite churchmen, the poor, the helpless, the impoverished, the suffering, and the stranger to your house. According to your means, feed them and give them drink, warm them, and give them alms accrued through your own righteous labors. Whether they are at home, in the marketplace, or on the road, people cleanse themselves in this way from their sins. For the unfortunate bear witness to our actions before God.

My child, behave justly and with sincere love toward everyone.[15]

Do not judge others; ponder your own sins and how to avoid them. Do nothing to another that you yourself would dislike. Keep your

---

on the variations between monastic and church practice, see Fedotov, *Russian Religious Mind*, 2:252–253; Ware, *Orthodox Church*, pp. 272–273.

12. Somewhat self-serving, as Sil'vestr himself was a priest, but probably he saw it only as proper moral behavior. The injunction is standard and based on the Orthodox liturgy.

13. The Ecumenic Prayer, again. See note 2 to first Chapter 10.

14. Here, Sil'vestr seems to refer to Anfim's parents as though he were not one of them. But all sources on Anfim attest to Sil'vestr's being his father (as does the "Epistle" in its opening paragraphs). Sil'vestr may be using "parents" here in the more general sense of ancestors or older relatives.

15. These strictures are based on Romans 12:9–10, 12:16–21, 13:10 and 14:13: "Love in all sincerity. . . . Care as much about each other as about yourselves . . . do not seek revenge, but leave a place for divine retribution. . . . 'Love your neighbour as yourself' . . . Let us therefore cease judging one another."

chastity above all. Watch your conscience as though it were a wicked enemy, but hate it no more than you would a dear friend attuned to you in spirit.[16]

For the Lord's sake, refuse alcohol, for in it lies drunkenness, from which all wicked customs derive. In preserving you from drunkenness, the Lord gives you much that is good and useful. You will be honored by others; you will turn the light of your soul to good deeds. Remember, child, the apostle's words:

> Make no mistake: no fornicator or idolater, none who are guilty either of adultery or of homosexual perversion, no thieves or grabbers or drunkards or slanderers or swindlers, will possess the kingdom of God. [1 Corinthians 6:9–10]

If passion does conquer you, child, or you fall into sin, have faith. Run to God with your confession; go to your father-confessor and weep bitterly for your sins. Repent truly, so you will not do that again. Keep the commandments of your father-confessor and fulfill the penance he sets. For,

> The Lord is merciful. He loves the righteous, He pardons the sinful, He calls all to salvation.[17]

Again, keep a Christian life, in the law of righteousness.

> Then keep your tongue from evil and your lips from uttering lies. [Psalms 34:13]

Refrain from speaking falsehood, flattery, or slander. Do not puff yourself up in any way.

> Humble yourself before God and he will lift you high. [James 4:10]

Do not mock anyone, child, who is in need. Remember, my son, how we lived all these years. No one went out of our house in want

---

16. This charming turn of phrase is uniquely Sil'vestr's.

17. The probable biblical source for this is Psalm 103:8–11: "The Lord is compassionate and gracious. . . . For as the heaven stands high above the earth, so his strong love stands high over all who fear him." The passage does not originate in the liturgy—the other obvious possibility.

or suffering. As much as possible, and for the sake of God, we gave whatever each person needed. At a minimum, we used words to help those who suffered.

When a person was capable of work, and we helped him for God's sake, loaning him what he needed, Christ, although invisible to us, sent abundantly, from His mercy, all good things. If a misunderstanding arose, we did not judge the other person harshly; we gave him the benefit of the doubt.

My child, be kind to monks and strangers and feed them in your house. Go to monasteries, too, with alms and food. Visit the poor, the sick, and those in prisons. Give them alms according to your means. Feed and clothe your servants sufficiently.

Love your wife and live with her within the law, according to the Lord's commandments. On Sunday, Wednesday, and Friday, on the Lord's holy days, and during Lent, live in chastity, in fasting, in prayer and repentance.

> The Lord knows each day of the good man's life, and his inheritance shall last for ever . . . [but] the Lord sets his face against evildoers. [Psalms 37:18, 34:16]

Teach your wife, child, to act as you do yourself.[18] She should fear God and know good manners, crafts, needlework, domestic management, and organization. She should know how to bake, cook, manage her household, and perform all tasks appropriate to a woman. When she knows everything herself, she can teach her children and servants. She can organize their work and instruct them in whatever they need to know.

Your wife should never take alcohol. If she refrains, her children and servants will follow her example. Nor should she sit idle even for an hour, unless she is ill; her servants should mimic this, too.

If your wife is a guest or has guests herself, she should not get drunk. When she converses with guests, she should discuss needlework, domestic management, and lawful Christian living. She should not laugh or gossip at social occasions.

She should allow no Devil-inspired songs, lascivious speech, or foul-

---

18. This section on women's responsibilities has particularly strong parallels to the middle part of the *Domostroi*. The ideas are not, however, presented in exactly the same order.

mouthed messages in her house. She and her servants should neither speak in such a way themselves nor listen to others do so.

Your wife should not pursue an acquaintance with wizards or sorcerers. She must not practice sorcery herself. She should not allow her male and female peasants into the household buildings.[19]

If she does not heed these recommendations, punish her, saving her through her fear. But you should not get angry with your wife, nor she with you.[20] Correct her when you are alone. When you are finished, soften your heart toward her, show favor toward her, and love her.

Teach your children and servants to fear God and to act well. You will answer for their behavior on Judgment Day.[21] If you remember our teachings and follow the recommendations in this letter, you and your servants will receive God's grace and inherit eternal life.

Keep, child, good people as servants of all ranks. Strive to imitate their good deeds. Pay heed to good words and act upon them. Read the Holy Scriptures often; place them in your heart for later use.

You have seen, child, how we lived our lives: deferentially, fearing God, in simplicity of heart, participating in church rites with due reverence, relying always on the Holy Scriptures.

You have seen how, thanks to God's mercy, I was revered by all and loved by all.[22] I cared for all those who came to me in need, giving

19. Does Sil'vestr intend a connection here? "Sorcery," i.e., folk magic or herbal medicine, flourished particularly in the countryside because villages were more remote from church control, so perhaps he considers peasants likely harbingers of sorcery. But the tone of the letter is such that he may simply be concerned about dirt or maintaining one's proper place in society.

20. This injunction strikes a particularly coldhearted note today. To beat someone deliberately after tempers have cooled seems worse than to strike out in fury. It was, however, typical of the sixteenth century. The advice also underscores the subordinate position of women, who were equated with children and servants.

21. Sil'vestr means by this that the master bears responsibility for teaching his children and servants, not for their actions. If dependent people sin because they were not taught properly, the person in charge shares in the sinner's guilt. If, however, sinners know better but choose to act badly, the responsibility is theirs alone.

22. This is a very early example of the shift that occurred in the late sixteenth and early seventeenth centuries from writing hagiography to writing biographies. The best-known autobiographical saint's life, written in the late seventeenth century, is Avvakum's *Life*. But there are earlier instances as well, such as "The Life of the Blessed Yuliana Lazarevsky," written by her son. Here Sil'vestr, too, is presenting his claim to virtue. If taken literally, incidentally, this passage contradicts the rumors that Sil'vestr's retirement to a monastery was exile. But in a would-be saint's life, some exaggeration may be expected.

them work and placing them in service. I judged no one pridefully or from the desire to be contrary, but with humility. I did not ridicule, mock, or fight with anyone. If anyone gave us offense, we bore ourselves patiently for the sake of God and took the blame upon ourselves.[23] By this means enemies became friends.

If I committed a sin, whether spiritual or carnal, if I erred before God and before other people, I soon cried my fault to God and confessed to my father-confessor with tears, pleading forgiveness in a soft voice. Then I fulfilled the penance my confessor set.

If, through my sinfulness or my ignorance, I earned a reprimand or spiritual correction, if someone ridiculed or mocked me, I accepted the criticism with love and took note of my fault. If I confessed everything and did not commit such deeds in the future, God consoled me. If I was innocent, yet did not keep quiet concerning the fact, but indulged in insults, mockery, or blows, I made myself guilty.[24] If I did not publicly correct myself, God in His righteous mercy will correct me.

I remembered the words of the Gospel:

Love your enemies; do good to those who hate you; bless those who curse you; pray for those who treat you spitefully. When a man hits you on the cheek, offer him the other cheek too; when a man takes your coat, let him have your shirt as well. Give to everyone who asks you; when a man takes what is yours, do not demand it back. [Luke 6:27–30] If a man in authority makes you go one mile with him, go two. [Matthew 5:41]

I also remembered the communion prayer:

O Lord, give me mercy for those who hate me, those who act against me, and those who curse me. Let no one among them suffer for my sake, in either the present or the age to come. May the Lord purify them with His mercy and cover them with His grace.[25]

23. The sudden shift to "we" here makes no sense. It is unclear whether Sil'vestr means himself and his wife or, more likely, himself and Anfim.
24. This contradicts the previous sentence, in which he claims to have accepted any criticism that came his way.
25. A prayer attributed to Cyril, twelfth-century bishop of Turov (*Tvoreniia sviatogo Kirilla episkopa Turovskogo* [Kiev, 1880], p. xcvii). It does not usually appear in the liturgy (see Raya and Vinck, *Byzantine Daily Worship*, pp. 247–404, for the services) but Sil'vestr may have included it among the prayers said privately by the priest.

With these good things I always comforted myself.

I never failed to attend church services from the time of my youth to the present, unless I was ill. I never overlooked a stranger or poor person, a sufferer or grief-stricken person, except on those occasions when I simply did not see him. According to my means I bought the sick and imprisoned out of jail and debtors out of slavery, fed the hungry and all those in need.

I freed all my workers and dowered them, bought others out of slavery and set them free.[26] All our workers are free and live in good houses, as you see. They pray to God for us and wish us well. If one has forgotten us, God will forgive him all. Now our domestic servants are all free; they live with us of their own free will.

You have seen, my child, the many abandoned ones, orphans and slaves and poor people—both male and female—to whom I have given food and drink until they reached full adulthood. I did this both in Novgorod and here in Moscow.[27] I taught each that craft for which he had ability. Many learned reading, writing, and singing; some icon painting; some the making of books; some silversmithing and other crafts.[28] Some I taught commerce, in all types of goods.[29]

Your mother too educated many poor and abandoned maidens and widows, instructing them well.[30] She taught them needlework and

26. This statement, besides casting an interesting spotlight on Sil'vestr's own life and thoughts, marks him as virtually unique in Muscovite Russia where (see Introduction) almost all domestic servants were slaves. (Where Sil'vestr got the idea of freeing his slaves is unclear.) Sil'vestr's philosophy also distances him from the *Domostroi*, which at times explicitly addresses slave owners.

27. This sentence is the source of the widespread belief that Sil'vestr, and consequently the *Domostroi*, came originally from Novgorod. As far as Sil'vestr is concerned, there is no reason to dispute it (although no reason to confirm it, either, as he could have been stationed in Novgorod for a time). The *Domostroi*, however, almost certainly originated in Moscow. See Introduction and Pouncy, "Origins of the *Domostroi*," for more discussion of these points.

28. These are all crafts related to the staffing and maintenance of churches, in which Sil'vestr had direct experience. Ivan IV placed him in charge of renovating the Kremlin cathedrals after the 1547 Moscow fire. (See another reference to this below: "I have known many craftsmen").

29. The "Epistle" contains the only references anywhere to Sil'vestr himself being engaged in commerce, so we know nothing of the extent or nature of his commercial contacts beyond the information given here. Anfim's trading career is better documented.

30. In these two paragraphs both the sex segregation and the differences between male and female roles are clearly illustrated.

every domestic skill and, having dowered them, arranged marriages for them. We married our male servants, too, to good women.[31]

God has granted that all these people live free in their own homes.[32] Many serve as priests and deacons, state secretaries (*d'iaki*) or under secretaries (*pod'iachie*),[33] or in other ranks. Each is in that rank to which he was born and in which God allowed him to be. Others work in various crafts; many trade in shops. Many serve as *gosti* in foreign lands trading various commodities.[34]

By God's mercy, we have been spared shame or quarrel among our agents and those who serve us.[35] We have not suffered from or inflicted fraud on others; we have had no trouble with anyone. In this God has watched over us while we were abroad. If an agent caused trouble for us with other people, by arguing, we took the fault on ourselves. No one noticed our good deeds; God made restitution for us. My child, imitate this behavior. Take others' wrongs upon yourself and bear them; God will recompense you doubly.

I knew no woman other than your mother; I fulfilled the vows I made with her. O God, perfect me, O Christ, that I may end my life

31. One of the obligations of slave-owning. See, for example, the following passage from Tsar Vasilii Shuiskii's decree on runaway peasants (1607): "Those individuals who have a slave girl under eighteen years old, or a widow of two years' widowhood, or a young single man under twenty, and allow them neither to marry nor be free, such maid, widow or young man should go and complain to the state treasury." If their claims were upheld, the slave would be freed because, according to the edict, the owner's behavior was opposed to divine law as well as a deterrent to increasing the population, a perennial state concern (translated and published in Basil Dmytryshyn, ed., *Medieval Russia: A Sourcebook, 900–1700*, 2d ed. [New York: Holt, Rinehart and Winston, 1973], p. 262).

32. A testament to Sil'vestr's charity. Manumitted slaves often resold themselves into slavery quickly because they lacked sufficient resources to support themselves. See Hellie, *Slavery*, pp. 133–134.

33. An example of the extreme fluidity in the sixteenth-century Muscovite bureaucracy, as well as the lack of social stigma against former slaves. State secretary and undersecretary were high-ranking positions (see Introduction). By teaching his former slaves to read, Sil'vestr allowed them to benefit from the shortage of literate personnel and such opportunities for rapid upward mobility as that shortage engendered.

34. *Gosti*, too, occupied high-status positions. These freed slaves became the social equals of Sil'vestr's own son, Anfim (who was both international merchant and state secretary).

35. Again, it is not clear whom Sil'vestr has in mind when he says "we"—most likely, himself and Anfim, although the penultimate sentence suggests he may have had another trading partner in mind.

in a Christian way, in accord with Your commandments.[36] Live, child, according to Christian law in all your habits, without guile or cunning. But do not trust everyone you meet. Admire a good man; do not love deceivers or lawbreakers of any sort. Guard your legal marriage carefully to the end of your life. Maintain the purity of your body; know no woman other than your wife.

Protect yourself also from the drinkers' disease.[37] From the depths of this pit evil beings carry the fallen one to Hell. A drunkard's house is empty of property, a shell. He will not receive God's blessing; he will be dishonored, a laughingstock, cursed by his parents. If, child, the Lord protects you from this evil, if you fulfill the law according to the Lord's commandments and do not indulge in alcohol,[38] you will live among those who do good deeds—that is, God-fearing people. You will be blessed by God and honored by others; the Lord will fill your house with abundance.

Remember to feed guests who come to your house. Treat your neighbors and acquaintances affectionately and hospitably, offering them good bargains and loans. If you visit someone, take small inexpensive gifts to show your regard.[39] When you travel, give food from your table to the master of the house and his guests. Seat them at your table and give them a little to drink. Give alms to the poor as well. If you do this, everyone everywhere will await you and come out to meet you. They will lead you along your way and protect you from all harm. They will not deliver you to the robbers' camp nor rob you on the road: because of your generosity, they will feed you instead. Good breeds good and evil, evil. Give back good every time, and you will

36. From the context, "in a Christian way" probably means "celibately." This suggests that Sil'vestr's wife was already dead (he always refers to her in the past tense). If so, by Orthodox custom, Sil'vestr would then be required to enter a monastery.

37. Sil'vestr is now repeating himself, either because he considers this topic particularly grave or because he has compiled his "Epistle" from several sources.

38. The Bible does not recommend abstaining completely from alcohol (quite the reverse, as in Paul's letter to Timothy, quoted in the additions to Chapter 11), although Proverbs and Ecclesiasticus, for example, inveigh against drunkenness. Sil'vestr's concern that his son not abuse vodka is getting the better of his religious training here.

39. This paragraph presumably reflects Sil'vestr's own experience during his years in commerce. Note the hazards of medieval travel in the reference to robbers, below. The Russian word for "gifts" here is reminders; there is no exact English equivalent, but in Scotland such gifts are called "wee mindings" because they remind the recipient of the giver's affection.

never lose, at least among honorable people. Bread, salt, good lending practices, and small gifts will bring you lasting friendship and warm praise.

While on the road, at a feast, or in the marketplace, do not ever begin a fight yourself. If someone hurls insults at you,[40] bear them patiently for God's sake and bow away from the quarrel.

> The Lord's curse rests on the house of the evildoer, while he blesses the home of the righteous. Though God himself meets the arrogant with arrogance, yet he bestows his favour on the meek. [Proverbs 3:34][41]

If your servants begin a fight, rebuke them. If the fight becomes serious, you should even strike the offender. Then your right arm will disperse the fight, and you will not suffer loss or enmity.

Again, give drink to him who loves you not and feed him with bread and salt, to replace enmity with friendship.

Remember, son, what softness of heart God has shown us and how He has interceded for us since I was a youth. I have never had to give surety for anyone, nor has anyone ever had to give it for me,[42] nor have I ever been sued by anyone, investigated, or called to defend myself. You yourself have seen that I have worked with many masters of different crafts—icon painters, book copyists, silversmiths, blacksmiths, carpenters, stone masons, bricklayers, and builders of walls.[43] I paid them, in advance, one, two, three, five, even ten or more rubles. Many of them haunted taverns and engaged in revelry. God has let me muddle along with such men for forty years, without myself being shamed, having to call the bailiff, or suffering any serious consequences. I treated all these people humbly, giving them bread and salt, drink and little gifts, doing good deeds for them, and trying to

40. The Russian word is the same as that used for a dog's howl.

41. This is the original, quoted with slight variation in James 4:6 and 1 Peter 5:5. Sil'vestr does not exactly match the wording of any of the three biblical passages.

42. Surety: *poruka*. The Muscovite state exacted monetary guarantees from the relatives, friends, and dependents of people whose loyalty it considered suspect. Sil'vestr's never having had to give or raise surety contradicts the view that he picked his friends poorly (from a political standpoint) or himself incurred Ivan IV's displeasure. On *poruka*, see Horace B. Dewey, "Political *Poruka* in Muscovite Rus'," *Russian Review* 46 (1987): 117–133.

43. This is again in connection with the restoration of the Kremlin cathedrals in the 1550s.

be patient. When I myself made a purchase, I paid for it quickly and kindly, offering my hospitality so that a friendship would be formed that would last forever. Once I had done this, the merchant would not sell to others behind my back, give me shoddy goods, or foreclose on me.[44] If anyone bought an item from me in good fellowship and genuinely did not like it, I would take it back and refund his money. So I had no quarrel nor difficulty with anyone, either as buyer or seller. Honorable people believed me in all matters, both here and among the foreigners.[45] I was never duped or enticed in anything by anybody, nor were payments due me delayed, either in handicraft production or in trade. Nor did I take out loans on myself[46] or lie to anyone about anything. You yourself have seen how many interactions I had with people, yet God granted that all my business ended without enmity. You know yourself that living with honorable men should not be based on wealth, pride, or deceit, but on righteousness, affection, and love.

My beloved son Anfim, since I have taught you and instructed you in good behavior and how to live a devout life, and have given you this crude work based on my poor understanding,[47] I pray you, child, for the sake of our Lord, the Immaculate Mother of God, and the great miracle workers: read it lovingly and attentively, and inscribe it in your heart. Asking for God's mercy and help, for understanding and strength, do everything recommended above, and do it with love. You should also teach and admonish your wife, your children, and the members of your household, so that they will fear God and live a life of good deeds. If you yourself act according to my recommendations and teach your wife, children, male and female slaves,[48] and other dependents to do likewise, if you organize your house well, God will send you all that is good, and you and all those dependent on you will inherit eternal life. If you do not heed my prayers and my admonition and do not live as instructed in this work, like the good and God-fearing people around you, if you do not follow the commands of your father-confessor, or take care of the members of your house-

44. Business is still done this way in Russia, *perestroika* notwithstanding.
45. On Anfim's reputation for honesty, see Pouncy, "*Domostroi* as a Source," p. 222.
46. Loans: *kabaly* (see note 4 to Chapter 62).
47. This downplaying of Sil'vestr's abilities is culturally determined: the church required humility, especially from its clerics.
48. Sil'vestr apparently does not expect Anfim to follow his example by manumitting his slaves.

hold, I will not share in your sin. You alone will answer for yourself, for your wife, and for the members of your household on Judgment Day. If, my most beloved child, you follow these few commandments that come out of my poor understanding, walk along the path we followed, listen to my words and translate them into deeds, you will be a son of the light, and an heir of the Heavenly Kingdom. God's mercy will grace you, and that of the Immaculate Mother of God, our intercessor, and of the great miracle workers Nicholas, Peter, Alexis, Sergius, Nikon, Cyril, Varlaam, Alexander,[49] and all the saints. You will merit your ancestors' prayers and my eternal blessing on you, now and forevermore. I bless you, my child, and say farewell. In this world and in the next, may God's mercy be granted to you, your wife, your children, and all those who wish you well, now and forevermore.

My beloved only child Anfim, God has willed, and our pious Orthodox sovereign tsar commanded, that you serve in the Royal Treasury, in the Customs Office.[50] So now I pray you, child, and tell you with tears in my eyes, for the Lord's sake remember the tsar's commands. Ask help and understanding from God, with your whole heart; always think ahead, so you may serve faithfully and righteously without guile or deceit of any kind. Do not use anything that is the sovereign's to reward your friends or to wreak vengeance upon your enemies. Do not cause anyone to suffer undue delay; act kindly toward everyone, do not quarrel. If you must delay, explain with kind words. Do not, however, release goods with undue haste.[51]

Keep an accurate account of your activities in the marketplace. Your service to the sovereign should not harm your soul in any way. Be satisfied with the salary our blessed sovereign has granted you. Keep good account of all that you have that belongs to the sovereign, both

49. With the exception of St. Nicholas, bishop of Myra—arguably the favorite saint among Russian Orthodox—these are all Muscovite saints. Peter, Alexis, Cyril, and Varlaam were metropolitans of Moscow between the fourteenth and sixteenth centuries. St. Sergius of Radonezh founded the great Trinity–St. Sergius Monastery (now part of what is known as the "Golden Ring" circling Moscow); on his death he was succeeded by St. Nikon. Alexander is Alexander Nevsky, hero of Novgorod's wars with the Swedes and Teutonic Knights (1240–1242), whose youngest son founded the Muscovite royal line.

50. For Anfim's career, see the Introduction.

51. The practices Sil'vestr decries in these two paragraphs were widespread among Muscovite bureaucrats. See, for example, Giles Fletcher's description of a hapless state secretary's return to Moscow after corrupt service in a neighboring province ("Of the Russe Commonwealth," p. 150).

as estimates and in writing, both income and expenditures. Be obedient to the Royal Treasurer, helpful to your colleagues, strong but compassionate toward the under secretaries, the master craftsmen, and the border guards. Welcome everyone who comes your way. Ensure justice, without undue delay, for the poor, the needy, the downtrodden, and captives everywhere. According to your means, feed them and give them drink and, based on your judgment of the person, alms. If you must give judgment, treat all alike—rich and poor, friend and enemy. If you fulfill your duty truthfully and righteously, without undue delay and without any guile, you will be as is described in the Gospel:

Do not judge superficially, [O Son of Man,] but be just in your judgements. [John 7:24] For as you judge others, so you will yourselves be judged, and whatever measure you deal out to others will be dealt back to you. [Matthew 7:2]

Glory to God our Creator, now and forevermore. Amen.

64. *Books That Tell What Foods People Put on the Table throughout the Year*

From Easter onward, on meat days, people serve swan, swan giblets, crane, heron, duck, black grouse, hazel grouse, roast hare's kidneys, salted chicken served with the gizzards, necks and livers, salt mutton, baked mutton, chicken soup, thick kasha, salt meat, baked split fowl, tongue, elk, pan-fried hare, pickled hare, hare gizzards, roast chicken served with the gizzards, lark, lark giblets, crown roast of mutton, pork, ham, carp, mushrooms, meat dumplings, and two kinds of cabbage soup.

And for supper, aspic, hazel grouse, baked hare, duck, roast hazel grouse, black grouse, mutton, baked split fowl, pickled hare, roast chicken, pork, and ham.

This chapter is from the Long Version of the *Domostroi*.

During Easter they serve the following fish dishes:[1] steamed herring, pike, and bream; smoked pink salmon, white salmon,[2] and sturgeon; sterlet spines; smoked beluga; beluga spines; white salmon spine stew; poached bream; fish soup spiced with saffron; soup made from perch, roach,[3] bream, and carp.

Also these pickled fish dishes: white salmon, sterlet, sturgeon, heads of pike seasoned with garlic, loach, grilled sturgeon,[4] braised sturgeon.

During St. Peter's Fast [eight days after Pentecost–June 28],[5] they serve steamed herring, pike, and bream; smoked pink salmon; white salmon; sturgeon; sterlet spines; beluga kebabs; white salmon spine stew; pike soup spiced with saffron; bowls of black fish soup;[6] baked perch; bowls of roach stew; soup made from gudgeon,[7] bream, carp, sturgeon, and sterlet.[8]

Salted foods: white salmon, lightly salted sterlet, heads of pike seasoned with garlic, loach, dried sterlet, grilled sturgeon, braised sturgeon, boiled, baked, and dried mushrooms, cabbage soup, carp, and crab.

Beginning with the Feast of St. Peter [June 29],[9] on meat days they serve swan, swan giblets, crane, heron, hare kidneys, roast joints of meat, roast beef tongue, roast saddle of mutton, salted chicken, chicken gizzards, chicken necks, baked mutton, chicken soup, corned beef, chipmunk, corned beef cooked with garlic, corned beef seasoned

---

1. There are no fast days during Easter week, even on Wednesdays and Fridays, so these fish dishes must be intended as supplements or voluntary substitutes for the meat mentioned above. On Orthodox fasting, see Ware, *Orthodox Church*, pp. 306–307.

2. Described in Fletcher, "Of the Russe Commonwealth," p. 122.

3. Here and throughout: roach (a fish), not roach as short for cockroach.

4. Grilled: *shekhonskaia*. This word is not found in any of the standard Old Russian dictionaries. "Grilled" is a guess, assuming that *shekhonskaia* is derived from *zhegnut'*, *zhegonut'* (to scorch, to burn).

5. Usually called the Fast of the Apostles, or the Fast of Saints Peter and Paul. See *Festal Menaion*, p. 42. Richard Chancellor, in his account of his 1553 voyage, refers to it as St. Peter's Fast; apparently this was its common name in the sixteenth century (Berry and Crummey, eds., *Rude and Barbarous Kingdom*, p. 36).

6. The word order here is garbled and what the author means by "black fish soup" is unclear.

7. Gudgeon is another kind of fish.

8. This last is a guess. The text says "*tavranchiuk*" of sturgeon and sterlet. V. I. Dal', *Tolkovyi slovar' russkogo iazyka*, 4 vols., Moscow, 1978–1980), defines *tavranchiuk* only as an archaic word for a fish dish. The context suggests a soup or a stew.

9. This is usually called the Feast of Saints Peter and Paul, whose joint feast day is June 29.

with herbs, goose seasoned with garlic, goose cooked with herbs, baked split goose, baked split smoked duck, aged corned beef, smoked beef tongue, elk tongue, elk, pan-fried hare, hare served with noodles, pickled hare, pickled hare kidneys, hare gizzards, hare liver, young roast chicken, hare paté, chicken pies, puff pastry, buckwheat kasha mixed with mutton fat, biscuits, beef cooked with garlic, sweetbreads, wild boar, ham, chitlings, ribs, kasha, two kinds of rennet, crooked burbot, pea noodles, noodles, carp, dumplings, cabbage soup with kasha, cheese blintzes, pies, patties, jellies, kasha, plums, soft cheeses, boiled milk pudding, milk with horseradish, butter, pancake (i.e., melted) butter, whipped butter, or peppered oil.[10]

During Our Lady's Fast [August 1–14],[11] they put these fish dishes on the table: There is sour cabbage and herring, with caviar of every sort standing nearby. There is roast beluga back, pink salmon seasoned with garlic, grilled sturgeon, white salmon, dried pink salmon, sturgeon spines, sterlet spines; steamed herring, pike, sterlet, and bream; pink salmon spines, and stewed fish spines. They serve winter soups spiced with saffron and chilled black perch soup that they had baked in the oven. There is ordinary hot fish soup, as well as soup made from pike, sterlet, carp, perch, roach, bream, and sturgeon. Along with the soups are offered butter, sterlet, fish cakes, pies—little turnovers cooked in nut oil with dried peas; sourdough patties mixed with peas and cooked in the same nut oil; sourdough pies, stuffed with peas and baked in the hearth; big poppyseed pies cooked in hempseed oil and stuffed with peas; big pies cooked in poppyseed broth. Also pies stuffed with hempseed cakes,[12] fish spines, pink salmon, sheatfish, and herring. Among these they strew piles of pancakes.

And salted dishes: pike covered with garlic, pike preserved in brine, lightly salted pike, roast beluga preserved in brine, white salmon preserved in brine and served with a sauce, sturgeon preserved in brine

10. The Russian is "korovai attskie." The Academy of Sciences' Slovar' russkogo iazyka XI–XVII vv. identifies attskii as a variant of adskii, from ad (Hell); korovai means butter or oil.

11. This is usually called the Dormition Fast because it ends with the Feast of the Dormition on August 15. See Festal Menaion, p. 42.

12. Hempseed cakes: soshni (variant of sochen', plural sochni). A thin unleavened bread, like tortillas, cooked in hempseed juice for fast days, or stuffed with kasha and served with berries, sour cream, or cottage cheese on meat days. Nowadays they are sometimes stuffed with potatoes as well.

and served with a sauce, pink salmon preserved in brine and served with a sauce, red salmon preserved in brine and served with a sauce.[13]

During Our Lady's Feast [August 15],[14] they put on the table swan, swan giblets, crane, heron, duck, roast saddle of mutton rubbed with saffron, roast joints of beef, roast tongue, pork loin, salted chicken, chicken soup, beef, salt pork, chipmunk, elk, corned beef cooked with garlic and herbs, pan-fried hare, hare stuffed in a turnip, pickled hare, roast chicken, the liver of a white ram cooked with pepper and saffron, pot-roasted beef,[15] pot-roasted pork, sausages, stuffed stomach,[16] ham, ribs, sweetbreads, pot-roasted chicken, carp, dumplings, cabbage soup.

For supper during Our Lady's Feast, they serve baked hare, ham cooked in hay,[17] sour aspic, pigs' heads and feet, baked split fowl, pickled hare, pork, and ham.

After St. Simeon's Day [September 1],[18] people do not serve chipmunk, sheep liver, or saddle of mutton.

After the Feast of the Veil [October 1],[19] they serve roast goose and pot-roasted goose.

During Our Lady's Feast, people put on the table the following fish dishes: steamed herring, pike, and bream; smoked fish—pink salmon, white salmon, sturgeon, beluga; sturgeon, beluga, and sterlet spines. Also saffron soup, black fish soup, perch soup baked in the oven, and soup made from roach, bream, carp, and sterlet.

And these pickled dishes: white salmon, pink salmon, fresh and lightly salted sterlet, pike heads seasoned with horseradish and garlic, lightly salted pike, pickled loach, loach in sour cabbage soup, dried

13. The *Domostroi* lists five or six types of salmon (pink salmon, red salmon, sig, and so on). For simplicity, I have reduced these to pink salmon, white salmon, and red salmon.

14. That is, the Feast of the Dormition.

15. Literally, beef cooked in a pot suspended over the hearth.

16. That is, the Russian equivalent of haggis; here, probably a cleaned pig's stomach filled with sausage stuffing.

17. *Buzhenina*: a dish that is still served. For a recipe, see Goldstein, *A la Russe*, pp. 134–135.

18. St. Simeon Stylite (see note 9 to Chapter 23). This feast marked the beginning of the Russian New Year during the Muscovite period.

19. The Feast of the Protective Veil of the Mother of God took on particular importance in the Russian countryside, where it merged with pagan rituals. On this day, peasant girls asked Mary for a happy marriage and for her protection in their new households (Hubbs, *Mother Russia*, pp. 79, 115–116).

sterlet, grilled sturgeon, braised sturgeon, baked mushrooms, boiled mushrooms, cabbage soup, and cracked crab.[20]

After St. Simeon's Day, people do not serve dried fish. But after St. Simeon's Day whole suckling pigs with butter and whole duck appear.

After St. Demetrius's Day [October 26],[21] you will see fish on the table and winter soups of all sorts.

During St. Philip's Fast [November 15–December 24],[22] they put these foods on the table: steamed and fresh chilled herring, steamed bream, white and pink salmon spines, steamed sterlet, freshwater salmon, steamed lodog,[23] winter soup, butter, whole suckling pig,[24] whole duckling, saffron soup, black fish soup, burbot soup, liver, milk flavored with burbot; soup made from perch, roach, bream, carp, beluga, sturgeon, and sterlet; soup thickened with wheat flour,[25] soup with bread,[26] sterlet soup, pike-perch soup, soup made from sturgeon guts.

And these salted foods: white salmon, pink salmon, sterlet, sturgeon, sterlet heads, pike heads cooked with garlic and horseradish, round fish cakes, fried sterlet, boiled pike, tench, perch, roach, pickled bream, lightly salted pike, horn-shaped rolls, ribs of beluga,[27] fried herring, grilled sturgeon, braised sturgeon, long strips of sturgeon,

20. Cracked crab: *raki kashenovye*. Dal' has no definition for *kashenovye*, while the *Slovar' russkogo iazyka XI–XVII vv.* identifies it only as a cooking method, supplying this quotation as its source. "Cracked" is a guess based on the dictionary references to *kashenovye* as related to *skashivat'/skosit'* (to cut, to chop).

21. St. Demetrius of Salonika, a sixth-century Christian martyred during the reign of Emperor Maximian, transformed during the ensuing centuries into a warrior saint like St. George. In the West, his feast day is October 8.

22. This refers to the Christmas fast, which begins on St. Philip's Day. The fast is called Advent in the West. For its Russian name, see, for example, Chancellor (Berry and Crummey, eds., *Rude and Barbarous Kingdom*, p. 36).

23. *Lodog, lod'ba*: a white-fleshed fish found in northern Russia.

24. Technically, suckling pig, like the ducklings mentioned next, violate the rules of fasting. Medieval diners sometimes convinced themselves that infant animals did not count as meat, but the Orthodox were usually more scrupulous about such rules than their Western neighbors.

25. The phrase here is *ukha s meshechkimi*. The standard Old Russian dictionaries do not offer a definition for *meshechki*, although Dal' (*Tolkovyi slovar'*) identifies the adjectival form (*meshechnyi*) as "the highest quality," applied to flour or caviar. The author could have either in mind, but he usually lists caviar by name, so I selected "flour" instead.

26. Soup with bread: *ukha s tolchaniki*. Dal' defines *tolchenik* as "a type of round loaf served with fish, especially in fish soup" (*Tol'kovyi slovar'*).

27. Ribs: *skhaby*, a Polonism.

two sorts of cabbage soup—with fresh fish stock and with sturgeon stock.

During the great Christmas feast [December 25–January 6],[28] they put these foods on the table: swan, swan giblets, roast goose, black grouse, partridge, hazel grouse, roast suckling pig, salt mutton, baked mutton, pickled suckling pig, suckling pig innards, chicken soup, corned beef seasoned with garlic and herbs, elk, pickled elk heart, chopped elk heart, elk lip, liver, and brains, pan-fried hare, pickled hare, roast chicken, goose giblets, pot-roasted beef, pot-roasted pork, ham, sausages, stuffed stomach, pot-roasted goose, pot-roasted chicken, crooked burbot, pea noodles, noodles, carp, dumplings, cabbage soup.

And during the great Christmas feast, people set out these fish dishes:[29] steamed and fresh chilled herring, steamed bream, white salmon spines, pink salmon spines, steamed sterlet, steamed lodog, winter soup, butter, suckling pig, whole duck, saffron soup, black fish soup, burbot soup, roe, burbot liver, pike soup spiced with pepper; soup made from perch, roach, bream, carp, beluga, and sterlet; soup thickened with wheat flour, soup served with bread, sterlet soup, pike-perch soup, soup made from sterlet guts.

And these pickled dishes: white salmon, pink salmon, sterlet, sturgeon, sterlet head, pike head cooked with garlic, fish cakes, boiled pike, perch, pickled roach, bream, pickled pike with horseradish, lightly salted pike, horn-shaped rolls, ribs of beluga, fried herring, grilled sturgeon, braised sturgeon, long strips of sturgeon, cabbage soup.

During Shrovetide,[30] people set out the following dishes: pastry straws, nuts, bread shaped like pine trees, shelled nuts, yeast dough, figs, semisoft cheese, boiled milk pudding, soft cheese.

During Lent, people put these dishes on the table:[31] the little loaves used during a fast, pressed caviar, caviar gleaned from sturgeon during

28. The Christmas feast extends from Christmas Day to Theophany (January 6).

29. As with Easter week, there are no fast days during the Christmas feast. These fish dishes are intended to supplement the menu.

30. The week before Lent, called "Butter Week" in Russia. Best known in the United States as Mardi Gras.

31. In fact, Orthodox diets during Lent were much more restricted than this. For most of "the Great Fast," as it was known, the faithful could eat only grains and vegetables—no fish, eggs, meat, or dairy products. The fish dishes may have been intended for the few "cheese fare" or "meat fare" days, or they may reflect the more relaxed rules found in Russia's Catholic neighbors.

the autumn, fresh caviar from sturgeon and sterlet, liver of pike spiced with saffron, white salmon casserole, pink salmon liver, black pike liver, pike-perch casserole, sterlet casserole, fresh sturgeon casserole, fresh white salmon casserole, fresh sturgeon liver, pickled beluga liver, dried sturgeon, beluga liver, smelt, dried smelt, layers of carp and ide,[32] boiled caviar, mixed caviar, dried sturgeon bellies, pickled fish bellies, fish spines stewed in vinegar, boxed sterlet, boiled tongue, dried sterlet, smoked sturgeon bellies, smoked beluga bellies, beluga tongue, grilled sturgeon, noodles made from dried peas, groats with poppyseed oil, split pea soup, mashed peas, two kinds of cabbage soup, and pancakes.[33] Also, onion tarts, fritters, pies stuffed with poppy seeds, sweet jellies, and unleavened bread.[34]

A note for those making flour: If you take ten measures of wheat to be ground into flour, you will get back three and a half measures of fine meal, three measures of white flour, five measures of coarse flour, and three measures of unsifted grain. From each measure of meal you can make twenty loaves, and each measure of white flour and coarse flour will make twenty loaves also. People typically give out two bags of salt for each measure of finely ground flour and one bag of salt for each measure of coarse flour.

65. Recipes for All Sorts of Fermented Honey Drinks: How to Distill Mead; Make Juice, Kvass, and Beer; Brew with Hops and Distill Boiled Mead

Boiled mead.[1] Take one part honey to seven parts warm water. Strain the honey carefully through a fine sieve, making sure no wax gets

---

32. Ide: Another kind of fish.

33. Pancakes are not fast dishes by most people's standards because they use milk, butter, and eggs. On the contrary, the week before Lent was traditionally a "pancake holiday" all over Europe (England's Shrove Tuesday, French Mardi Gras [Fat Tuesday], Russian Maslenitsa ["Butter Week," during which round pancakes symbolized the sun]), as cooks tried to use up all their forbidden ingredients before Lent began.

34. This contradicts the addition to Chapter 23, which proscribes use of unleavened bread by the Orthodox.

Chapter 65 is from the Long Version of the *Domostroi*.

1. *Obarnoi med*: mead made from scalded honey.

through. Put the strained honey into a pot with a half-measure of hops and boil it carefully. While you boil it, skim it with a fine sieve, till the mixture in the caldron is clear. When you have reduced the mixture by half, take it from the caldron and cool it by adding it to the warm water. Put the honey and warm water in a clean jar, free of wax, and cover it with yeast bread and honey. Warm it on the stove, then place it in another jar to ferment. When it has fermented properly, put it in a cask immediately so it will not spoil.

White mead. To distill white mead, choose clear, light-colored honey. Pound it well so there will be no bits in the mead. Mix one part honey to four parts warm water. Add one-quarter measure of hops to the brew. Then ferment it with yeast. When the mead has fermented, strain the yeast from the mead with a fine sieve until the mixture is clear. Then pour it into a cask.

Honey mead. To distill honey mead, take five parts honey to one part warm water and strain it until it is clear. Place it in a jar and add three measures of hops. Ferment it with yeast. When it is ready, strain the yeast from the mead with a fine sieve until the mixture is clear. When you are done, pour it into a cask.

Ordinary mead. To distill ordinary mead, add honey to six parts warm water and strain it until it is clear. Place it in a jar with a half-measure of hops. Ferment it with yeast. When the mead is ready, strain the yeast from the mead with a fine sieve until the mixture is clear, then pour it into a cask.

Boyars' mead. To distill boyars' mead, take the wax from six parts honey and mix it with hot water. Add a measure of hops to the brew and ferment it with yeast. Strain it so it is clear of wax and ferment it in the jar for a week. Then place it in a cask and let it stand in the cask for another week. Then strain the mead clear of yeast and place it in a second cask. Fill the cask up with honey.

Mead with spices. To add nutmeg and cloves to brewed mead, pour ordinary mead into small casks and top them off with honey. Place the spices in small bags and put the bags into the little casks with the mead. Cork the casks tightly so the air from inside will not escape.

Berry mead. To make berry mead, place berries of any type in a caldron with ordinary fermented mead. Cook the mixture slowly and for a long time so the berries will boil but not burn. When the berry mixture boils, let it stand overnight. Separate the berry mead carefully from the dregs and pour it into a cask. You must decide which mead to use as a base and how much to thicken the berry mixture. But when you decide the berry mead is finished, place it in a cask you have not used for mead before so there will be no yeast either in the casks or in the mead.

Berry juice. To make ordinary berry juice, take any sort of berries and put them, with water, in a caldron. Cook the mixture slowly and for a long time so that the berries will boil but not burn. When the berries boil, let them stand overnight. Then carefully separate the berry juice from the dregs and put it in a cask that has not had yeast in it.

Ordinary kvass. To brew ordinary kvass, take four parts honey and strain it until it is clear. Put it in a jar and ferment it using an ordinary soft loaf, without additional yeast. When it is done, pour it into a cask.

Imitation beer. To supplement ordinary beer that is sitting in a cask, strain the yeast from it and pour it into another cask that has no yeast. Put a bucket of beer in a caldron and add honey. For every bucket of beer you take from the cask, add a measure of honey. Heat the honey and the beer in the caldron to boiling point, until the two are thoroughly blended. Chill the mixture thoroughly and pour it into a new cask.

Baked turnip pudding. Take a turnip in good condition and cut it into thin slices. Thread them in a line so that the slices do not touch one another as they dry, and hang them in the sun or in a warm oven where bread has just been baked. They should not be watery; let them dry out well. Mash the dried slices and push the puree through a sieve. Put the turnip puree in a clay pot.

Take clear, light-colored honey (make sure it has not fermented) and boil it, skimming off any foam. Pour the boiled honey into the turnip puree—as much honey as you have puree. Add nutmeg, cloves, pepper, and saffron in such measure that no one spice dominates, nor is it overspiced. Seal the clay pot with dough, and steam it in the oven for two days and two nights. Then it will be good to eat. But if it is too liquid, add more turnip puree. It should be the texture of a lump of caviar.

Turnip as prepared in Constantinople. Rub moist turnip through a sieve. Soak it for a little while in water, then drain it and boil it. Pour it all out in a sieve so that the water drains away. It will be hot, so pour cold water on it to cool it. Drain it again in the sieve until it is dry. Then boil it again and drain it in the same way. When you have dried mashed turnip that has been boiled three times, make the puree into pellets and gently rub these through a coarse sieve. Drain them clear of all water, then add honey and pepper, enough to keep it from being bitter, but not so much as to obscure the taste. Add herbs, too, then bake it. When it is liquid, rub the turnip puree through a sieve again. Boil and drain more turnip in the same way. Dissolve honey in the water and pour it into a third pot. Add pepper to this as you did to the turnip pellets.

66. Recipes for Various Vegetables, Including Turnips

Boiled turnip. Take mashed turnip, or turnip rubbed with a piece of iron, and let it dry out. Soak it for three days, with three changes of water. Then cook it, adding honey and spices.

Watermelons. Strain watermelon puree through a fine sieve. Let it ripen in an alkaline solution. When it is ripe, do not cook it, but let it purify itself.

Take a watermelon and cut it in layers. Take out the seeds. Cut about two fingers width from the skin, leaving a little of the green flesh. Peel off strips a little thicker than paper. Put the strips in the juice and let them sit, changing the juice halfway through. Add honey and cook the mixture over a slow flame. Skim off any foam that appears. When the mixture is clear and no more foam appears, the syrup is ready. To the hot mixture, add spices—pepper, ginger, cloves, cinnamon, mace, or nutmeg—and simmer it. Put the syrup in a bowl so it will not burn. When it is ready, put watermelon pieces in the syrup.

Other people say you should cook the watermelon in a lime solution, then cool it before adding it to honey cooked with spices.

Melons. Peel melons thinly. Cut the body of the melon in half, then place it in an alkaline solution for a day and a night. Put the pieces in a spiced syrup like the one used for watermelons and let them sit. Stir the pieces, turning them over, from time to time.

Others say that you should leave the melons in the syrup for a while, then pour it off and replace it, leaving it there for a week

This chapter is from the Long Version of the *Domostroi*.

altogether. When the syrup has evaporated, add honey with spices—pepper, ginger, and cloves.

Kuzmin apples. Take whole apples, not bruised, not wormeaten. Place them on racks, one layer per rack. Pile the racks on top of one another, then pour three measures of honey syrup over all.

Ripe apples and quinces. Put ripe apples and quinces which are clean and unbruised in crates inside small buckets, five quinces per apple. Arrange them with your hands. Pour four measures of honey syrup over them. When you cover the bucket, leave space for a funnel so that air can escape as the mixture ferments.

Mozhaisk cream. Pure Mozhaisk cream is made of apples and pears that have not been mashed, but soaked in a blended syrup, without water. Put it in washed earthenware crocks.

Berry candy. To make candy from bilberries, raspberries, currants, strawberries, cranberries, or any other kind of berry, boil the berries well and for a long time. When they are boiled, strain them through a fine sieve. Add honey and steam the mixture until it is thick. While you steam it, stir the mixture constantly so that it will not burn, but will be very thick. Then pour it onto a board. Smear the board repeatedly with honey. As the mixture sets, pour a second layer, then a third. Do not put it to sit in the sun, but dry it opposite the stove. As the triple-layered mixture sets, twirl it around a tube.

Apple candy. To make apple candy, put apples in a small colander, so that, resting in the colander, they will steam for a long time. Then strain them through a fine sieve, and add some honey, and steam them again, stirring constantly. Mash them and knead them as you stir. When the mixture is thick, pour it onto a board that has been smeared with honey. Rub it well three times with honey. When it has cooled, put it in bowls—but make sure they are copper or tin (we put it in little tubs)—that have been smeared with honey. From the tubs it can be removed like cheese and placed in dishes on the table.

Another Translation concerning the Foods
That People Put on the Table throughout the Year

During Our Lady's Feast: they put out black hare throughout, pig's head seasoned with garlic after the Feast of the Veil, and ham cooked in hay after Our Lady's Feast.[1]

From Our Lady's Fast to St. Simeon's Day: cow's feet, black grouse rubbed with saffron, swan basted with honey, stew spiced with saffron. After the Feast of the Veil: swan giblets mixed with saffron and croutons, swan neck spiced with saffron. They put croutons on the swan's neck also; around here, the croutons are made of white bread and fried in butter.

They serve wild goose, as well as swan, and domesticated goose after the Feast of the Veil. After the Feast of the Veil, they also serve black grouse with a saffron sauce, crane with a saffron sauce, and roast duck with a simple sauce. They set out roast saddle of mutton rubbed with saffron until St. Simeon's Day, also roast joints of beef and roast tongue with a simple sauce. Pork ribs with a simple sauce are served after the Feast of the Veil. They serve hare kidneys with a simple sauce throughout the year. These dishes are also served throughout the year: pickled hare, chicken served with cheese and saffron, hare served on a bed of noodles, hare in a turnip, chicken with noodles, heart, fish soup served in the breast of a wild animal, steer, or elk. Goose giblets, roast chicken, black grouse, duck, sweet pies stuffed with cheese, and baked meat pies are set out with blintzes. Big sourdough pies are blended with butter and cheese and big baked pies served with cheese blintzes. Big fritters are served with honey and pancake butter, pies made from unleavened pastry stuffed with cheese. Pies and butter are set out among the tureens of fish soup. These foods are cooked on the hearth: beef seasoned with garlic, chicken, and pork. For dessert, people offer sweet fritters.

1. The content of this section suggests it was probably originally a separate text, for it has no connection to Chapter 66. In the manuscripts, however, it is always treated as a subsection of Chapter 66. Dates for the holidays are provided in Chapter 64 (Long Version).

Fish Dishes served during Our Lady's Fast: they put out sour cabbage with herring, with caviar of all sorts standing nearby. They serve roast beluga spine, pink salmon (with the teeth) seasoned with garlic, grilled sturgeon, white salmon, dried red salmon, sturgeon spine, sterlet spine, steamed herring, steamed pike, steamed sterlet, steamed bream, red salmon spine, and the spines of other fish.

These winter fish soups, spiced with saffron, are set out: chilled black perch soup; ordinary hot soup; soup made from pike, sterlet, carp, perch, roach, bream, and sturgeon. Amid the tureens of soup, they serve butter made from a heifer's milk, sterlet, and fish cakes.

People serve these sorts of pie: little turnovers stuffed with peas and cooked in nut oil, little sourdough fritters cooked in nut oil, baked sourdough pies stuffed with peas, big pies stuffed with poppy seeds mixed with hempseed oil and peas, big pies cooked in poppyseed oil with hempseed cakes, big pies stuffed with viziga,[2] pink salmon pies, sheat-fish pies, herring pies, pies with hempseed cakes. Amid the pies they strew piles of pancakes.

These salted foods are served: pike cooked in garlic, perch preserved in brine, lightly salted pike, roast beluga preserved in brine, white salmon preserved in brine and served with a sauce, sturgeon preserved in brine and served with a sauce, red salmon preserved in brine and served with a sauce, pink salmon preserved in brine and served with a sauce. After St. Simeon's Day, people do not set out dried fish, but do serve butter, suckling pig, and whole duck. After St. Demetrius's Day, winter soups are served.

During Lent, these fast dishes should be in the bakery: pancakes,[3] onion tarts, fritters, pies stuffed with poppy seeds, sweet jellies, and unleavened breads.

And these sweets are set out during those days [Lent]: watermelon, melon, apples, and pears in honey; cherries;[4] puddings made with ginger, saffron, and pepper;[5] honey mixed with ginger, saffron, and

2. Viziga is the dried spinal cord of a cartilagenous fish.
3. See note 33 to Long Version Chapter 64, above.
4. Russians would have had to strain to find any of these sweets during Lent (February–March), but fresh cherries would have posed a particular challenge. In Italy, maybe, or Astrakhan (but transport from Astrakhan would make them prohibitively expensive).
5. Puddings: *maziuny*, the same word used for turnip pudding in Chapter 65.

pepper; simple sweet and sour cooked cereals with raisins and millet; figs; berry candy; radish in honey.

On Saturdays and Sundays throughout Lent, people put out caviar, pike caviar, pressed caviar, fresh sturgeon caviar, caviar preserved during the autumn; liver of black and white pike, of sturgeon and beluga (dried and fresh); groats with pink salmon, pike-perch, sterlet, sturgeon, and beluga; bread;[6] dried mushrooms, mushrooms fried in butter; pies stuffed with millet, viziga, and peas; carp stuffed with fish, millet, and viziga; fritters, onion tarts, pancakes stuffed with poppy-seed-flavored cottage cheese and served with butter; pastry crust with sturgeon caviar; caviar simmered in vinegar and poppy juice; caviar patties.

During the Easter Feast, people set out swan, swan giblets, crane, heron, duck, black grouse, hazel grouse, roast hare's kidney, salted chicken, chicken gizzards, necks, and liver, salt mutton, baked mutton, mutton pies baked on the hearth, black and white chicken soup spiced with saffron, pies baked on the hearth, fritters, biscuits,[7] stuffed sour-dough pies, simple corned beef with savory, chicken halves, tongue, elk, pies stuffed with eggs and cheese, cottage cheese pancakes with eggs and cheese, pan-fried hare, pickled hare, hare bones, hare sweetbreads, roast chicken with the innards, giblets, and liver, lark, sheep innards,[8] pork, ham, carp, morels, dumplings, and two types of cabbage soup.

And for supper: aspic, hazel grouse, baked hare, duck, roast hazel grouse, black grouse, mutton, chicken halves, pickled hare, roast chicken, pork, and ham.

During Easter on fast days they serve steamed herring, dried pink salmon, dried white salmon, dried sturgeon, sterlet spine, dried beluga, sturgeon spine, beluga spine, steamed white salmon spine, steamed bream, saffron fish soup, black fish soup, pike soup, perch soup, roach soup, bream soup, and carp soup.

Also these pickled fish dishes: white salmon, sterlet; pies stuffed

---

6. The text adds here *kbaniki* (*kobon'ki*), a kind of fish.

7. Russian *kotlomy* (bread made of flour, butter, and eggs).

8. The text adds here *sandriki*. *Sandrik* is the word used for the cornice over the window on a traditional Russian house. Presumably a food (probably a bread or pastry) that reminds the author of this cornice, but the dictionaries offer no enlightenment.

with millet, viziga, and peas; carp mixed with millet and viziga or another fish.

During St. Peter's Fast, these foods are set on the table: steamed herring, dried fish—pink salmon, white salmon, sturgeon. Sterlet spine, beluga kebabs, sturgeon spine, beluga spine, steamed white salmon spine, pike soup spiced with saffron, bowls of black pike soup, baked perch, bowls of roach stew, and soup made from gudgeon, bream, carp, sturgeon, and sterlet.

Also these pickled fish dishes: white salmon, sterlet; pies stuffed with millet, viziga, and peas; carp mixed with millet and viziga or another fish; lightly salted sterlet, sturgeon, lightly salted sturgeon, lightly salted pike, pike head cooked in garlic, loach, dried sterlet, grilled sturgeon, braised sterlet; simmered, baked, and dried mushrooms; cabbage soup and crab.

During St. Peter's Feast, these foods are served: swan, swan giblets, crane, heron, duck, chicken halves, pieces of roast hare, roast beef tongue, roast saddle of mutton, salted chicken, chicken gizzards and necks.

67. Wedding Rituals

Set up a seat for the bridal couple. Cover the seat with a rug, and place on it a pillow made of satin or gold-colored velvet. Next to the seat two men should stand holding forties[1] of sables. Place a table next to the place set up for the bridal pair and cover it with two tablecloths. Put dishes on the table. Fill one platter with sweet bread and rolls and add cheese and a knife to cut it. Load a second platter with hops and gold coins, Muscovite and Novgorodian,[2] for sprinkling on the bride and groom.[3] Also place here nine sables, along with lengths of brocade

This chapter is from the Long Version of the *Domostroi*.

1. A bag holding forty sables, this became a standard unit of value in Muscovite times. Numerous engravings show Russians holding these bags (often offered as gifts to visiting dignitaries) during ceremonies.

2. After Novgorod's annexation to Moscow (1470–1471), its local currency was integrated into the Muscovite one but not eliminated. Novgorodian rubles were worth twice as much as Muscovite rubles.

3. See below, note 13.

and taffeta. On a third platter, pile the ceremonial towels.[4] On a fourth platter place the parts of the bride's headdress, with the *kika* on top.[5] Place a gold or silver wedding cup on this dish also. Fill the cup with mead that is slightly alcoholic and add two poppyseed heads. Finally, put a comb on the platter next to the headdress.

Against the walls, near the place where the bridal couple will sit, place two small benches. The thousandman[6] will sit on one bench and the matchmaker[7] on the other. Two men should stand near the bridal pair's place carrying trays holding loaves and cheese.[8] Cover the trays with satin or golden velvet. Trim the handles with bands of brocade or satin. A third man should hold a candle in a candlestick wrapped in satin or golden velvet, trimmed with the same. Two other men should hold torches. All these people should be dressed in velvet (or brocade, satin, or cloth-of-gold) caftans and jackets and should wear hats of black fox fur.

When the groom arrives with his retinue,[9] the people holding the

4. The ceremonial towels or cloths (*shirinki*) were distributed to guests and members of the wedding party as gifts.

5. *Kika*: the characteristic headdress of a married Russian woman, the *kika* resembled a large tiara, low at the sides and rising to a high point over the middle of the forehead. The *Domostroi* also lists the other pieces of the headdress: a clip to pin the bride's hair to the back of her head, a lace-trimmed cap that went under the *kika*, and a veil.

6. Thousandman (*tysiatskii*): originally the commander of the militia. In Novgorod, the *tysiatskii* became an important military and political figure, the man in charge of military operations (under the prince, who during Novgorod's period of independence was "called" from outside to assume command). Because weddings applied court terminology to every bride and groom, the thousandman here is the person in charge of the wedding, the one who makes sure that everything runs smoothly.

7. Russian weddings were arranged by matchmakers (*svakhi*), but during the ceremony these women served more as what we in the West would call matrons of honor. The bride had one female attendant from her own family and one from the groom's.

8. These loaves are *korovai*, as distinct from the *perepecha* (sweet bread) mentioned in the previous paragraph.

9. Bride and groom: the *Domostroi* names them the "young (or newlywed) prince" and the "young (or newlywed) princess." One of the most charming Russian wedding customs allowed everyone to be "prince for a day." The ingredients of this particular ceremony mark it as intended for real princes and princesses, but even peasant brides and grooms were referred to as "young prince" and "young princess" during their wedding rites (and their followers as "noblemen" and "noblewomen"). The "retinue," recalling the warrior companions of princes, is part of this fantasy, as well as a holdover from the days when young men abducted their brides. On this last, see, for example, Cross and Sherbowitz-Wetzor, trans. and eds., *Russian Primary Chronicle*, p. 56.

loaves, the candle, and the torches should enter also. When the time comes for the groom to be seated in his place, the matchmaker stays standing for a moment after the groom is seated. Then the bride and groom together seek her parents' blessing on their union.[10] Those who hold the sables pass them three times over the heads of the bride and groom. At this time the best man[11] blesses the sweet bread and cuts the cheese and offers them to all present: to the bride's mother and father, to the bride and groom, to their entire retinue, to all seated guests, and to everyone in the room. He should also send someone to take some of the bread and cheese to the groom's parents' house, where it is served to them and their guests.[12]

When the time comes for the bride to don her headdress and her veil, the matchmaker should stand and ask the bride's parents to sprinkle the coins and hops on the couple to be wed.[13] At this point the best man brings the platter piled with ceremonial towels to present to the groom and his retinue. The bride sends some of these, too, to the groom's parents.[14] Then, God willing, the bridal couple rise from their seats and go to the entrance hall. At this time, those present spread the lengths of brocade and taffeta along the path where the bride and groom will walk, as far as the groom's horse and the bride's sleigh. (For the bride drives to her wedding in a sleigh.) The sleigh should

10. Literally, "seek her parents' permission to comb their heads." As detailed in the next wedding ritual, combing the hair of bride and groom marked one stage in the wedding ceremony.

11. *Druzhka.* The closest English translation is "best man" but the *druzhka's* duties went far beyond those of the best man, as this chapter illustrates. There were also two best men in a Russian wedding, one working on behalf of the groom and his family, one appointed by the bride's father.

12. As Daniel Kaiser ("Symbol and Ritual in the Marriages of Ivan IV," *Russian History* 14 [1987]: 252) notes, during pre-Christian times the cutting of the bread and cheese, and its acceptance by both families, solemnized the marriage. Although by Muscovite times, church ceremonies were traditional, at least in urban areas, the rites that surrounded them were filled with pagan fertility rituals. The *Domostroi* itself barely touches on the religious ceremony, which was the priest's concern; all its attention is on the three days of customary celebration. On the tension between Christian and pagan ritual, see Levin, *Sex and Society*, p. 87.

13. The shower of "blessings" represents the family's desire for a fertile bride and underlines the fact that in pagan days the couple was, by this time, already wed. In modern Western weddings, bride and groom are showered with rice or confetti for the same reason.

14. It is not actually stated in the *Domostroi* whose parents receive the cloths from the bride. The author may have intended her to send them to her own parents. But since her parents are present and his are not, and since bread and cheese have already been sent to the groom's parents, I assume that his parents are meant.

"When the time comes for the bride to don her headdress and her veil, the matchmaker should stand and ask the bride's parents to sprinkle the coins and hops on the couple to be wed" (Chapter 67). The rite of sprinkling, like the comparable Western custom of throwing rice or confetti, preserved a pre-Christian fertility ritual: it blessed the newlyweds with wishes for good fortune, wealth, and many children. From Adam Olearius, *Vermehrte Moscowitische und Persianische Reisebeschreibung* (Schleszwig, 1656). Courtesy of the Princeton University Library, Department of Rare Books and Special Collections.

be lined with satin or taffeta, with a velvet cushion, or a small pillow of gold satin. Put a rug in the sleigh, also, and a pillow of crimson cloth. A forty of sables is hung on the sleigh while the bride is being driven to the wedding.

When the groom dismounts from his horse at the church door, and the bride leaves her sleigh, those present again spread brocade and taffeta for them to walk on. Within the church, they adorn the place where the ceremony will occur with brocade or gold satin as well and put two sables under the bride's and groom's feet.

When the groom leaves the church to remount his horse, and the bride returns to her sleigh, those present again spread the cloth for them to walk on. They do this too when the groom dismounts from his horse and the bride leaves her sleigh, as they return to their place at the table for the wedding feast. When they rise from the table and leave the main hall, the cloth is again spread before them. And when, having arrived at their own estate, the groom again dismounts and the bride leaves her sleigh, once more the guests spread the cloth before them as far as the [outdoor] staircase.[15]

Another Wedding Ritual

When the young groom arrives at the house, the bride is already sitting in her place, with the matchmaker seated at her side.[16] Her parents, with the boyars and noblewomen,[17] are also seated in readiness. The boyars sit waiting to greet the young groom in the courtyard. When the groom enters the main hall, the bride's parents, the matchmaker, and the noblewomen all rise, but the bride does not; she stays in her seat, but hides herself. The young groom seats himself next to the bride, and the bride's father and mother, the thousandman, and the boyars resume their places. They all sit for a moment. Then the best man comes to ask the bride's parents for their blessing, and the matchmaker stands up. At that moment the matchmaker must not say anything or leave the table. She and the best man bow to the icons in all four corners of the room. She takes the veil from the platter holding the headdress[18] and uses it to screen the bride from the groom. On one side of the screen she removes the bride's hat. On the other side of the screen she combs the groom's hair, and after that she combs the bride's hair three times. As the matchmaker begins to comb the hair of both bride and groom, the best man cuts the cheese and the sweet bread.

15. In the Muscovite period, the staircase generally ran up the outside of the house and was covered with a wooden roof. See, for example, Giles Fletcher's description in "Of the Russe Commonwealth," p. 126.

16. Although these rituals are presented as alternate forms (and do show some variation), they complement rather than duplicate one another. By the time the fifth ritual is reached, details for the whole three-day ceremony have been given.

17. Throughout this chapter, "noblewomen" translates "boiaryni." In the wedding rituals, the term means the couple's female relatives, friends, and important contacts and is therefore more general than "boyars' wives."

18. The arrangement of the platters is presumably the same as in the preceding ritual.

When the bride's hair has been combed, they separate the strands and braid her hair.[19] The bride twirls around, and as she twirls, they cover her with the veil. On the veil a cross is sewn.[20] Once the bride is veiled, the best man and the matchmaker bow to the icons again and ask the bride's parents to sprinkle the bridal pair. After this they pass out the ceremonial towels, and the priest unites the bride and groom. Then the steward supplies everyone with something to drink, and the boyars, sitting in the outer rooms, honor the newlyweds with a toast.

A Wedding Ritual

When negotiations begin, the prospective groom, with his relatives, visits his prospective father-in-law at his home.[21] All should be wearing clean clothes. He should take with him his father or eldest brother; one of these should go ahead of the prospective groom and the other behind him. They are met as they dismount, or at the foot of the stairs, or in the entrance hall. The bride's father meets them and seats them, according to rank, at the table. Those who accompany the groom sit on one bench, and those who speak for the bride take another bench. The bride's father brings red wine in cups. At that time, the man who speaks on the groom's behalf—that is, his father or eldest brother— begins the negotiations, calling the prospective father-in-law politely by name and saying, "It is time now to begin the business that has

19. The bride's new status is marked by a change in hairstyle: from the single braid of the unmarried girl, she now assumes double braids pinned close to her head and hidden by the headdress. (For speculation on the meaning of this change, see Matossian, "The Peasant Way of Life," p. 15. Matossian is quoting S. A. Tokarev, an ethnographer. The nineteenth-century peasant wedding described by Matossian [pp. 25–29] is very similar to the rites in the *Domostroi*, although in the *Domostroi* the bride assumes her headdress before the church ceremony, and in the peasant wedding she does this afterward.) Another pre-Christian survival: before the wedding, the bride dedicated a ribbon representing her braid to the birch tree, home of the *rusalki*. For more information, see Hubbs, *Mother Russia*, pp. 83–85.
20. This seems to be at least in part wishful thinking. Brides' veils were often embroidered with stylized images of the Great Mother Goddess (sometimes disguised as Mary or St. Paraskeva). For more information, see Hubbs, *Mother Russia*, pp. 24–28 and passim.
21. The signing of the contracts takes place before the wedding day; in other words, this ritual begins at an earlier point in the proceedings than the two previous ones. On prenuptial agreements, see Levin, *Sex and Society*, pp. 91–93.

brought us here." The bride's father commands a priest to speak; it is fitting for the priest to remember our forefather Abraham and his wife Sarah,[22] Joachim and Anne,[23] the Emperor Constantine and St. Helena.[24]

Once the priest has finished, and has blessed the assembled company with the cross, the two sides begin to talk and to draft the marriage documents. When they have agreed on the contract and the size of the dowry, and have affixed their signatures to the contract, and have checked the documents, the priest sings, "In you, O woman full of grace, all creation exults."[25] Then each takes his own copy of the contract, as they drink a measure of mead[26] to celebrate and congratulate one another. At this time they give gifts. The bride's father gives gifts to his new son-in-law: first, a blessing; then a cup or a ladle, velvet, brocade, or a forty of sables.

After the gifts have been presented by whomever the bride's father

22. Presumably, the reference is to Sarah's barrenness, discussed in Genesis 16:1–6 and cured by divine intervention (Genesis 17:15–18:15, 21:1–3). Like the following entry, this underlines the aristocratic bride's main function: to produce male heirs for her new lineage.

23. The Virgin Mary's parents. The Bible has little to say about Mary and her family, but her history quickly became the subject of apocryphal tales (see "The Protevangelium of James," Montague Rhodes James, *The Apocryphal New Testament* [Oxford: Clarendon Press, 1924, corrected 1953, reprinted 1960]). Like Sarah, Anne was believed barren until God granted her Mary. The story is adapted from Hannah's miraculous bearing of Samuel (1 Samuel 1:1–2:11). For a fully developed Orthodox ritual concerning Mary's birth, see *Festal Menaion*, pp. 98–130.

24. A reference to Emperor Constantine I the Great (ruled 306–337) and his mother, St. Helena, whose joint Orthodox feast day is May 21. Helena, according to some legends the daughter of British King Coel ("that merry old soul") and according to others a Greek innkeeper's daughter who rose to be empress, converted to Christianity late in life, and reportedly discovered the True Cross while on pilgrimage in Jerusalem. Constantine established Christianity as the state religion of the Roman Empire, founded the city of Constantinople, and moved the imperial capital there. Why the author considered their story particularly relevant for married couples is unclear: perhaps because it emphasized the importance of motherhood. Helena, Emperor Constantius's first, unofficial wife, was set aside so her husband could make a political marriage; Constantine restored her position and ordered her to be venerated after ascending the throne.

25. "*O tebe raduetsia.*" As quoted here, this is a reference to the Magnifical Hymn, sung to the Virgin Mary during the Liturgy of St. Basil the Great. See Raya and Vinck, comps. and eds., *Byzantine Daily Worship*, p. 331. Among her many responsibilities, the Virgin was patroness of weddings. See note 19 to Long Version of Chapter 64, above, and Marina Warner, *Alone of All Her Sex: The Myth and the Cult of the Virgin Mary* (New York: Knopf, 1976), pp. 274, 277–278.

26. The *Domostroi* does say "mead" here, although earlier the bride's father had brought wine.

ordered to present them, all kiss one another and drink toasts. Those present congratulate the groom, then the bride's father. Then they enter the rooms where the new mother-in-law is waiting with the noblewomen. The mother-in-law greets the groom's father and embraces him, placing a ceremonial towel around his neck.[27] Then she does the same with the groom, and with the others present. The noblewomen do this too. The bride is not present. (But among those of middle rank the brides do attend. They stand beside their mothers, do not greet anyone, and leave after a short time.)[28] Then the parents provide a buffet supper.

The next day, or a little later if the families prefer, the groom's mother visits the new bride's father's house. There she looks over the bride and gives her presents of brocade and sable.[29] She gives the bride a ring and on the next day sends a female relative with a cross, or a panagia,[30] and vegetables. Usually this woman receives a kerchief and cap for her services.

Once both sides have agreed on a date for the wedding, they make up a list that same evening. The groom sends his prospective father-in-law a list of which relatives will attend from his father's and mother's families, and which boyars and noblewomen will attend, who will be his thousandman, who will make up the wedding train, who will be his best man and his matchmaker. The bride's father sends a similar list to the groom, stating which boyars and noblewomen he will invite, who will be the best man and matchmaker for his side, who will be there to help the groom dismount, who will take care of the horses, and who will prepare the bride for bed.

When the wedding day arrives, the guests should sit down to eat on both sides of the table, in whatever place is assigned to them.[31]

27. A mark of honor. See, for example, Olearius, *Travels*, p. 159.
28. This notation underlines that "those of middle rank" are not this author's prime audience, as they were for the author of the first sixty-three chapters.
29. Only husbands and close male relatives were allowed in the women's quarters; prospective grooms did not qualify, so the groom's mother and aunts visited the bride to check on her suitability. As Nancy Shields Kollmann has noted ("Seclusion,"), this gave women an indirect but powerful say in Muscovite political alliances, which were based on family ties.
30. Panagia: an oval medallion of the Virgin Mary, worn on a chain around the neck.
31. Places would be assigned by rank. A reference to the precedence disputes that often arose over seating arrangements—that is, a note to be on one's best behavior and not fight because someone perceived as having lower standing has

Men and women eat at separate tables. The bride and the groom, however, should not eat. This is the time when they are instructed in the canons concerning marriage.[32]

At the proper time, the bride's father sends his oldest servitor to the groom to tell him that his best man and matchmaker are coming with the bed. The servitor says, "Please order your servants to show me where the granary is."[33] He is taken to the place where the bedding ceremony will take place (usually a ground-floor storeroom). He determines how to get there and returns to tell his party.

The best man arrives dressed in cloth-of-gold, accompanied by five or six boyars on horseback, also dressed in cloth-of-gold, with eight others in clean clothes walking beside the horses. Behind them come the people with the bed; they use a sleigh to transport it even in summer. The headboard should face the coachman's box and the bed be covered with a blanket. The sleigh should be pulled by two gray carriage horses; boyars in clean clothes should walk beside it. A elderly man dressed in cloth-of-gold stands, holding an icon, on the bed, behind the headboard.

Behind the bed comes the matchmaker in her costume: a yellow jacket,[34] a knee-length coat of the softest fur,[35] a kerchief, a beaver collar, and—if it is winter—a fur hat. She rides alone in another sleigh.

When they arrive at the groom-to-be's estate, the men on horseback dismount. They walk in pairs and enter the courtyard before the best man, who rides in on his horse. The best man dismounts at the stairway and waits for the bed to arrive. When the bed reaches the stairway, the groom's best man greets the party and tells the groom's servants to take the bed. These servants collect others to help them, then go to the sleigh and carry the bed away, holding it high over their heads. The noblewomen, meanwhile, greet the matchmaker as she arrives in

---

been given a better seat. On the precedence system, see Crummey, *Aristocrats and Servitors*, pp. 135–138.

32. For Orthodox rules on marriage, see Levin, *Sex and Society*, pp. 79–135.

33. This sounds strange, but the idea is to create privacy for the newlyweds by temporarily converting an unused storeroom or outbuilding into a bedroom for them.

34. *Letnik*: a light overgarment cut close to the figure and with long, wide sleeves.

35. *Shubka chervchata*: a knee-length coat made of fur from an animal's belly, considered the softest fur. *Chervchata* also means crimson (as in the pillow of crimson cloth, above), so the author may intend a crimson coat, but this reading seems more probable because *shubka* usually means "fur coat." (This outfit would be very hot in summer, but so would the other costumes.)

her sleigh. The noblewomen are dressed in fancy jackets and fur coats. The matchmaker gets out of the sleigh and, with the noblewomen, follows those who are carrying the bed. She walks behind the man carrying the icon.

The groom's matchmaker is waiting on the first flight of stairs. Behind her stand more noblewomen, dressed in fur coats like the first group. The two best men walk in front of the bed and the two matchmakers behind it. When they enter the granary, a priest sprinkles water in every corner and in the place where the bed will rest. Then they strew twenty-seven sheaves of rye on the floor. The rug that was brought from the bride's house is placed on top of the strewn rye, the bed placed on top of the rug and again covered with the blanket. They place the icon at the head of the bed. At each corner of the room, sables, in pairs, lie on arrows; a small roll made from finely ground flour also sits in each corner. A sideboard stands nearby, holding a dozen mugs containing different drinks made from mead and kvass. The sideboard should also hold a ladle and a single small cup, one with no handles or ring, or a large round goblet without a spout.[36]

In the room, near the head of the bed, they set up a table, covered with a veil, on which are placed candles and round loaves. A second small table sits atop the first. The small table has two plates, one for the cross that hangs round the groom's neck[37] and the other for the bride's necklace; it also holds two bowls, one for the groom's hat and the other for the bride's headdress.

At the foot of the bed, a third table is set up to receive the couple's robes. At one corner of this table a sheet [to screen the bride] is arranged, and behind the sheet they put a feather pillow, on top of a rug, a small wedding pillow,[38] a big covered pot[39] containing warm water, two basins, a large washtub, and two bedsheets. On this table they also set out a shirt, a chemise, a scrubber, a little washtub, a towel, and two skin tunics.[40]

36. Goblet: *bratina*, a loving cup.

37. Nowhere is the Orthodox church's ambivalent attitude toward sexuality more evident than in the custom that a man must remove his cross before engaging in sexual intercourse. Levin, among others, mentions this in *Sex and Sexuality*, p. 168.

38. Someone was usually appointed to carry two pillows like these during the processions. See below and Kaiser, "Symbol and Ritual," p. 257.

39. *Kumgan*: a covered metal pot with a long spout and handle, somewhat like the pots used by chefs to pour oil.

40. Skin tunics: *shuby nagol'nye*. Literally, a coat or tunic made from pelts or

When all this has been prepared, the best men and matchmakers send everyone else out of the room, then leave themselves. The granary is locked, and the best men seal it with their own seals. The two oldest grooms of the chamber, dressed in cloth-of-gold, stay to guard the room while the best men and matchmakers leave. Beside the grooms of the chamber stands a table without a tablecloth.

The bride's best man and matchmaker lead the way to her father's house. There the best man greets the groom's best man as he dismounts from his horse and the matchmaker greets the groom's matchmaker as she reaches the outside staircase. The bride's noble attendants greet the groom's as they disembark from their sleighs. The newly arrived best man and matchmaker do not, however, enter the main rooms of the house, nor are they greeted by the boyars and noblewomen seated there.

During the time that the bed is being set up, the people who accompany the best men and matchmakers to deliver the bed should be doing honor to one another in the courtyard (the tables and chairs for this should have been set up previously). Thus, when the best man and the matchmaker, being finished with the bed, go to collect the groom, they will find, already set out in the groom's chambers, a large table with a tablecloth and dishes holding bread and rolls, one for each guest. The groom's father sits at the end of the table, the thousandman in one corner, and the groom in the center, with his mother next to him. The noblewomen sit below the mother, all dressed in yellow jackets and knee-length coats of the softest fur. They wear kerchiefs on their heads and headdresses of beaver fur, or fur hoods[41] in winter. The boyars sit on benches opposite the women. The other members of the retinue sit on benches opposite the high table.[42] The man holding the candles should wear a girdle of gold, a long tunic,[43] a gold or

---

sheepskins from which the fur or wool has been removed (that is, untanned leather); sometimes, a coat constructed so the fur/wool is inside instead of outside. See also skin hats (*shapki nagol'nye*) elsewhere in this chapter.

41. *Kaptura*: a large fur hat that covers the neck and shoulders—a combination of hat and hood.

42. In the Middle Ages, the usual arrangement for a banquet (or for everyday meals on a large estate) was to have a "high" table, for the estate owner's family and most honored guests, and long tables running down the hall for everyone else. Guests were placed at table according to rank. People of higher rank sat "above" (closer to the high table), with their social inferiors "below" them.

43. Long tunic: *feriaz*, a tunic with long, tight sleeves, worn over the shirt and

brightly colored caftan, and a hat of soft fur.[44] Across his shoulders he should have a sash of velvet, or brocade, or a bag in which he keeps the candles. Each candle should weigh forty-five pounds.[45] The two men who hold the bread should be likewise attired, with long tunics and sashes across their shoulders. The loaves and the trays that hold them should both be wrapped in velvet or brocade. The wrapped loaves should be covered with a small pillowcase or a golden sash. Put a loaded sideboard here and another in the entrance hall. Last, make the horses ready in their finery—chains jingling under gold coverlets.[46]

When all is ready, the servants send a message to the best man, who bows in all directions, then approaches the groom's father. Together, the best man and the groom's father order the wedding party to make an obeisance to the bride's father on their behalf. Then the thousandman, the boyars, and the entire retinue, including the best man, set out. Five or six men, mounted and dressed in cloth-of-gold, precede them, and many servants, dressed in bright colors, run beside the horses.

When they reach the bride's estate, the men dismount from their horses at the gates. Those who came on foot enter first. At the bride's house, the family will also have prepared a high table, set against the back wall, with a tablecloth and dishes. The bride's father sits at the head of the table, and her mother on a bench, with the noblewomen massed behind her. The boyars sit opposite the women on benches. They arrange a place in the center of the room, opposite the doors, enclosing two wedding pillows, one for the groom and one for the bride. A table stands there, with two tablecloths on it, holding dishes, a loaf, and sweet bread. Another loaf, set in a tureen, sits on the table; a second tureen holds cheese. At the end of this table sits the thousandman. The two matchmakers sit behind the bride. Opposite the bridal couple's bench sit two to four members of the retinue. The best

---

trousers, particularly on ceremonial occasions. See, for example, Olearius, *Travels*, p. 128.

44. Literally, the fur from an animal's throat. The *Domostroi* is quite specific about fur: note the reference to fur from an animal's belly, worn by the matchmaker and noblewomen, in note 35.

45. A *pud* and a quarter. One *pud* is approximately thirty-six pounds.

46. Olearius describes horses outfitted in this way to greet his ambassador on the party's first arrival in Moscow (*Travels*, p. 57). Again, this emphasizes the high court rank of the readers addressed in these wedding rituals.

men sit opposite the matchmakers. The priest's place is at the end, behind the platters.

Several noblewomen stand near the center of the room. One holds the platter with the main part of the bride's headdress, another a platter containing the veil, a third, the cap and other parts of the headdress. A fourth holds a platter with items for sprinkling: hops, twenty-seven sables, twenty-seven lengths of brocade and taffeta of various colors, and twenty-seven small coins, both gold and silver.[47]

There should be another table set out, sufficient for the retinue, and a filled sideboard. The man holding the candle should wear a girdle round his waist, a long tunic, and a hat of throat or lynx fur. He carries the candles in a bag of velvet or taffeta. Each candle should weigh twenty-seven pounds.[48] The two men holding the bread should be likewise attired, with long tunics and sashes across their shoulders. The loaves and trays should be wrapped in velvet or brocade. The wrapped loaves should be covered with a small pillowcase or a golden sash.

In the entrance hall stands a sideboard, and in the courtyard tables with benches, but without tablecloths, holding beer and mead. On the table stand flasks of wine.[49]

When the groom's best man arrives, the servants greet him at the gates, in the middle of the courtyard, and again at the stairs. The bride's best man greets the groom's as he reaches the first flight of stairs. When the groom's man enters the house, he bows to the icons on all four walls. Then he says to the bride's father, "My lord N. has commanded me to make obeisance to you," naming the groom's father and bowing. He repeats this, greeting the bride's noble guests on behalf of the groom's, the bride's mother on behalf of the groom's mother and noblewomen, and the bride's noblewomen on behalf of the groom's mother and noblewomen. He names each person on whose behalf he proffers greetings. When he is finished, he makes obeisance to the bride's father and boyars on behalf of the thousand-man and the retinue, saying, "N., the thousandman, has commanded

---

47. The setup of the platters differs from that used in the first ritual.
48. A *pud* minus a quarter. See note 45.
49. The author may mean vodka instead of wine (in the sixteenth century the same word was used for both). Red wine was usual, however, in elite weddings. For the symbolic associations of red and weddings, see Kaiser, "Symbol and Ritual," pp. 258–259.

us to say, that N., the groom, is ready to set out." The bride's father answers, "When it is time, we too will come." Then the groom's man rides away.

When the groom's best man returns home, the groom's family sends their matchmaker off in her sleigh. She wears a yellow costume. When she arrives at the bride's estate, the noblewomen greet her as she dismounts from her sleigh, and the matchmaker as she reaches the first flight of stairs. When she enters the house, the noblewomen who previously remained seated leave the table and embrace her.

All the women go to the place where the bride is sitting behind the screen. The bride wears a crown, a yellow jacket, and a knee-length coat of softest fur. The matchmaker kisses her and says, "It is time for your lord to come." The bride's mother then blesses her, fastening a necklace or panagia around her neck and kissing her. The bride weeps and at this time sings her wedding songs.[50]

When the bride has finished her lament, they go to the place that has been set up for the wedding. The bride's mother goes first. The bride comes behind her, with the groom's chief matchmaker on her right and her own matchmaker on the left. The noblewomen come last. When all have entered the room, the bride and the matchmakers bow in all directions. The bride's parents and the noblewomen go to their places. The priest pronounces all worthy; he blesses the bride with his cross and sprinkles [holy] water on the place where the bridal couple will sit.

The best man, at this time, says to the bride's father and mother, "N., bless your daughter and the place she sits." The bride's father and mother reply, "May God bless her." Then they light the candles set before the icons.

The priest prepares two candles, made from twisted wax. When the candles are set up, the best man is sent to fetch the groom. When he arrives at the groom's estate, he follows the same procedure that he followed when he delivered the bed. Then he enters the house and

---

50. Brides were supposed to weep bitterly to demonstrate their love for their parents and their reluctance to leave their natal home to live among strangers. The wedding songs, many of which have been preserved, express the bride's grief at length and often with great beauty. For examples, see Matossian, "Peasant Way of Life," pp. 26–27, and N. P. Kolpakova, *Lirika russkoi svad'by*, nos. 199–203. (Kolpakova records songs for all phases of the wedding cycle.) On the social context that produced the reluctant bride, see Hubbs, *Mother Russia*, pp. 79–86.

bows in all directions. He offers greetings from the bride's father to the groom's father, from the bride's noble guests to the groom's, from the bride's mother to the groom's mother and from the bride's noble-women to the groom's, and to the thousandman. He then says to the thousandman, "N. (giving the bride's father's name) has ordered me to tell you that it is time for the groom to begin his good work." Having said this, the bride's best man returns to her estate.

When he is gone, the thousandman and the groom's retainers rise and bow. The thousandman speaks to the groom's father and mother, calling them by name, saying, "They have given permission for your son to enter the state of lawful matrimony. It is for you to bless his going to that place." The father and mother come from behind the table and bow to the icons on all four walls. They tell their son, "May God bless you and have mercy upon you. May He grant you a most proper affection, health, and prosperity."[51] They bless him, giving him a cross or relics to wear on a chain round his neck. They place their hands on his head, and the mother places a ring on his finger. Then they leave the room: the best man first, then the retainers, two by two, the youngest first and those more venerable toward the back. Last comes the groom, with the thousandman on his right; these two mount their horses ahead of the retinue.

Once the groom has mounted his saddle horse, all over the courtyard men leap onto their saddle horses and steeds.[52] They ride out of the courtyard two by two. As they leave the gates, their servants, dressed in cloth-of-gold, run before them. They should have a man running beside every stirrup. The candleholder and the holders of loaves go first, then the priest with his cross, then (after a little wait) the best man with the servants nearby. Then come the retainers, two by two.

51. Before the eighteenth century, most marriages were made for political or economic reasons; love and affection were expected to follow marriage, not precede it. (Among Russian boyars, who did not see their brides before the wedding, no other course was possible.) Still, personalities might clash and affection not always result. For devout Christians, an "excessive" attraction between spouses posed almost as great a threat because passion directed toward one's marriage partner was considered to detract from one's duty to God. The wish, therefore, is that the newlyweds will find a way between the two extremes. For a speculative but thought-provoking study of changes in affective relationships within the family, see Lawrence Stone, *The Family, Sex and Marriage in England, 1500–1800* (New York: Harper & Row, 1977).

52. The distinction here is between battle horses (destriers, *koni*) and saddle horses (*argamaki*).

Behind them run more servants with cloaks and horse blankets and the like, whatever the members of the wedding party have brought with them. Before the groom and the thousandman walk two masters of horse, dressed in cloth-of-gold and carrying small batons. Behind them come men carrying covers for the horses. Near the groom and the thousandman walk men finely dressed in bright colors. This is how people customarily arrive at the bride's estate and ascend the stairs to the house.

When they arrive, the priest uses a cross to bless the wedding party. The bride's best man greets the party on behalf of the bride's father, walking before the groom and the thousandman. The bride's father and the seated boyars do not greet the new arrivals, but wait inside, where they line up against both walls. When the groom and the thousandman arrive, they bow to the icons on all four walls. At that moment, the groom's best man finds a boy sitting beside the bride in the place set up for the new couple. He summons the boy, saying jokingly, "There is a horse for you in the Horde; the golden ones are at the Ugra."[53] The priest blesses the groom as he takes his place.

The thousandman and the groom's retainers take their places. The two priests (the one who accompanied the groom and the one already present at the bride's house) command that the pair of candles near the bridal couple's seat be lighted. The groom's candleholder stands opposite the groom, and the bride's opposite the bride. The men holding the bread stand together, bearing their trays. When all are in place, the betrothal rite begins.[54] After the ceremony, the groom kisses the

53. This fascinating statement recalls Russia's long domination by the Mongols. The "Horde" refers to the Mongol government (the so-called Golden Horde or one of its offshoots); the Ugra River, south of Moscow, was the site of an abortive battle between Mongol and Russian forces in 1480, after which the Russians considered the "Mongol Yoke" to have been formally lifted (although effective Mongol rule had ended some hundred years earlier). Roughly translated, it means, "Get lost, kid," but the boy was usually bribed to leave with a small gift (not unlike the Mongols themselves, whose administration consisted primarily of collecting tribute).

54. The *obruchan'e*, or church-administered engagement ceremony, marked by an exchange of rings and distinct from the more secular *rukobit'e* (handfasting). Since the contracts have already been signed (with monetary penalties for dishonor exacted if they are broken) and the wedding ceremony follows immediately, the ecclesiastical betrothal rite is in this instance a formality. It was not always so, however. For more on secular and church betrothal ceremonies, see Pushkareva, "Women in the Medieval Russian Family," pp. 31–32; Levin, *Sex and Society*, pp. 89, 93–94.

bride. The two matchmakers, without leaving the area of their seats, stand and bow to the icons in all directions. The matchmakers say to the bride's father and mother, giving their names, "Give your blessing to your children who are now being wed, and let us comb your daughter's hair." The matchmaker for the bride's family then combs the girl's hair, braids it, and places the headdress on her head. The senior best man[55] cuts the loaves and the cheese, taking pieces from all four corners, and places the pieces on one dish. Then he cuts thin slices of bread and cheese, which he spreads among the dishes. To the first platter, the best man adds some ceremonial towels. This dish he carries to the groom, giving his name and saying, "The bride, N., shows her respect for you with this bread, cheese, and cloth." The groom takes one towel and wraps it around himself. The best man repeats this ceremony with the thousandman and each retainer who was on the list.[56] He also offers a plate containing a piece of bread, a chunk of cheese, and a towel to each person whose name is in his written orders.[57] Then the servants give platters to the bride's father and mother and to all the guests. Finally, more servants take platters to the groom's parents and the guests waiting at their house. These dishes, too, contain bread, cheese, and towels. The bride and groom also send bread, cheese, and cloth to any relatives who could not attend the ceremony.

At the moment when the thousandman and the retainers receive the bread, the bride's father stands and offers them red wine. He orders his servants to bring wine to the seated boyars. The boyars' servants—whether there in the house, in the entrance hall, on the stairs, or in the yard—toast the newlyweds and give out towels to whomever the bride's father commands.

While the wedding party veils the bride and carries her crown on a platter around the house, the senior matchmaker sprinkles the bride and groom. The thousandman stands and helps the groom to rise,

---

55. Elsewhere in the text, the context suggests that the senior best man is the one selected by the groom's family. The junior best man would therefore be the one representing the bride's family. The text makes a similar distinction between the two matchmakers.

56. That is, the list given to the bride's father when the contracts were signed.

57. The word here is *iarlyk*, a Mongol word usually used for the document certifying a prince's right to rule over and collect taxes on a particular principality. Here it has the more general sense of orders written down, in this case by the bride's father.

"When the bride's hair has been combed, they separate the strands and braid her hair" (Chapter 67). In Muscovite Russia, only maidens wore their hair loose; combing the bride's (and groom's) hair symbolized their new status as an adult, married pair. A comb like the one above would be used for such ceremonial occasions; made of carved bone, this is seventeenth-century work from Kholmogory, the center of Russian craftsmanship in ivory. Courtesy of the Walters Art Gallery, Baltimore.

and the priest begins to sing, "All my hope. . . ."[58] The best man asks the blessing of the bride's parents, saying, "Allow your children to go to their wedding." The groom bows, making obeisance to the bride's father and mother according to custom. Then he takes his bride by the hand and sets off with her for the church. (The retainers precede them as before.)

The retainers mount their horses, which stand in front of the groom's saddle horse. The bride sits in her sleigh, on a seat by herself, with the two matchmakers opposite her. The noblewomen do not attend the church ceremony.

During the ceremony, a pair of sables is placed under the couple's

58. It is unclear exactly which prayer the author means. The most likely is "You are our hope, a stronghold and refuge for Christians," a prayer to the Mother of God (Raya and Vinck, comps. and trans., *Byzantine Daily Worship*, p. 225), said during Terce. Other, less probable, sources include "O Lady, Bride of God . . . only hope of the hopeless (ibid., p. 118) and "The Father is my hope, the Son my refuge" (ibid., p. 119).

feet—one sable for the groom and another for the bride. The cup from which they drink during the ceremony should have no handle, so that, once they have drunk from it, it can be broken. The bride should not fling herself down when she prostrates herself to the groom, and he should help her up with outstretched hand, for he has previously broken the cup with his foot.[59]

After the church ceremony, the wedding party returns to the bride's father's house. The seated boyars greet the retainers as they dismount from their horses and begin to ascend the stairs. The bride's father himself comes out to meet them as they arrive in the entrance hall; he kisses the groom. The groom has walked back from the church, holding his bride by the hand. He is accompanied by the thousandman and she by the matchmaker. As they walk into the entrance hall, the bride's mother greets them. Then they enter the main room and, having bowed to the icons, resume their seats. The bride's father brings wine to the groom, the servants bring out red wine, and the groom is first to eat some of the bread and cheese. [Then the dinner begins.]

The servants first bring out a swan,[60] which they present to the groom. He places his hand on it in token of his acceptance of it and orders that it be carved. The servants put the swan on the table. They send pieces of the meat to the bride's parents and all the noble guests, placing bits on each plate.[61] The servants should also dispense old

59. This paragraph is a list of things to watch out for during the wedding ceremony, not a description of the ceremony itself. Apparently the author assumed either that the ceremony was familiar to his readers or that the priest would instruct them in the proper procedure. The loving cup he mentions contained red wine; after sharing it with his bride, the groom stepped on it and broke it. For varying interpretations of the broken cup and its multiple symbolic meanings, see Kaiser, "Symbol and Ritual," p. 254; and Pushkareva, "Women in the Medieval Russian Family," pp. 36–37. The *Domostroi* seemingly preserves the older version of this ceremony, not the "playful action in the struggle for authority within the family" that Pushkareva describes as usual for the sixteenth century.

60. Swan, considered a delicacy, conferred a special cachet on any feast (see chapters 64 and 66, for example) but had a particular association with weddings. Nineteenth-century recreations of Muscovite life (and twentieth-century movies, also, like Eisenstein's *Ivan the Terrible*) often included scenes of the swan—plucked, cooked, and reconstituted—at the wedding feast.

61. Until the Italians introduced earthenware plates to European tables (in most places, sometime in the seventeenth century), plates and bowls were scarce. Among the rich, the usual standard was one dish for each pair of diners. Roast meat was carved into large pieces and placed on these platters; diners (who brought their own knives and spoons) then carved small pieces of meat from the platter and put them on their individual trenchers—bread squares that served as plates. Soups,

wine and fowl. After the third course, the groom stands, and his thousandman and best man with him. The groom calls out, and the best man says to the bride's father, "N., the groom requests that you feast with him tomorrow." He invites the bride's mother also, and all the seated guests, by name. While the best man speaks, the groom, wearing a skin hat, bows.

When he has finished making the invitations, the best man grasps the upper tablecloth and the dish containing the pieces of bread and cheese. Having rolled the tablecloth up, he hands it to the groom's servants, and tells them to take it to the room at the groom's estate where the bed was set up. The retainers leave the house and mount their horses. The bride's father takes his daughter's hand and goes to the door. There he sprinkles his son-in-law, saying kindly, "By God's design my daughter has married you, N. You are the one chosen to love her and to live with her in lawful matrimony, as did our fathers and our fathers' fathers." The groom hugs his father-in-law, then leaves with the bride, mounting his horse according to the procedure described above. The bride sits in her sleigh with the two matchmakers, and they proceed to their own home in the same way as they went to the church.

When they reach the groom's estate, they enter the granary (or, among people less well-off, the cellar). There the groom's parents sprinkle them as they walk clockwise.[62] Then the bedding ceremony begins. The thousandman unveils the bride, saying to the couple, "May the Lord grant you a good rest." The candles and the loaves of bread are set out in the places prepared for them. The groom's hat and the bride's headdress are taken off and put in the places arranged for them. At that time, all stand and sing vespers.

After the service, the bride undresses behind the curtain. Then the thousandman and all the retainers go into the main house, where the groom's father waits. The following people stay with the groom: the two best men, the two matchmakers, the groom of the chamber, and any noble relatives (male and female) whom he asks to remain. These people remove his robe. The groom wears, on top of his undertunic,

---

stews, and other wet foods were served in bowls, again shared by two people. Even cups were often shared.

62. Literally, "in the direction of the sun," a sign that they are married, probably of pre-Christian origin.

a skin tunic.[63] The bride wears a quilted jacket. Both have hats of soft fur.[64]

At this point, the couple dismisses the best men and the match-makers. Only those who will serve them later remain in the vicinity [but outside the room]. The thousandman, the retainers, the senior best man, and the senior matchmaker go to the room where the groom's father waits. They tell him, "God has arranged that your children, N. and N., be married, that they lie together and rest well, and now they restore their strength." Then the other best man and matchmaker visit the bride's father, saying that the couple has arrived and are now bedded together.[65]

The two grooms of the chamber stay near the doors of the bridal chamber. When the groom has lain with the bride for a while and has known her, he calls out to the groom of the chamber, commanding him to fetch one of his female relatives. He goes behind the screen and washes himself, then dresses in the shirt and one of the skin tunics. The bride comes in with the female relative (sometimes two) that the groom summoned. They wash her there. Both nightshirts are placed in the tureens. Then the bride dons the chemise and the other tunic. The groom summons the best man then, and awaits him in the great bed, while the bride waits on the pillow behind the screen.

When the best man arrives, he sends a message to the groom's parents, saying that God has granted that all go well. Then they send a message to the matchmaker, and the thousandman, and those rel-

---

63. Russian boyars dressed in layers of clothing: shirt and trousers, covered by a *zipun* (here translated as undertunic), caftan, *feriaz* (here, long tunic), *okhaben* (another tunic with long sleeves and a cape), *odnoriadka* (used only when going outside), and in winter, a fur coat on top of all. The "skin tunic" seems to take the place of the caftan in these rituals. For a description, see Fletcher, "Of the Russe Commonwealth," pp. 242–243. Boyars wore several layers of hats, also, beginning with a skullcap.

64. Literally, fur made from an animal's throat.

65. Like the groom's family earlier, the bride's parents remained at their own estate but were kept apprised of the stages of the ceremony as they occurred. The bedding ceremony was crucial to both sides. Although the Orthodox church, unlike its Western sister, did not consider consummation necessary to bind the marriage (see Levin, *Sex and Society*, pp. 59–65), the honor- and dynastic-minded Russian courtiers did not share this view. For them, marriage existed to produce new members for the clan; a nonconsummated (or barren) match would soon be dissolved. In this sexist world, the bride bore the blame for any failure to reproduce; she would also suffer if she proved nonvirgin because this impinged on her family's honor (and, just as important, the paternity of her children).

atives who feel concern for the groom. The groom's mother and her noble attendants come to see the bride. They bring food with their own hands: aspic made from chopped chicken, with plums, lemons, and cucumbers. The thousandman feeds the groom, while the groom's mother and noblewomen feed the bride behind the screen.

The groom's family, meanwhile, sends the best man with a message to the bride's parents. Having called the bride's parents by name, the best man says to them, "The groom, N., has sent me to tell you that by means of God's mercy and your bestowal of your daughter on him and your care of her, all has come out well for us. I give you my thanks for that bestowal."

The bride's father kisses the best man, giving him a little drinking cup. The bride's mother gives him a towel. Then, joy and festiveness reign in both households.

The two ceremonies—the betrothal [at home] and the crowning [at church]—and the vespers sung in the groom's granary, as well as the prayers and matins, public services, and singing of the hours on the second day when the groom comes from the bathhouse are church events, to be conducted according to the canonical rule. All who are eligible and permitted to attend should attend.

When the groom's parents, the best man, and the matchmaker leave the granary, the newlyweds may do as they wish. Near the granary and under the stairs, they tether colts and fillies. For the colts, seeing the fillies, will neigh at them.[66]

After this is done, the retinue, the guests, both best men, and the two matchmakers all return to their own homes. Relatives of the couple, if invited, stay overnight. The candles burn all night. Toward morning, the bathhouse is readied.[67] The best men and the matchmakers from both sides arrive. The junior best man sends, on behalf of the bride's father, servants carrying bathing utensils to the senior best man. These servants carry two bowls, four towels (two for drying

66. The fertility-ritual aspects of this are striking, but the custom also serves to contribute to the general noise and diversion.

67. The bathing ritual described below had a dual meaning. Most obviously, it purified the couple following the sexual intercourse that solemnized their marriage. But the bathhouse was also the home of pagan spirits, the *rozhanitsy* (female) and *banniki* (male); the bathing ritually introduces the groom in his new role to these protective clan spirits. On the *rozhanitsy*, see Hubbs, *Mother Russia*, pp. 15–16. The bathhouse spirits also ruled childbirth. On childbirth, see Levin, "Childbirth."

and two for washing), and a copper caldron with a lid. The junior best man also asks that he be informed when the groom stirs.

When the groom is ready to get up, he summons his groom of the chamber and orders that the best man be brought to him. The people in charge of the bath are sent to the bathhouse, and when all is ready, the best man appears. The groom rises and is dressed in boots, a skin tunic, and a fur hat. He puts on his sleeves before he sets off.

Meanwhile, the bride stays in bed, covered by a blanket. When the groom is gone, the matchmaker comes to her, accompanied by the noblewomen. Together they begin to help her up. At this moment, a fife sounds, trumpets and tambourines play. When the bride has risen, her attendants dress her in a white jacket, a golden tunic, and a hat made of soft fur.[68] She covers herself with a cloak, then enters the main part of the house. There they have prepared a little bed for her behind a screen, and she lies down.

The best man sends a man to the bride's father's estate, to tell the bride's best man that the groom has gone to the bathhouse and that the bride has awoken. The matchmaker then journeys to the groom's estate to see the bride. The bride's father dispatches his best man to the groom with gifts. The best man rides dressed in cloth-of-gold, following the procedure detailed above. Behind him, in a sleigh, travel the gifts, packed in boxes and covered with a lap robe.

When the bride's best man arrives at the bathhouse, he distributes the gifts to the servants so that they may hold them for the groom. [The groom puts on the gifts]: a shirt, trousers, two girdles (one with a pouch containing gold coins), leggings, linen foot cloths,[69] boots, tunic, skin coat, and hat made of fur from an animal's belly. Even before this, while the groom is still in the bathhouse, the servants give him an undershirt and boots.[70]

The retainers, the thousandman and his comrades, now arrive at the bathhouse. Here tables with drinks have been set up; whoever wishes may drink and give drink to his servants. The new arrivals play the tambourine and pass ceremonial towels out to those who

68. Literally, fur from an animal's throat.
69. *Chetygi* (variant of *chedygi*), a kind of footwear, here probably describing the linen cloths wrapped around the feet in place of socks. See Fletcher, "Of the Russe Commonwealth," p. 243.
70. The *Domostroi* definitely says "boots" twice. Perhaps the groom exchanges one pair when the new ones arrive.

washed the groom. Then the groom leaves the bathhouse and returns to his room, where he sleeps for a while.

The bride is not taken to the bathhouse but is washed inside the main house. When it is time to put on her headdress and robe, the matchmakers accompany her to the granary. At that time, the groom retires to his own rooms, along with all his attendants. There he attires himself in cloth-of-gold.

[When they are both dressed,] they sit on the bed, as they sat in their places during the betrothal ceremony. The matchmakers veil the bride, and the groom, accompanied by his entire retinue, returns to the granary and takes his place on the bed next to the bride. The thousandman and the guests also sit, in order of their rank. The groom's father enters, with his boyars, and kisses his son, congratulating him on his marriage. He unveils the little bride and congratulates her, also. Then all offer their congratulations. The groom's father then blesses his son and daughter-in-law, on the occasion of her unveiling, using an icon or cross or panagia, and giving them *votchina* lands.

Then the servants bring chicken and kasha, and the groom eats. The groom, his father, and the retinue then go into the main house. The bride, still unveiled, and the matchmakers go to the women's quarters to see the groom's mother. She and her guests kiss the bride and congratulate her. They bless her using a cross or panagia and give her rings. Then they order food be prepared.

When the food is ready, all the women go into the main hall. On the table, vegetables have been set out directly on the tablecloth, without plates or bread. A gold robe lies there, too. If it is summer, light coats[71] are placed on the table; if winter, skin tunics. The noblewomen wear white jackets and knee-length coats of the softest fur.[72] During winter these should have fur hoods.

The groom's father and mother sit at the end of the table and the newlyweds in the place of honor. The matchmakers and noblewomen sit near the bridal couple, the thousandman and boyars on benches, and the retainers at the table opposite. Then the food is brought in. The bride's father sends his best man with gifts; these are now brought in on platters. The groom's father receives a shirt and trousers. As

71. Light coats: *okhabni* (see note 63).
72. The *Domostroi* adds, "with *spuski*." The meaning here is unclear; it may be a scribal error. Two possibilities are "with false sleeves" (from *pusk, pusto*: empty) or "with trimming" (from *pushok*: fluff).

they are brought in, the best man calls him by name, saying, "The bride, N., honors you." As the groom's father receives the gifts, the bride bows to him; then all stand.

The groom's mother receives brocade and her noble attendants taffeta, also brought in on platters. Again, the best man speaks, and the bride bows. Among those of lower rank, the groom's mother receives taffeta (but of the more expensive kind) instead, and her noblewomen get chemises, kerchiefs, or caps.

The thousandman and noble guests also receive shirts and trousers, but no gifts are given to the retainers.

When the assembled company has eaten the vegetables, the gifts are carried from the chamber. Then, the groom's father and mother bless their son, using an icon, giving him the golden robe, as well as a tunic, dishes, horses (in festive attire), slaves, and *votchina* lands. The groom's mother also blesses her new daughter-in-law in the same way, bestowing clothes and dishes on her. The thousandman and the noble guests give the bride and groom whatever they wish.

The bride and groom then go to their own rooms.[73] The men command that the horses be got ready. When the time comes, they deck themselves in cloth-of-gold and go to the estate of the bride's father, following the procedure described earlier. The priest is in the front, holding his cross, followed by the retainers, then the thousandman with the groom. When they arrive at the estate, the bride's father has a fanfare played on trumpets and tambourines. He also arranges a formal ceremony of greeting, with servants in the courtyard, mounted on steeds, and on the stairs. The bride's father himself, with his relatives, wait in the entrance hall to welcome the groom, the thousandman, and the retainers. In the main rooms the bride's mother and the noblewomen sit at the high table. This table is set with a tablecloth, but no dishes; it holds vegetables.

When the bride's father and his noble guests have greeted the groom, they enter the dining room and stand in the places assigned to them. Then the groom enters with his thousandman. One of the best men precedes him into the room, and the other remains close by. The retainers file in behind the groom. The bride's mother moves a little away from the table in order to greet her son-in-law, ask about

73. Presumably, back to the storeroom set up for them, although the bride and groom would probably be assigned a room of their own after the wedding.

his health, and embrace him while she wraps a ceremonial towel around his neck. Then the noblewomen leave the table to embrace the groom in the same way. The bride's mother then embraces the thousandman and the retainers in this way, and the noblewomen greet them as well, but without the towels.

The noblewomen then seat themselves on benches, in order of rank, and the groom sits next to his new mother-in-law. The thousandman sits at the corner, the bride's father at the end of the table, the boyars on benches, and the retainers at the table opposite.

The bride's father provides wine to accompany the vegetables. The servants bring in cooked food. The guests eat. When they are done, the servants clear the table and the guests change their attire. (But the noblewomen keep the same dress: white jackets and knee-length fur coats.)[74] Then a full breakfast is brought in.[75]

When the time comes, the groom and the thousandman rise. The best man also stands, inviting the bride's father and mother and each of the noble guests in turn, calling each one by name and saying, "The groom respectfully requests that you join him today at his house, to feast at his table." When all the invitations have been issued, the groom's party returns to the entrance hall, where they again don their golden robes. They then return to the groom's estate using the same protocol that they used earlier. When they arrive, they rest for a little while. During this time the meal is prepared.

When the meal is ready, the bride is dressed in her most elaborate costume and the best man is sent to summon her father and mother. The noble guests, male and female, go and seat themselves at the table.

The bride's father arrives dressed in cloth-of-gold. The boyars who accompany him, riding two by two, also wear cloth-of-gold. Their servants run behind them, staying close to the horses. The bride's mother, and the noblewomen who accompany her, wear golden jackets and travel in sleighs.[76]

When the party arrives at the groom's estate, the men go to one

74. Again, the *Domostroi* adds "with *spuski.*" See note 72.
75. Unless the newlyweds got up very early, this would probably be a late-morning meal, closer to what we might call lunch. Nonetheless, the original author of the *Domostroi* would not have approved. See his strictures on breakfast, Chapter 13.
76. Jackets with *spuski.* See note 72.

staircase and the women to another. There, on the stairs or in the entrance halls (depending on how the property is laid out), the groom's party greets them, the men welcoming the men and the women, the women.

On the table in the dining room, vegetables have been set out. [The guests now go to the table.] The noblewomen go first. The bride's mother sits in the place of honor, with the bride next to her. Then come the matchmakers, the noblewomen, and the other guests. The noblewomen from the groom's side sit below these, and his parents take the lowest places.[77] The bride's father sits at the end of the table, with the groom's father at his side. The boyars sit on benches; those from the bride's side sit below those from the groom's. The groom takes his place next to his father, and the thousandman and the retainers sit at the table opposite.

When all are seated, the groom's father gets up, as do the boyars, who have just come with the bride's family. They go over to the groom's mother and the noblewomen who sit with her. The men bow to the women, ask them how they are, and kiss them. Then they go out to the entrance hall and change their clothes. They return to the table, bringing wine. The assembled company eats.

The servants then clear the table and bring food for the banquet. The groom rises to pay his respects to his father and parents-in-law. He toasts them with beakers of red wine and mead. As the food is set out, the bride's father rises, and the best man from the bride's side. The best man speaks to the groom's father, saying, "N. (the bride's father) respectfully requests that tomorrow you will allow him to entertain you at his house." The best man repeats this invitation to the groom, the boyars, the groom's mother, and the noblewomen—naming each in turn. The bride's father bows, and the groom and the boyars raise their cups to him.

At the proper time, the servants bring in the gifts—a large beaker, or one with a spout, and velvet or brocade. When the cups have been filled with mead, the groom's father speaks to the bride's, saying, "O Lord, grant that our dear children (here he gives the names of his son and daughter-in-law) will live healthily and happily for many years."

77. That is, the place farthest from the seat of honor (see note 42). In this instance, the distinctions are minimal, as the groom's father still sits next to the bride's, even if he has taken a slightly less prestigious seat to honor his guests. Note that among the boyars, the groom's side takes precedence.

"When they have agreed on the contract and the size of the dowry, . . . the priest sings 'In you, O woman full of grace, all creation exults.' Then each takes his own copy of the contract, as they drink a measure of mead to celebrate and congratulate one another" (Chapter 67). After the contract signing came the wedding: three days of joyous celebration and feasting. From Adam Olearius, *Vermehrte Moscowitische und Persianische Reisebeschreibung* (Schleszwig, 1656). Courtesy of the Princeton University Library, Department of Rare Books and Special Collections.

The senior best man then rises and speaks to the bride's father, calling him by name and saying, "Your son-in-law N. respectfully asks that you accept this large beaker made of gold, this brightly colored velvet, and a forty of sables." The best man also presents gifts to the bride's mother—a goblet or wine cup, brocade, and a forty of sables. Calling her by name, the best man says, "Your son-in-law respectfully requests that you accept these gifts."

The noblewomen then accompany the bride to her own rooms, where, after a little while, they put on their traveling costumes. The bride's parents and the guests who came with them then return to their own home, in the same way they came. The groom's family escorts them to their horses or, in the case of the noblewomen, their sleighs. They cheer them as far as the gates; joy reigns on both sides. The matchmakers and best men, however, wait behind a while, until the newlyweds are again settled in the granary. Then they disperse to their own homes.

On the third day, a bath is again prepared. The bride's best man comes a second time with "gifts of the bath," removing the clothes that he brought the day before and replacing them with others. When the groom emerges from the bathhouse, the thousandman and the retinue ride up. The groom goes to his chamber and dresses. Then, accompanied by his entire retinue, he goes to his parents' rooms to pay his respects to them. There vegetables have been laid out as on the previous day. The groom's mother, the bride, the matchmakers, and the noblewomen are seated at the table and the boyars on benches. They all sit according to their rank and eat.

At that time, the best man from the bride's side addresses the company, inviting the groom's parents, the bridal pair, and all the guests to feast at the bride's family's house. Having shown him honor, they let him go, then change their clothes and eat breakfast. Meanwhile, at the bride's father's house, the servants prepare the table, arranging the places according to rank and setting out vegetables.

When the meal is prepared, the bride's father sends his best man to invite the guests to his table. The groom's father rides at his son's right side and the thousandman on the left. The retainers go in front of them, all arrayed in their costumes, as described earlier, and the boyars ride behind, also attired in their finery. The groom's mother rides in a sleigh, with the bride opposite her. The matchmakers and noblewomen enter their sleighs one at a time. The matchmakers sit opposite the noblewomen in the first sleigh.[78]

When they arrive at the house, they enter the main rooms, where they are greeted according to their rank. The bride's father greets the groom and his father, and the bride's mother greets her daughter and the groom's mother. All go to the place where the vegetables have been laid out. There the newly arrived boyars kiss the noblewomen from the bride's family. The servants then bring out wine and cooked food, and the guests eat these and the vegetables. At the proper time,

---

78. That is, the first not counting the one holding the bride and the groom's mother.

the noblewomen retire to the women's quarters, and the men distribute the dowry and sign the wedding contracts. (But if these are disputed, the distribution and signing should be left to another day.)[79]

After the contracts are signed, the men sit down to feast by themselves, and the women feast in the women's quarters. When the meal is done, the bride's father blesses the groom, using an icon. He wishes his son-in-law well and gives him presents—beakers, velvet, brocade, sables, horses in festival attire, and armor. The two of them drink a toast with the groom's father and the thousandman. Then all go and put on their costumes for the journey. The two fathers, the groom, the thousandman, and the senior boyars go to the women's quarters to say farewell. There the bride's father blesses his daughter and gives her icons, a dress, dishes, rings, *votchina* lands, and slaves.[80] The bride's mother blesses her son-in-law and gives him icons, a robe, and dishes, then gives her daughter a dress and a robe embroidered with precious stones, hemmed with pearls. Then the groom's party returns to their own home, traveling in procession as formerly. The feasting and visiting may continue for more days if the families are so inclined.

A Less Elaborate Wedding Ritual

It often happens that people cannot afford a wedding appropriate to their rank, either because their financial resources are insufficient, or because they fear that the wedding will bankrupt them. [In either case, they should proceed as follows.] When discussion of the marriage begins, the groom and his party visit the prospective bride's father. They agree on the marriage settlements and the dowry. When the documents are written up, the bride's family inflates the dowry slightly, but the two families have a verbal agreement that the groom will not take the whole. They write down a sum larger than the bride's family can afford so that the bride's father will appear more honorable before his relatives.[81] When the documents have been written up, the

79. So as not to disrupt the festivities.
80. Unlike women in the medieval West, Russian wives retained control over their dowries. See, for example, Sandra Levy, "Women and the Control of Property in Sixteenth-Century Muscovy," *Russian History* 10 (1983): 154–169.
81. One would go far to find a better example of an "honor" society in operation. (In an honor society, one's status depends primarily on one's birth and reputation.)

two sides exchange pleasantries and then go about their business. During this time, the bride's father gives his new son-in-law an icon, one without a very intricate frame, as well as some satin, silk clothing, or a bow. Then they visit the bride's mother, who greets the groom, wrapping a ceremonial towel about his neck. The bride embraces her father-in-law in the same way. In some places the groom even greets the bride. At this time the servants present a ceremonial towel on the bride's behalf. Then the groom's party returns home.

On the day of the wedding, the groom and his retinue visit his parents to ask their permission to dine at the bride's home that day. They send their best man first to the bride's house, to announce that the groom is on his way, so that all will be ready for him. The best man also asks where the groom will lie, inspects the bed (which is in a locked room), and installs his own groom of the chamber.

While all this is going on, the bride is escorted to her seat at the table. She is accompanied by her matchmaker and her relatives, who seat themselves according to their rank. Near the bridal couple's place is a tablecloth, on which are set out dishes, rolls, sweet bread, round loaves, cheese, grain, the bride's kerchief and other accoutrements, and a veil. Near the bride's father's seat the candleholder and a man carrying two loaves on trays stand waiting.

When the groom arrives, the candleholder and the man holding the loaves precede him into the room. There the two official loaf-carriers, one for the groom and one for the bride, take the trays with the loaves and go to their places. The groom's party enters in this order. First come servants in festive clothes, then the candleholder and man holding the loaves. Behind these, the priest walks, carrying his cross. Then the best man walks in, followed by the retainers. Last comes the groom and the thousandman. As each group enters the room, they bow to the icons.

With the permission of the bride's parents, the groom seats himself in the place of honor and his retainers take seats appropriate to their rank. The priest betroths them in the manner prescribed by the church. After this ceremony is complete, the groom kisses the bride. The matchmaker then stands, bows to the couple, and asks their permission to comb their hair. At the same time, the best man cuts the loaves

---

On Muscovy as an honor society, see Kollmann, *Kinship and Politics*; Crummey, *Aristocrats and Servitors*; and Kollmann, "Women's Honor."

and the cheese and places a ceremonial towel on each platter. He takes the platters around to the groom, the thousandman, and the retainers, saying, "The bride wishes to pay her respects to you with these gifts." Then the bride's father distributes drinks to the thousandman, and the retainers, to honor them.

When the bride is veiled, and the matchmaker has sprinkled her with grain, the families take some time to celebrate. When they are ready, they rise and set off for the church ceremony. When they return from the church, the bride's parents meet them at the outside stairway and again sprinkle them with grain. The rest of the bride's family likewise meets them on the stairs or in the entrance hall, where they embrace the groom, the thousandman, and the retainers. Then they all seat themselves at the table. The bride's father pours wine, the servants bring food, and all feast at their leisure. In this, less elaborate, wedding ritual, each platter of food is shared by three people and guests sit on both sides of the table because no one will depart for the groom's estate. The groom and the thousandman do not issue their invitation because everything is conducted at the bride's house.

When the groom retires for the bedding ceremony, the bride's father stands and escorts his daughter to the doors of the bedchamber. He speaks kindly to his new son-in-law, saying, "By God's will my daughter has married you, N. You have been granted the right to love her and live with her in lawful matrimony, as did our fathers and our fathers' fathers." The groom hugs the bride's father; then the couple enters the bedroom. And the bride's mother sprinkles grain on them again because the groom's mother is not present. After the newlyweds have sat for a little while on the bed, the bride's father goes in and unveils his daughter, then leaves. The servants bring chicken and kasha and the priest sings vespers. They remove the groom's robe and leave. After a while, the groom sends his best man to let the company know that all has gone well. The bride's mother then comes to feed the newlyweds, carrying the food in her own hands.

The next morning, the groom goes, at his leisure, to the bathhouse. The bride's father sends the "bathing gifts" there—a shirt and trousers. The groom returns to the bedchamber, where he is met by the thousandman and retainers. When the vegetables have been prepared and the noblewomen are seated at the table, the groom and his retinue arrive. The bride's parents ask how he does, and the women embrace him, wrapping ceremonial towels around his neck as before. The servants bring wine and cooked dishes, which the guests eat. The men then change their clothes, and the women retire to their quarters. At this time, the servants prepare the table for the second wedding feast.

When all is prepared, the guests seat themselves at the table according to their rank. Some people include the bride and the noblewomen at this feast, and others have them banquet separately. When they are done, the groom goes into his chamber with his retainers, to celebrate, but the bride stays with her mother. After a time, the thousandman and the retinue leave. Then the groom sends for the bride, and they rest.

On the third day, the groom again goes to the bathhouse and the bride's father again sends clothes for him to wear. When he is washed, he returns to his chamber, where he is joined by the thousandman and retainers. The groom's party goes to the bride's father's quarters, where they inspect the clothes that are part of the dowry, noting the number and the kind. Then they sign the marriage contracts, and each takes his copy. When this is done, the men join the women in their quarters. The bride is there, arrayed in her robes. Vegetables are set out, and the bride's mother pours wine for her son-in-law and his retinue. When they have eaten the food, they go out, change their clothes, and seat themselves at the table, where all has been prepared for the third wedding banquet.

After the meal, the servants pass around cups for the toasts. The bride's father toasts his son-in-law and gives him his blessing and whatever gifts he wishes to bestow. Then the guests go back to their homes. The bride's parents bless their daughter on the occasion of her departure from their home. They present her with whatever gifts they wish. Then the groom rides to his parents' home.

The groom's parents have invited to their house all the boyars (male and female) associated with their family. (The groom sends word in advance of his arrival.) When everyone has assembled, the groom and his retinue go to pay their respects to his father, and the bride to the groom's mother. In the women's quarters, the bride removes her traveling dress and the women dress her in a way appropriate to her rank. When she is dressed again, the groom's father arrives to greet his new daughter-in-law. She gives him a ceremonial towel and presents caps to the groom's mother and noblewomen. Then the groom comes in with his retainers, to pay his respects to his mother. She greets him. Then all go to the table.

The noblewomen seat themselves first, then the boyars. While this is going on, the servants bring in gifts from the bride to the groom's father, a platter holding a shirt and trousers. The best man displays the gifts, and the bride bows. Next the groom's mother receives brocade or taffeta, a shift, or a kerchief. The male friends and relatives also receive shirts and trousers, and the women shifts, kerchiefs, and caps. The best man displays each gift, and the bride bows. Afterward they sit at table as long as they wish, either men and women together or separated by sex. But if the newlyweds arrive at the house late in the afternoon, this feast can be delayed until the next day, or even the day after that.

When the meal is done, the groom's parents toast their son's health and give the couple icons and whatever else they like. The noble guests also toast the couple's health and give them icons; the noblewomen further gift the bride with crosses and rings. Joy reigns.

Additional Remarks on Weddings

The *candles*[82] should not be equal in size, whether they are large or average. The groom's candle is usually of average size, weighing about four and a half pounds and about twenty-one inches long.[83] The bride's candle weighs about three and a half pounds and measures about twelve inches.[84] Among those of rank, the bride's candle is usually smaller, thinner, and shorter, although people design them according to their own taste.

Two *loaves* are normally provided, one for the groom and one for the bride. The trays holding the loaves are sent in when the bride arrives and stay near the bride, but the cover on them is from the groom and has a cross sewn on it. The tray holding the loaf intended for the groom should be of average size—neither large nor small.

---

82. Emphasis, here and elsewhere in this section, is mine. The "additional remarks" seem to be just jotted-down comments based on the author's own experience, so the emphasis is to help identify the topic under discussion.

83. These measurements have been converted from the medieval Russian ones (five *funty* and about three-quarters of an *arshin* long), based on the values given in Blum, *Lord and Peasant*, pp. 621–622.

84. Seven *vershki*. One *vershok* is the width of a finger; there are sixteen to the *arshin* (twenty-eight inches).

As the party heads for the *church ceremony*, the bride sings and makes obeisances.

People usually send sweets and *gifts* to the groom's parents. Sometimes they send the sweets but not the gifts.

During the *betrothal rite*, before the church ceremony, the groom and the bride exchange rings. They clasp hands and exchange small, well-made bands, stamped with gold or silver. Elaborate rings and rings with stones are not used in the wedding ceremony.

When the bridal pair go to the church, there should not be a *carpet* spread between the horses (or sleighs) and the church. They step directly on the ground as they traverse the road from the place where they dismount. But when they get to the church, the couple should walk on a carpet from the church porch to the doors, and from the doors to the center of the church, and should stand on a carpet during the ceremony as well. And the floor covering will be whatever the bride's parents choose to donate—usually taffeta or cotton.

When the bridal couple leaves the church to return to their horse and sleigh, no carpet is spread before them. But when they reach the bride's parents' house, when the retainers go into the house and the couple is escorted to the bedchamber, then a carpet is spread before them—from the bride's sleigh up the stairs, through the entrance hall, into the bedchamber, and up to the bed. If the bedding ceremony takes place in the groom's parents' house, then a carpet is spread there, also. This floor covering is usually made of brocade, taffeta, or cotton, but sometimes of broadcloth.

As the bride and groom move along, the servants should roll up the carpet behind them, then run ahead to roll it forth again.

When the bride and groom arrive for the *bedding ceremony*, their mother sprinkles them with grain as they approach the doors.[85] She should wear her coat turned inside out while she does this. When she is finished, the mother goes into the main house, and the newlyweds enter the chamber and sit on the bed. With them go the matchmaker, the best man, and several noblewomen from each family. Stewed chicken and kasha are brought for the groom. He tears the chicken to pieces and distributes it, then eats a little kasha and gives some to the

85. This could be the groom's mother or the bride's, depending on whether the full or "less elaborate" ritual is used.

bride. They bring kasha again in the morning and send some to the bride's parents.

The best man makes the groom comfortable, then leaves the bed-chamber and enters the main house. The matchmaker and the noble-women undress the bride and put her to bed with the groom, then they too leave.

The grooms of the chamber wait near the storeroom, to safeguard the newlyweds.

Then the groom remembers his duty, by means of which children are born. After half an hour, the best man comes and asks the groom how things are going. He then goes to report to the groom's parents, offering his respects and asking about their health. Then the parents send the best man back to the groom, commanding the groom to come himself and report on his progress. So the best man leaves, with the matchmakers and the noblewomen who undressed the bride, to ask the groom to report to his parents. The groom gets up and puts on his shoes and a skin tunic or whatever he wishes to wear. Then the noblewomen help the bride to get up and dress. They do not put shoes on her; she wears a fur coat and a hat of black fox. When dressed, she sits on the bed and does not get up even when the groom's parents appear.

When they arrive, the parents embrace the newlyweds and give them food. Then the best man goes to the bride's parents' house, to pay the groom's respects and to let them know that all has gone well.

When, early the next morning, the best man goes to the bride's parents' house, to bring them the kasha that was first taken to the bride and groom in their chamber, he also brings the couple's night-shirts. The bride's mother should keep these in a sealed container.[86]

86. The nightshirts, stained with blood, served as proof of the bride's virginity if this were later questioned.

Appendix

Contents in the Short Version

The book called *Domestic Order* has in it much that Christian men and women, children, manservants, and maidservants will find useful. Here is a list of its contents.

Xerox

65–68
71 – 74
80 – 85
8 9 –91
95 –98
118 – 120
124– 127
141 –145
155 – 157
204 – 239

Contents in the Mediate and Long Versions

---

1. The text actually says, "how to go on" (*kak priluchitsia*), but this is probably a copyist's error for *kak pir luchitsia* (when there is a feast).

Glossary

Boyar	Literally, those men, usually heads of the oldest Muscovite princely and nontitled service families, who were granted the title *boiarin* (pl. *boiare*) and who served as the tsar's chief counselors; in the sixteenth century, approximately forty men. More generally, "boyar" meant "magnate," i.e., a male member of the dominant nonprincely families. The wife of a boyar was a *boiaryna* (pl. *boiaryni*).
Chetvert'	One-quarter of a *desiatina*, about half an acre. Also a measure of grain, the equivalent of about three bushels; the amount varied from place to place, like the medieval bushel.
D'iak	State secretary, one of the highest-ranking officials in the Muscovite chancery system. Each chancery was headed by a *kaznachei*, under whom served the *d'iaki*. The state secretaries' subordinates were the undersecretaries (*pod'iachie*).
Druzhka	One of two men (one from the groom's family, one from the bride's) who assisted at a wedding ceremony. Roughly translated as "best man" but actually a far more substantial role.
Dvorianstvo	Gentry, more properly, the middle ranks of the military service classes: middle-level army officers whose families entered service with the Muscovite tsar during the sixteenth and seventeenth centuries and who were therefore excluded from the highest court ranks and from the system of precedence (see *mestnichestvo*) that conferred them.
Gost'	One of a small number of merchants appointed by the state and licensed to trade internationally on behalf of the crown (pl. *gosti*). The elite of Russian merchants.

Kabala	A written contract. By the later sixteenth century, usually associated with *kabal'noe kholopstvo* ("limited service contract slavery," to borrow Richard Hellie's term): a contract that bound the borrower to serve the lender until his debt was paid or until the death of one of the parties. In the *Domostroi*, a written contract guaranteeing the terms of a loan in which property provided collateral.
Kanun, kanon	A drink used to commemorate the dead in Orthodox church services. Usually, beer mixed with mead or honey.
Kasha	Any grain cooked slowly in liquid, but most often buckwheat groats mixed with a little onion, then simmered in broth.
Kika, kyka	A married woman's headdress.
Kut'ia	Food used to commemorate the dead during Orthodox church services. Frumenty (porridge mixed with fruit and spices).
Kvass	A slightly alcoholic drink, similar to beer, made by fermenting rye bread in water. This is the generally accepted anglicized spelling (Russian *kvas*).
Mestnichestvo	The Muscovite system of precedence, begun in the fourteenth century as a way of reconciling rival princes and boyars to service with the house of Moscow. Male members from a select number of clans were ranked in relationship to one another, and positions and honors (even seating arrangements) were assigned on the basis of rank. As the number of descendants of the original families increased, *mestnichestvo* became increasingly difficult to determine; Peter the Great's elder brother, Tsar Fedor Alekseevich, abolished it in 1682.
Oprichnina	Originally, the portion of an estate granted to a widow on her husband's death. In 1564, Ivan the Terrible divided his realm into an *oprichnina*, in which he instituted a reign of terror with the help of his *oprichniki*, and a *zemshchina* ruled by a puppet tsar. The division lasted until 1572, after which use of the word was banned.
Osmina	Half a *chetvert'*.
Panagia	Oval medallion of the Virgin Mary, worn around the neck.
Pomest'e	Service estate (pl. *pomest'ia*). Originally, land granted to military servitors to support them during their service and to be returned to the crown on the holder's death. By the end of the seventeenth century, any landed estate. The holder of a *pomest'e* was a *pomeshchik*, which eventually (late eighteenth century) meant any member of the gentry class.
Poruka	Surety. A payment required of servitors suspected of disloyalty to the crown, which would be forfeit if they dis-

	pleased the tsar or tried to escape punishment. More generally, a guarantee of good behavior.
Pud	A unit of weight, the equivalent of approximately thirty-six pounds.
Svakha	Matchmaker. During the wedding ceremony, one of two women (one from the groom's family, one from the bride's) who served as the bride's attendants.
Tiaglo	Literally, "burden." In the sixteenth century, a collective term for taxes and obligations paid directly to the prince (pl. *tiagla*), as well as the capacity to meet such obligations. Clerics and state servitors were exempt from *tiagla*. In the eighteenth century and later, the peasant labor unit (usually a husband and wife). In the *Domostroi*, *tiaglo* usually means specifically those obligations imposed on owners of urban households; other specific terms (*pozem*, *dan'*, *obrok*, etc.) describe taxes and obligations on shops or rural landholdings.
Tysiatskii	Thousandman. Usually commander of the militia (a high government official). In weddings, the master of ceremonies.
Votchina	Patrimony, i.e., property owned outright and in perpetuity by a particular clan. *Votchina* lands could be sold only with the consent of the kin group; sales could be undone if another member of the clan repurchased the land. The Muscovite tsars disliked the independence ownership of *votchina* lands conferred on their servitors; over the course of the sixteenth and seventeenth centuries, the privileges of *votchina* ownership were eroded. The owner of a *votchina* (pl. *votchiny*) was a *votchinnik*; the same person might hold both service estates and patrimonial lands.

Suggestions for Further Reading

Alef, Gustave. *Rulers and Nobles in Fifteenth-Century Muscovy*. London: Variorum Reprints, 1983.

Anderson, Bonnie S., and Judith P. Zinsser. *A History of Their Own: Women in Europe from Prehistory to the Present*. 2 vols. New York: Harper & Row, 1988.

Andreyev, Nicholas A. *Studies in Muscovy: Western Influence and Byzantine Inheritance*. London: Variorum Reprints, 1970.

Ariès, Philippe. *Centuries of Childhood: A Social History of Family Life*. Translated by Robert Baldick. New York: Vintage Books, 1962.

Atkinson, Dorothy, Alexander Dallin, and Gail Warshofsky Lapidus, eds. *Women in Russia*. Stanford: Stanford University Press, 1977.

Baron, Samuel H. *Muscovite Russia*. London: Variorum Reprints, 1980.

Berry, Lloyd, and Robert O. Crummey, eds. *Rude and Barbarous Kingdom: Russia in the Accounts of Sixteenth-Century English Voyagers*. Madison: University of Wisconsin Press, 1968.

Billington, James H. *The Icon and the Axe: An Interpretive History of Russian Culture*. New York: Vintage Books, 1970.

Birnbaum, Henrik, and Michael S. Flier, eds. *Medieval Russian Culture*. California Slavic Studies, vol. 12. Berkeley: University of California Press, 1984.

Blane, Andrew, ed. *Russia and Orthodoxy: Essays in Honor of Georges Florovsky*. The Hague, 1975.

Blum, Jerome. *Lord and Peasant in Russia from the Ninth to the Nineteenth Century*. Princeton: Princeton University Press, 1961.

Bornstein, Diane. *The Lady in the Tower: Medieval Courtesy Literature for Women*. Hamden, Conn.: Archon Books, 1983.

Boxer, Marilyn J., and Jean Quataert, eds. *Connecting Spheres: Women in the Western World, 1500 to the Present*. Oxford: Oxford University Press, 1987.

Brown, Peter Bowman. "Early Modern Russian Bureaucracy: The Evolution of the Chancery System from Ivan III to Peter the Great, 1478–1717." Ph.D. dissertation, University of Chicago, 1978.

Brown, William Edward. *A History of Seventeenth-Century Russian Literature.* Ann Arbor: Ardis Books, 1980.

Bushkovitch, Paul A. *The Merchants of Moscow, 1580–1670.* New York: Cambridge University Press, 1980.

Clements, Barbara Evans, Barbara Alpern Engel, and Christine D. Worobec, eds. *Russia's Women: Accommodation, Resistance, Transformation.* Berkeley: University of California Press, 1991.

Cross, Samuel Hazzard, and Olgerd P. Sherbowitz-Wetzor, trans. and eds. *The Russian Primary Chronicle, Laurentian Edition.* Cambridge, Mass.: Medieval Academy of America, 1953.

Crummey, Robert O. *Aristocrats and Servitors: The Boyar Elite of Russia, 1613–1689.* Princeton: Princeton University Press, 1983.

——. *The Formation of Muscovy, 1304–1613.* New York: Longman, 1987.

——. *The Old Believers and the World of Antichrist: The Vyg Community and the Russian State, 1694–1855.* Madison: University of Wisconsin Press, 1970.

Dewey, Horace W. *Muscovite Judicial Texts, 1488–1556.* Ann Arbor: University of Michigan Press, 1966.

——. "Political *Poruka* in Muscovite Rus'." *Russian Review* 46 (1987): 117–133.

Dewey, Horace W., and Ann M. Kleimola. "Muted Eulogy: Women Who Inspired Men in Medieval Rus'." *Russian History* 10 (1983): 188–200.

Dmytryshyn, Basil, ed. *Medieval Russia: A Sourcebook, 900–1700.* 2d ed. New York: Holt, Rinehart and Winston, 1973.

Fedotov, George P. *The Russian Religious Mind.* 2 vols. Belmont, Mass.: Nordland, 1975.

Fennell, John L., trans. and ed. *The Correspondence between Prince A. M. Kurbskii and Tsar Ivan IV of Russia, 1564–1579.* Cambridge: Cambridge University Press, 1955.

——. ed. *Kurbsky's History of Ivan IV.* Cambridge: Cambridge University Press, 1965.

Fennell, John. L. I., and Anthony Stokes. *Early Russian Literature.* Berkeley: University of California Press, 1974.

Florovsky, Georges. "The Problem of Old Russian Culture." *Slavic Review* 21 (1962): 1–15.

Forster, Robert. "The Provincial Noble: A Reappraisal." *American Historical Review* 68 (1962–1963): 681–691.

Gerschenkron, Alexander. *Continuity in History and Other Essays.* Cambridge, Mass.: Belknap Press, 1968.

——. *Economic Backwardness in Historical Perspective.* Cambridge, Mass.: Belknap Press, 1962.

Gies, Frances, and Joseph Gies. *Marriage and Family in the Middle Ages.* New York: Harper & Row, 1987.

——. *Women in the Middle Ages.* New York: Crowell, 1978.

Goldstein, Darra. *A la Russe: A Cookbook of Russian Hospitality*. New York: Random House, 1983.

Grobovsky, Antony N. *The "Chosen Council" of Ivan IV: A Reinterpretation*. Brooklyn: Theo Gaus's Sons, 1969.

Grossman, Joan Delaney. "Feminine Images in Old Russian Literature and Art." *California Slavic Studies* 11 (1980): 33–70.

Gudzii, N. K. *History of Early Russian Literature*. New York, 1949.

Halperin, Charles J. "Master and Man in Muscovy." In A. E. Presniakov, *The Tsardom of Muscovy*. Gulf Breeze, Fla.: Academic International Press, 1978.

——. *Russia and the Golden Horde: The Mongol Impact on Medieval Russian History*. Bloomington: Indiana University Press, 1985.

Hamm, Michael, ed. *The City in Russian History*. Lexington: University Press of Kentucky, 1976.

Hellie, Richard. *Enserfment and Military Change in Muscovy*. Chicago: University of Chicago Press, 1971.

——. *Slavery in Russia, 1475–1725*. Chicago: University of Chicago Press, 1982.

——. "Women and Slavery in Moscow." *Russian History* 10 (1983): 213–229.

Henisch, Barbara. *Fast and Feast: Food in Medieval Society*. University Park: Pennsylvania State University Press, 1976.

Herberstein, Sigismund Freiherr von. *Notes Upon Russia*. Translated by R. H. Major. 2 vols. London: Hakluyt Society, 1851–1852.

Herlihy, David. *Medieval Households*. Cambridge, Mass.: Harvard University Press, 1985.

Hittle, J. Michael. *The Service City: State and Townsmen in Russia, 1600–1800*. Cambridge, Mass.: Harvard University Press, 1979.

Hubbs, Joanna. *Mother Russia: The Feminine Myth in Russian Culture*. Bloomington: Indiana University Press, 1988.

Huizinga, Jan. *The Waning of the Middle Ages*. New York: Doubleday, 1954.

Hull, Suzanne. *Chaste, Silent and Obedient: English Books for Women, 1475–1640*. San Marino, Calif.: Huntington Library, 1982.

Hunt, David. *Parents and Children in History*. New York: Basic Books, 1970.

Kaiser, Daniel. "Symbol and Ritual in the Marriages of Ivan IV." *Russian History* 14 (1987): 247–262.

Kaplan, Marion A., ed. *The Marriage Bargain: Women and Dowries in European History*. New York: Haworth, 1985.

Karlinsky, Simon. "The *Domostroi* as Literature." *Slavic Review* 24 (1965): 497–502.

Keenan, Edward L. *The Kurbskii-Groznyi Apocrypha: The Seventeenth-Century Genesis of the "Correspondence" Attributed to Prince A. M. Kurbskii and Tsar Ivan IV*. Cambridge, Mass.: Harvard University Press, 1971.

——. "Muscovite Political Folkways." *Russian Review* 45 (1986): 115–181.

——. "Putting Kurbskii in His Place, or: Observations and Suggestions Concerning the Place of the 'History of the Grand Prince of Moscow' in the History of Muscovite Literary Culture." *Forschungen zur osteuropäischen Geschichte* 24 (1978): 131–161.

———. "Vita. Ivan Vasilevich, Terrible Tsar: 1530–1584." *Harvard Magazine* 80, no. 3 (1978): 48–49.

Klapisch-Zuber, Christiane. *Women, Family and Ritual in Renaissance Italy.* Translated by Lydia Cochrane. Chicago: University of Chicago Press, 1985.

Kleimola, Ann M. "The Changing Face of the Muscovite Aristocracy. The Sixteenth Century: Sources of Weakness." *Jahrbucher für Geschichte Osteuropas* 25 (1977): 481–493.

———. "Military Service and Elite Status in Muscovy in the Second Quarter of the Sixteenth Century." *Russian History* 7 (1980): 47–64.

———. "Patterns of Duma Recruitment, 1515–1550." In *Essays in Honor of A. A. Zimin.* Columbus: Ohio State University Press, 1985.

———. "Status, Place, and Politics: The Rise of Mestnichestvo during the *Boiarskoe Pravlenie.*" *Forschungen zur osteuropäischen Geschichte* 27 (1980): 195–214.

Kliuchevskii, V. O. *A Course in Russian History: The Seventeenth Century.* Translated by Natalie Dunnington, introduction by Alfred J. Rieber. New York: Quadrangle, 1968.

Kollmann, Jack Edward. "The Moscow *Stoglav* ('Hundred Chapters') Church Council of 1551." Ph.D. dissertation, University of Michigan, 1978.

———. "The *Stoglav* Council and Parish Priests." *Russian History* 7 (1980): 65–91.

Kollmann, Nancy Shields. *Kinship and Politics: The Making of the Muscovite Political System, 1345–1547.* Stanford: Stanford University Press, 1987.

———. "The Seclusion of Elite Muscovite Women." *Russian History* 10 (1983): 170–187.

Levin, Eve. "Infanticide in Pre-Petrine Russia." *Jahrbucher für Geschichte Osteuropas* 34 (1986): 215–222.

———. *Sex and Society among the Orthodox Slavs.* Ithaca: Cornell University Press, 1989.

Levy, Sandra. "Women and the Control of Property in Sixteenth-Century Muscovy." *Russian History* 10 (1983): 154–169.

Lewitter, L. R. "Women, Sainthood and Marriage in Muscovy." *Journal of Russian Studies* 37 (1979): 3–13.

McNally, Susanne Janosik. "From Public Person to Private Prisoner: The Changing Place of Women in Medieval Russia." Ph.D. dissertation, State University of New York at Binghamton, 1976.

A Manual of Eastern Orthodox Prayers. Crestwood, N.Y.: St. Vladimir's Seminary Press, 1991.

Meyendorff, John. *Byzantium and the Rise of Russia.* Cambridge: Cambridge University Press, 1981.

Miller, Alice. *For Your Own Good: Hidden Cruelty in Child-Rearing and the Roots of Violence.* Translated by Hildegarde Hannum and Hunter Hannum. New York: Farrar, Straus and Giroux, 1983.

Miller, David B. "The Viskovatyi Affair of 1553–1554: Official Art, the Emergence of Autocracy, and the Disintegration of Medieval Russian Culture." *Russian History* 8 (1981): 293–332.

The New English Bible with the Apocrypha. New York: Oxford University Press, 1976.

Nicholas, David. *The Domestic Life of a Medieval City: Women, Children and the Family in Fourteenth-Century Ghent*. Lincoln: University of Nebraska Press, 1985.

Okenfuss, Max. *The Discovery of Childhood in Russia: The Evidence of the Slavic Primer*. Newtonville, Mass.: Oriental Research Partners, 1980.

Olearius, Adam. *The Travels of Olearius in Seventeenth-Century Russia*. Translated and edited by Samuel H. Baron. Stanford: Stanford University Press, 1967.

Ozment, Steven. *When Fathers Ruled: Family Life in Reformation Europe*. Cambridge, Mass.: Harvard University Press, 1983.

Patterson, Orlando. *Slavery and Social Death*. Cambridge, Mass.: Harvard University Press, 1982.

Paul of Aleppo. *Travels of Macarius, 1652–1660*. Selected by Lady Laura Ridding. New York: Arno Press, 1971.

Pintner, Walter M., and Don Karl Rowney, eds. *Russian Officialdom: The Bureaucratization of Russian Society from the Seventeenth to the Twentieth Century*. Chapel Hill: University of North Carolina Press, 1980.

Pouncy, Carolyn Johnston. "The *Domostroi* as a Source for Muscovite History." Ph.D. dissertation, Stanford University, 1985.

——. "The Origins of the *Domostroi*: An Essay in Manuscript History." *Russian Review* 46 (1987): 357–373.

Presniakov, A. E. *The Tsardom of Muscovy*. Gulf Breeze, Fla.: Academic International Press, 1978.

Raya, Archbishop Joseph, and Baron José de Vinck, eds., comps,. and trans. *Byzantine Daily Worship*. Allendale, N.J.: Alleluia Press, 1969.

Russell, Jeffrey Burton. *Witchcraft in the Middle Ages*. Ithaca: Cornell University Press, 1972.

Shahar, Shulamith. *Childhood in the Middle Ages*. London: Routledge, 1990.

——. *The Fourth Estate: A History of Women in the Middle Ages*. London: Methuen, 1983.

Skrynnikov, R. G. *Ivan the Terrible*. Edited and translated by Hugh Graham. Gulf Breeze, Fla.: Academic International Press, 1981.

Smith, R. E. F. *The Enserfment of the Russian Peasantry*. Cambridge: Cambridge University Press, 1968.

Smith, R. E. F., and David Christian. *Bread and Salt: A Social and Economic History of Food and Drink in Russia*. Cambridge: Cambridge University Press, 1984.

Stevens, Carol B. "Belgorod: Notes on Literacy and Language in the Seventeenth-Century Russian Army." *Russian History* 7 (1980): 113–124.

Stone, Lawrence. *The Family, Sex and Marriage in England, 1500–1800*. New York: Harper & Row, 1977.

Tannahill, Reay. *Food in History*. New York: Stein and Day, 1973.

Thompson, Ewa M. *Understanding Russia: The Holy Fool in Russian Culture*. Lanham, Md.: University Press of America, 1987.

Von Staden, Heinrich. *The Land and Government of Muscovy: A Sixteenth-*

Century Account. Translated and edited by Thomas Esper. Stanford: Stanford University Press, 1967.

Voyce, Arthur. *The Art and Architecture of Medieval Russia.* Norman: University of Oklahoma Press, 1967.

Vucinich, Wayne S., ed. *The Peasant in Nineteenth-Century Russia.* Stanford: Stanford University Press, 1968.

Ware, Timothy. *The Orthodox Church.* London: Penguin, 1963.

Zenkovsky, Serge A., trans. and ed. *Medieval Russia's Epics, Chronicles and Tales.* Revised and enlarged ed. New York: Dutton, 1974.

Zguta, Russell. *Russian Minstrels.* Philadelphia: University of Pennsylvania Press, 1978.

———. "Witchcraft and Medicine in Pre-Petrine Russia." *Russian Review* 37 (1978): 438–448.

Printed Editions of the *Domostroi*

Domostroi. Translated and edited by V. V. Kolesova. Moscow: 1990. The Long Version, in sixteenth-century and modern Russian, accompanied by Sil'vestr's epistle. Also includes related works (agricultural manuals and herbals)—most notably, *Rafli,* mentioned in *Domostroi,* Chapter 23.

Domostroi po spisku Imperatorskogo Obshchestva Istorii i Drevnostei Rossiiskikh. Edited by I. E. Zabelin. *Chteniia Imperatorskogo Obshchestva Istorii i Drevnostei Rossiiskikh* [Chteniia OIDR] (1882), bk. 1. Reprinted with an introduction by W. F. Ryan. Letchworth, Herts.: Bradda Books, 1971. The oldest Long Version manuscript.

Le Domostroi (Ménagier russe du XVIe siècle): Traduction et commentaire. Translated and edited by M. E. Duchesne. Paris: Picard et fils, 1910. Translation of the Short Version, as presented by Orlov.

Golokhvastov, D. P. "Domostroi blagoveshchenskogo popa Sil'vestra." *Vremennik Imperatorskogo Obshchestva Istorii i Drevnostei Rossiiskikh* (1849), bk. 1. The oldest Short Version manuscript, known as the "Konshin" copy.

Iakovlev, V. A. *Domostroi. Po rukopisiam Imperatorskoi publichnoi biblioteki.* St. Petersburg, 1867; 2d ed., Odessa, 1887. A mixture of versions based on the various manuscripts belonging to what is now the Russian National Library in St. Petersburg.

Orlov, A. S. *Domostroi. Issledovanie.* Part 1 (part 2 never printed). Moscow, 1917. Reprinted, The Hague: Europe Printing, 1967. Survey of Long Version manuscripts; includes the only copy of Mediate Version and limited discussion of the Intermediate Version.

——. *Domostroi po Konshinskomu spisku i podobnym.* 2 vols. Moscow, 1908–

1910. Reprinted, The Hague: Europe Printing, 1966. Survey of Short Version manuscripts; printed text of the Konshin copy and variations from other MSS.

Weiner, Leo, comp. *Anthology of Russian Literature from the Earliest Period to the Present Time*, vol. 1 (Tenth to Eighteenth Centuries), pp. 126–130. Translated excerpts from the *Domostroi*.

Index

Birds, 100, 120, 149–150, 153; for hunting, 118
Bomelius, Eleazar, 50
Books, 47, 184, 187; domestic, 43; magical/medical, 50, 112–113
Boyars, 6–11, 13, 22–23, 42, 45–46, 49, 62, 71–72, 75, 78, 86, 115, 172, 174, 177; and precedence (*mestnichestvo*), 9, 35; at weddings, 205, 208–239; wives and daughters of, 7–8, 41, 133
Boyars' sons. *See* Gentry
Bread, 34, 64, 125–126, 131, 146, 150–151, 161, 163–165, 187, 197–198; communion, 66–67, 80; menus including, 194–196, 201–203; unleavened, 119, 192, 196, 202
Breweries, 23, 156–157
Brewing, 32, 125–126, 155; directions for, 156, 196–198; supplies for, 145, 151–152, 156, 164, 166, 196–198
Broth, 125, 148–149, 151, 162–163, 195

Candles, 22, 73–74, 205–206, 213, 215–217, 219, 223, 225, 237
Candy and sweets, 125, 131, 150–152, 154, 158, 161; menus including, 196, 201–203; recipes for, 200; storing, 165, 176
Cattle, purchasing slaughtered, 148–149
Caviar, 151, 198; menus including, 192, 195–196, 202–203; purchasing, 25, 148
Chanceries, 10–12, 48; language used in, 40, 169; personnel, 10–12, 22–23, 42–46, 49, 111, 120–121, 123, 145, 148, 170, 174, 185, 189–190; private, 10, 120–121, 145, 170
Charity. *See* Alms
Chastity, 17, 27, 32, 68, 88, 96–98, 106–107, 111–112, 124, 181, 185–186
Cheese. *See* Dairy products; Weddings: bread and cheese at
Chess. *See* Games
Chicken. *See* Birds; Poultry
Childbirth, 29–31, 86, 100, 155
Children, 20, 27–33, 41, 48, 63–65, 72, 85–86, 88, 93–100, 102, 119, 140, 143–144, 163, 167, 172, 175, 181–182, 188, 239. *See also* Daughters; Sons
Christians: duties of, 20, 48, 62–63, 65–75, 77–81, 83, 85–92, 98–101, 103–104, 110–112, 116, 121–122, 178–183; self-destruction of, 77, 80, 101, 109, 114
Christmas, menus for, 195

Chrysostom, St. John, 118
Churches: attending, 7, 20, 74, 83, 86–87, 106, 111, 140, 178, 182, 184, 225; proper behavior in, 87
Churching, after childbirth, 31, 86
Cleanliness, 34–35, 73, 101, 105–106, 124, 131–132, 140–143, 157, 159–160, 163–168, 170, 174–176
Clothing, 72, 129; care of, 105–106, 125, 132, 140, 166, 173, 176; for children, 33, 128; making of, 34, 107, 126–128; for servants, 35, 105–106, 128, 163. *See also* Weddings: clothing for
Coel, king of Britain, 210
Confession, of sins, 20, 63, 68–70, 74, 92, 106, 111–112, 180, 183. *See also* Sins: remission of
Conspicuous consumption, 16, 50
Constantine I the Great, emperor of Rome, 210
Constantinople, 130, 198, 210
Constantius, emperor of Rome, 210
Contracts: debt-slavery, 16, 120, 175; loan, 37, 175; marriage, 95, 209–210, 231, 233
Conversations, good and bad, 77, 80, 88, 101, 133
Cooking, 101, 125–126, 131, 162–163
Cooks, 158–159
Corporal punishment, 16, 30–31, 93, 96, 106, 109, 143–144, 171–172, 174, 182; restrictions on, 143–144
Crab, 191, 194, 204
Crafts, 34, 47, 101, 129, 184. *See also* Artisans
Credit, commercial, 12, 122
Cross: as liturgical object, 62, 66–67, 75, 78–79, 112, 115, 177, 179, 210–211, 213, 217–219, 227, 234, 237; sign of, 75, 79, 87, 89–91, 101, 118
Cyril, bishop of Turov, 183
Cyril, metropolitan of Moscow, 189

Dairy products, 35, 145, 150, 152, 164–165, 196; menus including, 161–162, 192, 194–195, 201–203
Daughters, 17, 27, 29–32, 41–42, 93–96, 143. *See also* Children
David, king of Israel, 88
Death, 68, 113, 116, 120; of children, 23, 30–31, 94–95; life after, 67, 80, 94, 100, 102, 104, 122, 138, 163, 188; of parents, 70, 97, 179; rituals following, 75, 78–79, 95, 97, 179
Debt, 122, 174–175

Dement'ev family, 45
Demetrius, St., of Salonika, 194, 202
Desserts. *See* Candy and sweets
Devil, devils, 77, 80, 83–84, 91, 101–102, 109–110, 112–114, 135, 181, 186
Dice. *See* Games
Dishes. *See* Utensils: eating
Dishonor, 50, 76, 83–85, 99, 112, 123–124, 186, 219; among women, 108, 139
Distilling, 125–126, 156–157
Divination, 113, 117–120. *See also* Magic
Dmitrii, son of Ivan IV, 32
Domostroi: author of, 37–38, 41–44; editors of, 38, 44–45; owners of, 45–49; textual history of, 37–40
Dowries, 30, 42, 95, 185, 210–211, 233, 236
Drunkenness, 34, 36, 40, 48, 68–69, 81–83, 88, 92, 104, 106, 111–113, 132, 138, 160, 180, 186
Druzhina-Osoryin, Kallistrat, 27
Duck. *See* Birds; Poultry

Easter, menus for, 191, 203–204
Eggs, 148, 150, 162, 165, 196, 203
Elders, behavior toward, 72, 98–100
Entertainment, 77, 80
Equals, behavior toward, 72, 103, 190
Erasmus, 38

Fabrics, 12, 25; cutting, 126–128; storing, 127–128, 147, 166, 176
Family, definition of, 23
Fasts, 83, 88, 113, 116, 181; behavior during, 111; menus for, 161–163, 191–192, 194–196, 202–204; preparation for, 125, 151–152
Fathers: rights and responsibilities of, 26, 30–32, 93, 95–100; at weddings, 206–239
Fear: of God, 65–66, 68, 87, 93, 95, 97, 104, 107, 112, 124, 136, 145, 152, 177, 181–182, 188; saving through, 63, 93, 95, 182; of superiors, 69, 71, 105, 109, 126, 143–144
Feasts, 34–35, 37, 108, 141; behavior at, 76–78, 80–85, 160; memorial, 70, 75, 78–79, 84, 155; menus for, 191, 193, 195, 201, 203–204; among women, 36, 85, 132–133, 138–139, 181. *See also* Weddings: feasts at
Fedor Ivanovich, tsar of Russia, 144
Fences, care of, 36, 153, 173
Fields. *See* Agriculture

Fire, preventing, 22, 170, 173–174
Fish, 120; cooking, 125, 151, 158–160, 162–163; menus using, 162, 191–196, 202–204; preserving and storing, 64, 148, 151–152, 164–165, 175; purchasing, 24–25, 145, 148, 151–152, 158
Flour, 125, 149, 152, 164, 194–196, 213
Food: presentation, 159; preservation, 24–25, 148–154, 164–170, 175–176; suitable for servants, 159, 161–163, 172
Fools, holy, 116
Foreigners, 4, 19–20, 43–45, 84, 177, 188. *See also* Russia: commercial relations; Trade: international
Friends, 36–37, 126, 131, 133, 138, 186–188
Fruit, 152, 225; growing, 24, 153–154; juices from, 152, 154–155, 165, 176, 198; menus including, 192, 195, 202–203; preserving, 152, 154, 159, 165, 175–176; recipes for, 199–200
Frumenty, 67, 74–75, 78

Games, 32, 77, 80, 97
Gardens, 24, 41, 153–154; pests in, 153
Gemstones, 22, 95, 129–130
Gentry, 9–10, 13, 22–23, 42, 45–46, 49, 174
George, St., 14, 194
Gifts, 36–37, 186; to churches and monasteries, 50, 74, 110–111, 179, 181; to merchants, 146, 187. *See also* Weddings: gifts given at
Gluttony, 69, 85, 106, 112–113, 135, 139
Goddess, great mother, 107, 209
Godunov, Boris, tsar of Russia, 32
Golden Horde. *See* Mongols; *entries for individual khanates*
Gorbatov-Shuiskii, Prince A. B., 41, 69
Gossip, 28, 35–36, 109, 129, 131, 133–137, 139, 181
Grains, 150, 234; cooking, 125, 149, 162; menus using, 161–163, 190, 192, 196, 203–204; purchasing, 24–25, 145, 148; storing, 151–152, 164
Grouse. *See* Poultry
Guests, 34, 106, 110, 126, 151–152, 155–156, 158, 162; proper treatment of, 48, 84–85, 132–133, 141, 160, 181, 186; responsibilities of, 81–82, 132–133, 138–139, 181
Gur'ev family, 11

Manners, 35, 76, 83–85, 132–136, 160, 181

Marriage, 7–9, 17, 31–33, 93–97, 106, 177, 185; age at, 23, 32–33, 128; canons concerning, 18, 212. *See also* Betrothals; Contracts: marriage; Weddings

Martyrs, 115–117

Mary, mother of Jesus, 109, 188, 209; as intercessor, 89, 143, 189; reverence for, 62, 66, 69, 77, 80, 90, 116, 177, 192–193, 201–202, 210–211, 221, 231

Masters and slaves, 25–28, 33–36, 104–111, 133–138, 160–161, 163, 169–172. *See also* Servants; Slavery

Maximian, emperor of Byzantium, 194

Mead, 125, 138, 164–165, 176; recipes for, 155, 196–198

Mealtimes, regulations concerning, 86, 88, 106, 112–113, 139, 229

Meat: cooking, 125, 148–149, 158–163; preserving and storing, 64, 148–149, 152, 164–165, 175; purchasing, 145, 148–149, 158

Meat days: menus for, 161–163, 190–195, 201, 203–204; preparation for, 125, 161

Medicine. *See* Healing

Men, responsibilities of, 25–28, 41, 50, 63–65, 76, 83, 85–87, 92, 103–104, 107, 124, 128, 140, 145, 147–157, 163, 168–175

Menus, 40, 44–45, 190–196, 201–204

Merchants, 12–13, 22, 25, 34–35, 42–48, 122, 131, 145–146, 148, 174; *gosti*, 12, 145–146, 171; as guests, 84, 146, 155, 162; as household employees, 145, 170–172, 185

Military service classes. *See* Boyars; Gentry

Monasteries and convents, 17–19, 42, 46, 70, 74, 80, 84, 86, 98, 110, 115, 154, 178, 181–182, 186

Money, 92, 127–128, 131, 134, 149–150, 152–153, 158, 187, 204

Mongols, 4–5, 177, 219–220

Moscow (city), 1–4, 11, 24, 47–48, 184, 189, 204

Mothers: as intercessors, 100; rights and responsibilities of, 27, 29–32, 93, 95–100; at weddings, 206–239

Murder, 82, 119–120, 163

Muscovy. *See* Russia

Musical instruments, 77, 80, 112, 226, 228

Needlework, 32, 34, 95, 101, 125–128, 131–132, 181

Neighbors, 35–36, 120–121, 124, 129, 133, 153, 186

Nicholas, St., 189

Nikon, patriarch of Moscow, 46, 90

Nikon, St., abbot of Trinity–St. Sergius Monastery, 189

Niphont, St., 85

Noodles, 151, 192, 195–196, 201

Novgorod the Great, 6, 47, 184, 204–205

Obedience, 20, 26–28, 33–34, 69–72, 92, 98–100, 103, 124, 132–133, 160–161, 189–190

Oil: cooking, 24, 150, 192, 196, 202; in liturgy, 75, 78, 112, 115, 179

Old Ritualists, 46, 89–90

Orchards, 24, 41, 153–154

Orphans, care of, 110, 125, 154, 184

Orthodox Eastern church, 19, 38, 40; beliefs, 20, 42, 49–50, 62–63, 66–70, 73–75, 77–81, 88–94; clergy, 18–20, 42, 44–46, 63, 69–70, 75, 77–80, 84, 86, 89–90, 92, 97, 106, 111–112, 115–116, 119, 148, 174, 179, 181, 185; controversies, 19–20, 90, 91, 103, 117; councils, 20, 47, 86, 90, 117–120, 178; excommunication by, 67, 117–120; and "first fruits," 154–155; restrictions on sexuality, 88, 106–107, 111–112, 181; rules for icons, 73; sacraments, 66–67, 75, 94, 111; services, at church, 79, 106, 115, 178, 225; services, at home, 74–75, 78–79, 85–87, 106, 158, 178, 223, 225, 235

Paganism: beliefs and practices, 99, 113–114, 117–120; survivals, in Russia, 30, 67, 174, 193, 196, 206–207, 209, 223, 225

Pancakes and blintzes, 34, 125, 150–152, 161, 192, 196, 201–203

Paphnutius, husband of Theodora, 109

Paraskeva, St., 209

Paul of Aleppo, 79, 87

Paul of Tarsus, St., 62, 71–73, 77, 82, 88, 104–105, 107, 117, 137, 191

Peasants, 12–15, 17, 25, 42, 49, 120–121, 145–146, 150, 182, 185, 205; enserfment of, 10, 13–15

Pelageia, wife of Anfim, 39, 65

Peresvetov, I. S., 20

Peter, metropolitan of Moscow, 189

Peter, of Damascus, 91

Peter, St., 191, 204
Philip, St., 194
Physicians, 50, 115, 119. *See also*
  Healing
Pickled foods, 159, 162–163, 165, 175–
  176, 191–196, 201–204
Pies and pastries, 34, 125, 150–152,
  158; menus including, 161–163, 192,
  195–196, 201–204
Pigs, slaughtering, 149
Poland-Lithuania, 43, 154, 159
Poor, caring for, 20, 23, 48, 50, 68–70,
  72, 74, 84–85, 104, 110–111, 140, 146,
  152–155, 163, 165, 176, 179–186, 190
Poultry: menus including, 190–195,
  201, 203–204; served at weddings,
  222–223, 225, 227, 235, 238
Prayer, 63, 65–69, 74–75, 83, 100, 106,
  111–112, 116, 122, 124, 127, 135, 158,
  181; behavior during, 86–87, 90–91,
  178; before meals, 77, 80; for tsar
  and others, 71, 75, 78, 86, 179;
  before work, 101
Prices, 17, 128–129, 146–150, 152–153,
  187
Priests. *See* Orthodox Eastern church:
  clergy; Weddings: priest's role at
Princes and princesses, 41, 62, 71, 89,
  111, 115–116, 133, 205
Printing, 19, 38
Property, 123, 178; justly acquired,
  122, 177; lost, through sin, 82–83,
  93, 97, 113, 131, 186; seized, by
  force, 108, 110, 113, 120

Quarrels, preventing, 34, 81, 84, 134–
  137, 144, 153, 160, 183, 185–187

Recipes, 40, 196–200
Rightering, 14, 174
Riurik, founder of Russian state, 6
Roman Catholic church, 64, 75, 155
Romanov clan, 1, 8; house belonging
  to, 1–4
Romodanovskii, Prince G. G., 45
Russia (Muscovy): commercial
  relations, 4, 159, 177, 202; economic
  conditions, 25, 148, 171; military
  campaigns, 4; political and social
  system, 4–20, 26–29, 33, 36, 42, 185–
  187, 224, 233

Sacred writings, 85, 90, 91, 112, 116,
  177, 182
Saints, 32, 69, 74, 83, 86, 89, 101, 116–

117, 188, 190; relics of, 62, 65–67, 75,
  78–79, 112, 115, 117, 218
Samuel, king of Israel, 210
Sarah, wife of Abraham, 210
Satan. *See* Devil, devils
Sauces, 192–193, 201–202
Sergius, St., of Radonezh, 32, 189
Servants, 41; definition of good, 33,
  104–107, 109–110, 133, 146, 170–171;
  education of, 48, 103–107, 125–126,
  133–138, 143–145, 150, 181–182, 188;
  and illicit sex, 106–107; as part of
  family, 15, 23, 136; proper treatment
  of, 33–36, 42, 63–65, 84, 88, 107,
  110–111, 123–124, 129, 131–133, 139,
  146, 159, 161–163, 181; punishment
  of, 35–36, 78, 106, 109, 131, 143–144,
  163, 169–172, 187; responsibilities of,
  20, 24, 28, 76, 84–87, 101–111, 125–
  126, 133–143, 151, 153, 158–176; at
  weddings, 212, 215, 218–219, 226–
  229, 232, 234
Shops, 171–172, 175, 185
Shuiskii, Tsar Vasilii, 185
Siberia, Khanate of, 5
Sil'vestr, priest of Annunciation
  Cathedral, 4, 20, 36–43, 46–49, 65,
  69, 131, 137, 176–190; slaves freed
  by, 47, 184–185; wife of, 184–186
Simeon Stylite, St., 115, 193–194, 201–
  202
Sins 183; punishment for, 76–78, 80–
  85, 88, 93, 97, 99, 101–102, 104, 113–
  114, 120–124, 131, 137, 145, 163, 186;
  remission of, 67, 70, 74, 80, 94, 114–
  115, 122, 138, 163, 179; responsibility
  for, 26, 35, 65, 93, 104, 107, 124,
  137–138, 182, 188–189
Slavery, 13, 15–17, 33–36, 47–48, 50,
  100, 104–105, 108, 111, 120, 123–124,
  163, 174, 184, 185; and
  manumission, 47, 124, 184–185; and
  peculium, 105. *See also* Masters and
  slaves
Slaves. *See* Servants
Songs, 32, 77, 80, 112, 181; wedding,
  29, 217, 238
Sons, 17, 30–32, 84, 93–96, 99–101,
  134–135, 143, 171. *See also* Children
Sorcery. *See* Magic
Soup, 148–152, 156, 160; menus
  including, 160–163, 190–196, 201–
  204; for servants' meals, 34, 161–163
Spices. *See* Herbs and spices
Stables, 23, 41, 160, 167, 169–170, 173

Wives. *See* Husbands and wives;
Women

Women, 13, 16–18; and alcohol, 107–
108, 132, 138–139, 181; and church
attendance, 7, 86–87; definition of
good, 27–28, 102–103, 124–127, 132–
133; and economic resources, 7, 17,
27, 124–127, 233; as household
authority, 7, 27–28, 107, 124–128,
131–132, 139, 143, 150, 169, 171, 181–
182; old, as bad influence, 107–109;
and pregnancy, 17, 29, 86, 101, 144;
responsibilities of, 20, 26–29, 85–87,
92, 102, 124–128, 131–133, 138–143,
147–157, 163, 169–171, 181–182;
seclusion of, 7–8, 18, 26–29, 32, 36,
42, 50, 85, 126, 138–139, 159, 211,
233, 236–237

Wood, 125, 143, 145, 147, 152, 168

Work, 74, 101, 181, 183; in the
household, 101–102, 125–129, 140–
143, 158–176

Xenophon, 48

Yeast, 24, 156, 164–166, 195, 197–198
Youths. *See* Children
Yuliana Lazarevsky, 27, 32, 182

Zeno, emperor of Byzantium, 109